THE

ADULT ONLY

JOKE
BOOK III

HB

HINKLER
BOOKS

The Adult Only Joke Book III
First published in 2004 by Hinkler Books Pty Ltd
17-23 Redwood Drive
Dingley Victoria 3172 Australia
www.hinklerbooks.com.au

First printed in 2004

Reprinted   2004

ISBN 1 7412 1653 2

Cover design: Sam Grimmer
Text by: Scribblers & Writers Pty Ltd

Printed and bound in Australia

CONTENTS

INTRODUCTION

First there was one, and then there was a second, now here's the third in the series of Adult Only Joke Books. It's a great collection of jokes from right across the board. There are blonde jokes, blue jokes, and redneck jokes. There are lawyer jokes, doctor jokes, and jokes about the madness of the military. There are sports jokes, religious jokes and ethnic jokes. There are jokes about the sexes. And jokes about sex . . . Plus there are some fascinating insights into the human condition – a nice way of saying, 'Gee, people do some crazy things!'

The joke has been around with us for a long time. Indeed, you will find Adam and Eve get plenty of mention in this book! From their sex lives to their diets. They also spawned the first interaction between man and woman, thus giving us the great jokes and lines today about the differences between the sexes – what men are really saying, what women really want, and so on.

From the days of the Garden of Eden, we have come through to the age of technology, with IT, a pretty dull business in itself, forming the basis of new gags. So from the beginning to now, we can all laugh at ourselves - and each other. Just like real adults.

So, sit back, pour yourself a coffee, open the book, and have a good laugh.

AND SO, TO THE BEGINNING . . .

Two little boys, Tommy and George are sharing a room in the hospital.

As they are getting to know each other a little bit, Tommy gets around to asking, 'Hey George, what're you in for?'

'I'm getting my tonsils out,' says George. 'I'm a little worried.'

'Oh don't worry about it,' says Tommy. 'I had my tonsils out and it was a blast! I got to eat all the ice cream and jelly I wanted for three weeks!'

'Oh yeah?' asks George. 'That doesn't sound too bad. How about you? What're you here for?'

'I'm getting a circumcision, whatever that is,' Tommy frowns.

'Oh my God! Circumcision?' cries George. 'Jeez, good luck. I got one of those when I was a baby and I couldn't walk for two years!'

You know you're in a redneck hotel when you phone the front office and say, 'I've got a leak in the sink.' And they say, 'Go ahead!'

What's the sex position that makes ugly babies?
Ask your parents.

What's grosser than gross?
Two Siamese twins connected at the tongue.

What's even grosser than that?
When one of them throws up.

Dean saw an advertisement for a blow-up doll called Life-Like Tina which claimed she was 'so realistic you can't tell the difference!' As Dean had not had a girlfriend for a long time he ordered one, and waited in anticipation.

The supplier got the order from Dean, and the bloke who was mailing it couldn't believe how realistic 'Life-Like Tina' looked. When no one was around he decided to blow her up. He then thought that as she was inflated he might as well give her a bit of a test run. He had sex with the doll, meticulously washed it afterwards, packaged it up and posted it out to Dean.

A month later Dean rang the supplier.

'You know that "Life-Like Tina" blow up doll? I can't tell you how happy I am.'

'That's great!' said the supplier.

'It was a totally unbelievable experience,' enthused Dean.

'Realistic then?' asked the supplier.

'So realistic . . . I got syphilis.'

Your butt is so big; you have more crack than a drug dealer.

The young blonde has long been infatuated with a popular local disc jockey and finally gets to meet him when the station holds an open house.

She is very excited about being in a radio studio with all the equipment and flashing lights.

The DJ seductively suggests they get better acquainted, and leads her into a vacant studio where he unzips his pants.

'I suppose you know what this is?' he whispers.

'I sure do,' she says, grasping it in her hand and putting it near her mouth. 'I'd like to say hello to Ricky, Bobby, Louise and the whole gang down at Danny's Pizzeria.'

A small tourist hotel was all abuzz about an afternoon wedding where the groom was 95 years old and the bride was only 23. The groom looked pretty feeble and the feeling was that the wedding night might kill him, because his bride was a healthy, vivacious young woman.

But the next morning the bride came down the main staircase slowly, step by step, hanging onto the banister for dear life.

She finally managed to get to the counter of the little shop in the hotel. The clerk looked really concerned, 'Whatever happened to you, honey? You look like you've been wrestling an alligator!'

The bride groaned, hung on to the counter and managed to speak, 'Oh God! He told me he'd been saving up for 75 years, and I thought he meant his money!'

An engineer dies and reports to the pearly gates. St Peter checks his dossier and says, 'Ah, you're an engineer – you're in the wrong place.'

So, the engineer reports to the gates of hell and is let in. Pretty soon, the engineer gets dissatisfied with the level of comfort in hell, and starts designing and building improvements. After a while, they've got air-conditioning and flush toilets and escalators, and the engineer is a very popular guy.

One day, God calls Satan up on the telephone and says with a sneer, 'So, how's it going down there in hell?'

Satan replies, 'Hey, things are going great. We've got air-conditioning and flush toilets and escalators, and there's no telling what this engineer is going to come up with next.'

God replies, 'What? You've got an engineer? That's a mistake – he should never have gotten down there. Send him up here.'

'No way. I like having an engineer on the staff, and I'm keeping him.'

'Send him back up here or I'll sue.'

Satan laughs uproariously and answers, 'Yeah, right. And just where are *you* going to get a lawyer?'

An English Bobby comes home from work early to find his wife in bed with three men.

'Hello, hello, hello!' he says.

His wife whines, 'What? No hello for me?'

You're so anally retentive, you could stick a piece of coal up there and have a diamond in a week.

An expectant couple were soon to have their first child. Their doctor told them of a new invention to relieve the mother's pain during childbirth. This invention could be attached to the mother and it would transfer the pain she experienced to the baby's father.

The couple talked it over and the husband was anxious to help his wife with her delivery. When the blessed time came, they opted to use the new invention. It was strapped to the mother and the dial was set at 10%.

With the mother's first contraction, the husband felt no pain. He asked that the dial be adjusted to 30%. With the next contractions, the mother felt less pain and the husband tolerated the experience well.

The husband, feeling courageous and noble, asked that the dial be turned to 100%. The nurse did so and the mother completed the entire labour and delivery with no pain. The husband did not feel any pain either, and was certain that women had overrated their plight in childbirth.

A few days later the happy new family returned home from

the hospital. They were shocked as they drove into their driveway to see the mailman lying dead on the front porch.

Your mama's so fat, when she stepped on the dog's tail we had to change his name to Beaver.

'I have good news and bad news as a result of the blood tests we ran on you,' the defence lawyer says to his client.

'OK, what's the bad news?' asks the client.

The lawyer says, 'Your blood matches the DNA found at the murder scene.'

'Friggin' hell!' cries the client. 'What's the good news?'

'Well,' the lawyer says, 'your cholesterol is down to 3.9, and your sugar levels show you're not a diabetic.'

A farm boy accidentally overturned his wagonload of corn. A farmer who lived nearby heard the noise, saw the mess, and yelled over to the boy, 'Hey Jimmy, forget your troubles. Come in and visit with us. I'll help you get the wagon up later.'

'That's mighty nice of you,' Jimmy answered, 'but I don't think Pa would like me to.'

'Aw come on boy,' the farmer insisted.

'No, Pa –'

'Forget about your Pa. You been working so hard, it was bad luck when that wagon fell over, so you come inside and set a spell and rest up.'

'Well OK,' the boy finally agreed, and added, 'but Pa won't like it.'

After a hearty dinner, Jimmy thanked his host. 'I feel a lot better now, but I know Pa is going to be real upset.'

'Don't be foolish!' the neighbour said with a smile. 'He's a very understanding man, your father. By the way, where is he?'

'Under the wagon.'

A guy walks into a bar with his dog on a leash.
A drinker turns, looks, laughs and says, 'Gee, that's a weird dog – he's stumpy-legged, doesn't have a tail, and is pink! I bet my Rottweiler would beat the crap out of it.'

The owner takes the challenge, and $100 is laid on the bar. Out in the yard, the fight starts, and in less than a minute the Rottweiler gets mauled to pieces. The owner pays up and slinks off into the night, crying.

A second drinker says his pit bull will win, with the bet at $500. They go out into the yard and when the fight is finished there are bits of pit-bull terrier all over the place. The drinker pays up, and leaves, with empty pockets and a broken heart.

A third punter puts a grand down, saying his mastiff-pit-bull-Rottweiler-Dingo-Doberman, brought up in the wild, will do the pink dog over. They go out in the yard. This challenger lasts even less time than the others. His owner, shocked, is carted home in the back of a ute.

When order is restored, the barman leans over and says to the victorious owner, 'Say what breed is that anyway?'

The owner says, 'Until I cut his tail off and painted him pink, he was the same breed as every other crocodile.'

You might be a redneck if you study for a blood test.

Frank works hard at the factory. His only joy is to spend most evenings bowling or playing basketball at the gym. His wife thinks he is pushing himself too hard, so for his birthday she takes him to a local strip club.

The doorman at the club greets them and says, 'Hey, Frank! How ya doin?'

His wife is puzzled and asks Frank if he's been to this club before.

'Oh no,' says Frank. 'He's on my bowling team.'

When they are seated, a waitress asks Frank if he'd like his usual VB.

His wife is becoming a little uncomfortable and says, 'You must come here a lot for that woman to know you drink VB.'

'No, darling, she's also in the Ladies Bowling League on Wednesday nights. We share lanes with them.'

Then, a stripper comes over to their table and throws her arms around Frank. 'Hi, Frankie,' she says, 'Want your usual table dance?'

Frank's wife, now furious, grabs her purse and storms out of the club. Frank follows and sees her getting into a cab. Before she can slam the door, he jumps in beside her and she starts going ballistic, screaming at him.

The cabby turns his head and says, 'Hey, Frankie, looks like you picked up a real doozie this time!'

A guy was standing in front of the gorilla cage at the zoo one day, when a gust of wind swept some dust into his eye. As he rubbed his eyelid, the gorilla went crazy, bent open the bars, and beat the guy senseless.

When the guy came around, he reported the incident to the zookeeper. Nodding, the zookeeper explained that pulling down your eyelid means 'screw you' in gorilla language. The explanation didn't make the victim feel any better – and he vowed revenge.

The next day, he purchased two large knives, two party hats, two party horns and a large sausage. Putting the sausage in his pants, he hurried to the zoo and went right up to the gorilla's cage where he opened up his bag of goodies. Knowing that gorillas were natural mimics, he put on a party hat. The gorilla looked at him, reached through the bars, grabbed a hat from the bag, and put it on.

Next, the guy picked up his horn and blew on it. The gorilla reached out, picked up the other horn, and did the same.

Then the man picked up his knife, whipped the sausage out

of his pants, and sliced it in half. The gorilla looked at the knife, looked at his own crotch, looked at the man, and pulled down his eyelid.

One fine morning in Eden, God was looking for Adam and Eve, but couldn't find them. Later that day, God saw Adam and asked where he and Eve were earlier.

Adam said, 'This morning Eve and I made love for the first time.'

God said, 'Adam, you have sinned. I knew this would happen. Where is Eve now?'

Adam replied, 'She's down at the river, washing herself out.'

'Damn,' said God, 'now all the fish will smell funny.'

AEROPLANES & FLYING

A man goes skydiving for the first time. After listening to the instructor for what seems like days, he is ready to go. Excited, he jumps out of the plane. About five seconds later, he pulls the ripcord.

Nothing happens.

He tries again. Still nothing. He starts to panic, but remembers his back-up chute. He pulls that cord. Nothing happens. He frantically begins pulling both cords, but to no avail. Suddenly, he looks down and he can't believe his eyes. Another man is in the air with him, but this guy is going *up*!

Just as the other guy passes by, the skydiver, by this time scared out of his wits, yells, 'Hey, do you know anything about skydiving?'

The other guy yells back, 'No! Do you know anything about gas stoves?'

D uring class the skydiving instructor always takes the time to answer questions.

One guy asks, 'If our chute doesn't open, and the reserve doesn't open, how long do we have until we hit the ground?'

The jumpmaster looks at him and in a perfect deadpan voice answers, 'The rest of your life.'

A blind man was describing his favourite sport – parachuting. When asked how this was accomplished, he said that things were all done for him. 'I am placed in the door and told when to jump. My hand is placed on my release ring for me, and out I go.'

'But how do you know when you are going to land?' he was asked.

'I have a very keen sense of smell and I can smell the trees and grass when I am 300 feet from the ground,' he answered.

'But how do you know when to lift your legs for the final arrival on the ground?'

He quickly answered 'Oh, the dog's leash goes slack.'

Q: What's the difference between God and skydivers?
A: God doesn't think he's a skydiver.

Q: What kind of crazy bird yells 'Polly wants a cracker' when he jumps from an airplane?
A: A parrot trooper.

Q: What's the difference between a skydiver and a golfer?
A: A golfer goes 'WHACK . . . Oh shit!' A skydiver goes 'Oh shit! . . . WHACK'

Flight 101 is coming in for a landing under the control of the co-pilot, and the pilot is freaking out. The sweat is jumping off his brow. The plane lands and screeches to a halt.

Relieved the pilot turns to the co-pilot and says, 'Man, that was the shortest runway I ever landed on.'

The co-pilot says, 'Yeah, which is weird because it's soooooo wide.'

One night, a Delta twin-engine plane was flying somewhere above New Jersey. There were five people on board; the pilot, David Beckham, Bill Gates, the Dalai Lama, and a hippie.

Suddenly the passenger cabin began to fill with smoke. The cockpit door opened, and the pilot burst into the compartment.

'Gentlemen,' he began, 'I have good news and bad news. The bad news is that we're about to crash in New Jersey.

The good news is that there are four parachutes, and I have one of them!'

With that, the pilot threw open the door and jumped from the plane.

David Beckham was on his feet in a flash. 'Gentlemen,' he said, 'I am the world's greatest athlete. The world needs great athletes. I think the world's greatest athlete should have a parachute!'

With these words, he grabbed one of the remaining parachutes, and hurtled through the door and into the night.

Bill Gates rose and said, 'Gentlemen, I am the world's smartest man. The world needs smart men. I think the world's smartest man should have a parachute, too.'

He grabbed one, and out he jumped. The Dalai Lama and the hippie looked at one another.

Finally, the Dalai Lama spoke. 'My son,' he said, 'I have lived a satisfying life and have known the bliss of true enlightenment. You have your life ahead of you, you take the last parachute, and I will go down with the plane.'

The hippie smiled and said, 'Hey, don't worry, pop. The world's smartest man just jumped out wearing my backpack.'

NASA planned a mission that involved keeping three astronauts in space for two years. Because of the extended duration of the trip, each was allowed to take 100kg of baggage.

The first astronaut decided to take along his wife. The second decided to take along tapes so he could learn how to speak Arabic. The third astronaut decided to take along 800 packets of cigarettes.

Two years later, when the space shuttle landed, there was a big crowd waiting to welcome them home. Out came the first astronaut and his wife, each with a baby in their arms. Next, came the second astronaut speaking fluent Arabic. They both gave their speeches and got a rousing applause.

Suddenly out came the third astronaut with a cigarette in his mouth. He walked up to the podium and snarled at the crowd, 'Has anyone got a match?'

10 SIGNS YOU'RE FLYING WITH A 'NO-FRILLS' AIRLINE

1. You can't board the plane unless you have the exact change.
2. A passenger from the previous flight has locked herself in the toilet and is hysterically refusing to come out.
3. Before you take off, the stewardess tells you to fasten your Velcro.
4. The captain berates the first officer for having lost the crank handle.
5. The captain asks all the passengers to chip in a little for petrol.
6. The captain yells at the ground crew to get the sheep off the runway.
7. You ask the captain how often their planes crash and he says, 'Just once.'
8. There's no movie, but your life keeps flashing before your eyes.
9. You see a man with a gun, but he's demanding to be let off the plane.
10. The bloke next to you is reading that book about the plane crash in the Andes and how the survivors ate each other.

An airline recently introduced a special half-price fare for wives accompanying their husbands on business trips. Anticipating some valuable testimonials, the publicity department of the airline sent out letters to all the wives of businessmen who used the special rates, asking how they enjoyed their trip.

Responses are still pouring in asking, 'What trip?'

GROUND CONTROL TO . . .

Pilot: November 123 on a very short final, understand I'm cleared to land?
Tower: Oh, who's talking?
Pilot: Me.

Radar: Flight 1234, for noise abatement turn right 45 degrees
Pilot: Roger, but we are at 35,000 feet, how much noise can we make up here?
Radar: Sir, have you ever heard the noise a 747 makes when it hits a 727?

Tower: N2234, are you a Cessna?
Pilot: No, I'm a male Hispanic.

Pilot: Request heading 110 to avoid.
Radar: To avoid what?
Pilot: To avoid delay.

Pilot: Radar, this is Cessna 4675.
Radar: Cessna 4675, go ahead.
Pilot: Radar, I don't seem to be making much progress here. How is my ground speed?
Radar: Well, all depends. If you are a hang glider, you are doing very well.

A plane took off from Sydney airport. After it reached a comfortable cruising altitude, the captain made an announcement over the intercom.

'Ladies and gentlemen, this is your captain speaking. Welcome to flight 293, non-stop from Sydney to Perth. The weather ahead is good and we should have a smooth and uneventful flight. Now sit back and relax – Oh my God!'

Then silence.

Shortly after, the captain came back on the intercom and said, 'Ladies and gentlemen, I am so sorry if I scared you earlier but while I was talking, the flight attendant brought me a cup of coffee and spilled the hot coffee in my lap. You should see the front of my pants!'

At the rear of economy a man muttered, 'You should see the back of mine.'

A large, twin-engine train was making its way across America. While crossing the western mountains, one of the engines broke down.

'No problem, we can make it to Denver and get a replacement engine there,' thought the engineer, and carried on at half power. Yet he had not gone further than a kilometre when the other engine broke down, and the train came to a standstill in the middle of nowhere.

Ever the optimist, the engineer made the following announcement, 'Ladies and gentlemen, I have some good news and some bad news. The bad news is that both engines have failed, and we will be stuck here for some time until the additional engines arrive. The good news is that you didn't make this trip in a plane!'

While cruising at 40,000 feet, the aeroplane shuddered, and a passenger looked out the window.

'Good Lord!' he screamed. 'One of the engines just blew up!'

Other passengers left their seats and came running over. Suddenly the aircraft was rocked by a second blast as another engine exploded on the other side. The passengers were in a panic and even the flight attendants couldn't maintain order.

Just then, standing tall and smiling confidently, the pilot strode from the cockpit and assured everyone that there was nothing to worry about. His words and his demeanour seemed to make most of the passengers feel better, and they sat down as the pilot calmly walked to the door of the aircraft.

There, he grabbed several packages from under the seats and began handing them to the flight attendants.

Each crewmember attached their package to their backs.

'Say,' spoke up an alert passenger, 'Aren't those parachutes?'

The pilot confirmed that they were.

The passenger went on, 'But I thought you said there was nothing to worry about?'

'There isn't,' replied the pilot as a third engine exploded. 'We're going to get help.'

The following announcement was heard over the cabin PA system on a packed trans-Atlantic flight.

'Ladies and gentlemen, we are overbooked on this flight. We are offering anyone $1000 plus a seat on the next flight if they are willing to give up their seat on this flight.'

After a short pause, the offer was loudly accepted by someone in the cockpit.

ACTUAL MAINTENANCE COMPLAINTS SUBMITTED BY PILOTS AND THE REPLIES FROM THE MAINTENANCE CREWS.

Problem:	Left inside main tyre almost needs replacement.
Solution:	Almost replaced left inside main tyre.

Problem:	Test flight OK, except auto-land very rough.
Solution:	Auto-land not installed on this aircraft.

Problem:	Something loose in cockpit.
Solution:	Something tightened in cockpit.

Problem: Evidence of hydraulic leak on right main landing gear.
Solution: Evidence removed.

Problem: DME volume unbelievably loud.
Solution: Volume set to more believable level.

Problem: Dead bugs on windshield.
Solution: Live bugs on order.

Problem: IFF inoperative.
Solution: IFF inoperative in OFF mode.

Problem: Friction locks causing throttle levers to stick.
Solution: That's what they're there for.

Problem: Number three engine missing.
Solution: Engine found on right wing after brief search.

A military cargo plane, flying over a populated area, suddenly loses power and starts to nose dive. The pilot tries to pull up, but with all their cargo, the plane is too heavy. He yells to the soldiers in the back to throw things out to make the plane lighter. They throw out a pistol.

'Throw out more!' shouts the pilot.

So they throw out a rifle.

'More!' he cries again.

They heave out a missile. The plane stabilises and the pilot regains control. With a sigh of relief they land safely at the airport.

They unload the plane and head off home. Pretty soon they meet a boy on the side of the road who's crying. They stop and ask why he is crying.

'I was riding my bike and out of the sky a pistol hit me on the head!'

They drive a little further, and meet a boy who's crying even harder. Again they stop and ask why the boy crying.

He says, 'I was walking to the shops when from nowhere a rifle hit me on the head!'

They apologise and keep driving until they come across a boy who is crying hysterically. They stop and ask him what the matter is.

'Nothing,' the boy replies, 'I'm crying from laughter – I just farted and a house blew up!'

A student was heading home for the holidays. When she got to the airline counter, she presented her ticket to Houston.

'I'd like you to send my green suitcase to Hawaii, and my red suitcase to London,' she told the agent.

The confused agent said, 'I'm sorry, we can't to that.'

'Really? I am so relieved to hear you say that because that's exactly what you did with my luggage last year!'

ANIMALS

Farmer McCarthy lived for many years with only his dog for a companion. One sad day he found his dog dead from old age. He went to his parish priest and asked if services could be said for his dog.

The good father said, 'Oh no, we can't have services for a dog here, but there's a new church down the street that might be willing.'

'Father, do you think $50,000 might be enough of a donation?' asked farmer McCarthy.

'Well man, why didn't you tell me your dog was a Catholic?'

There once was a farmer from Hay
Who found that his hens wouldn't lay
The trouble was Brewster
His champion rooster
You see, Brewster the rooster was gay!

Q: Did you hear about the duck who bought some lipstick?
A: She asked the chemist to put it on her bill.

Q: Did you hear about the naughty chicken?
A: It was eggspelled from school.

Q: Did you hear about the performer who specialised in bird impressions?
A: He ate worms.

A butcher is working when he notices a dog in his shop. He goes to shoo him away when he spots a note in the dog's mouth. The note reads, 'Can I have 12 sausages and a leg of lamb, please?', and wrapped inside the note is a $10 note.

So the butcher takes the money, puts the sausages and lamb in a bag, and places the bag in the dog's mouth. The dog trots happily out of the shop.

Intrigued, the butcher decides to close up shop and follow the dog. It walks down the street and comes to a crossing. The dog puts down the bag, jumps up and presses the crossing button. Then he waits patiently, bag in mouth, for the lights to change. They do, and he walks across the road, with the butcher following.

The dog comes to a bus stop, and looks at the timetable. Then he sits on one of the seats to wait for the bus. The butcher is in awe.

Along comes a bus. The dog walks to the front of the bus, looks at the number, and goes back to his seat.

Another bus comes. Again the dog checks the number and climbs onto bus. The butcher, mouth agape, follows him onto the bus.

The bus travels through town and out to the suburbs. Eventually the dog gets up, moves to the front of the bus and, standing on his hind legs, pushes the button to stop the bus.

The dog gets off, meat still in his mouth and the butcher follows. They walk down the road, and the dog approaches a house. He walks up the path, and drops the package of meat on the step.

Then he walks back down the path, takes a big run, and throws himself against the door. He goes back down the path, takes another run, and throws himself against the door again. There's no answer at the door, so the dog goes to the window and bangs his head against it several times. He sits at the door waiting.

The door swings open. A big bloke looks down at the dog.

'You stupid dog!' he yells.

The butcher is taken aback because, evidently, this dog is not stupid. So he runs up to the bloke and says, 'What the hell are you doing? This dog is a genius. He's so clever, he could be on TV!'

The guy responds, 'Clever? Yeah right. This is the second time this week he's forgotten his key!'

Customer: Have you got any dogs going cheap?
Pet Shop Owner: No, I'm afraid they all go woof.

'I play Scrabble with my pet dog every night.'
'He must be clever.'
'I don't know about that. I usually beat him.'

Q: What do you call a young goat who visits a psychiatrist?
A: A crazy mixed-up kid.

Q: What do you call a zebra without stripes?
A: A horse.

Q: What do you call cattle that always sit down?
A: Ground beef.

Q: Which bird succeeds?
A: A budgie without teeth.

Q: What kind of hen lays the longest?
A: A dead one.

Q: Which insects can tell the time?
A: Clockroaches.

A turtle is walking down an alley in New York when he is mugged by a gang of snails. A police detective comes to investigate and asks the turtle if he could explain what happened.

The turtle turns to the detective with a confused look and replies, 'I don't know officer. It all happened so fast . . .'

Bob was excited about his new rifle and decided to try bear hunting. He travelled up to Alaska, spotted a small brown bear and shot it. Soon after there was a tap on his shoulder, and he turned around to see a big black bear.

The black bear said, 'That was a very bad mistake. That was my cousin. I'm going to give you two choices. Either I maul you to death or we have sex.'

After considering briefly, Bob decided to accept the latter alternative.

So the black bear had his way with Bob.

Even though he felt sore for two weeks, Bob soon recovered and vowed revenge. He headed out on another trip to Alaska where he found the black bear and shot it dead.

Right away, there was another tap on his shoulder. This time a huge grizzly bear stood right next to him.

The grizzly said, 'That was a big mistake, Bob. That was my cousin and you've got two choices: Either I maul you to death or I have sex with you.'

Again, Bob thought it was better to cooperate with the grizzly bear than be mauled to death, so the grizzly had his way with Bob.

Although he survived, it took several months before Bob fully recovered from his run-in with the bear. By then, Bob was completely outraged, so he headed back to Alaska and managed to track down the grizzly bear and shoot it.

He felt the joy of sweet revenge, but then there was a tap on his shoulder. He turned around to find a giant polar bear standing there.

The polar bear looked at him and said, 'Admit it Bob, you don't come here for the hunting, do you?'

Two guys are out hiking. Suddenly, a bear starts chasing them. They climb a tree, but the bear starts climbing up the tree after them.

The first guy gets his sneakers out of his knapsack and starts putting them on.

'What are you doing?' asks the second guy.

'When the bear gets close to us, I thought we'd jump down and make a run for it.'

'Are you crazy? You can't outrun a bear.'

'I don't have to outrun the bear. I only have to outrun you.'

Q: What do you call a fish with no eyes?
A: A fish.

Q: Why did the fish cross the sea?
A: To get to the other tide.

Q: Why did the fish jump out of the water?
A: Because the seaweed.

Q: Why did the flies run across the top of the cling wrap box?
A: Because it read 'Tear along the dotted line.'

Q: Why did the zookeeper refuse to work in the elephant enclosure?
A: Because the work kept piling up.

Q: Why do chickens watch TV?
A: For hentertainment.

Q: Why do frogs like beer?
A: Because it's made from hops.

Q: Why does a stork stand on one leg?
A: It would fall over if it lifted the other one.

Q: How do dinosaurs pass exams?
A: With extinction.

Q: How would you feel if you saw a dinosaur in your backyard?
A: Very old.

Q: What's the scariest dinosaur of all?
A: The Terrordactyl.

Q: Where do dinosaurs go to the toilet?
A: In the dino-sewer.

Q: Which dinosaur does well in English exams?
A: Tyrannathesaurus Rex.

A guy is browsing in a pet shop and sees a parrot sitting on a little perch. It doesn't have any feet or legs.

The guy says aloud, 'Jeesh, I wonder what happened to this parrot?'

The parrot says, 'I was born this way. I'm a defective parrot.'

'Holy crap,' the guy replies. 'You actually understood and answered me!'

'I got every word,' says the parrot. 'I happen to be a highly intelligent, thoroughly educated bird.'

'Oh yeah?' the guy asks, 'Then answer this – how do you hang onto your perch without any feet?'

'Well,' the parrot says, 'this is very embarrassing but since you asked, I wrap my weenie around this wooden bar like a little hook. You can't see it because of my feathers.'

'Wow,' says the guy. 'You really can understand and speak English can't you?'

'Actually, I speak both Spanish and English, and I can converse with reasonable competence on almost any topic, including politics, religion, sports, physics and philosophy. I'm especially good at ornithology. You really ought to buy me. I'd be a great companion.'

The guy looks at the $200 price tag. 'Sorry, but I just can't afford that.'

'Psssssssst,' says the parrot, 'I'm defective, so the truth is, nobody wants me. You can probably get me for $20, just make the guy an offer!'

The guy offers $20, and this is gratefully accepted by the pet-shop owner. The man walks out with the parrot.

Weeks go by. The parrot is sensational. He has a great sense of humour, he's interesting, he's a great pal, he understands everything, he sympathises, and he's insightful. The guy is delighted.

One day the guy comes home from work and the parrot says, 'Pssssssssssssst,' and motions him over with one wing.

'I don't know if I should tell you this or not,' says the parrot, 'but it's about your wife and the postman.'

'What are you talking about?' asks the guy.

'When the postman delivered the mail today, your wife greeted him at the door in a sheer black nightie and kissed him passionately.'

'*What?*' the guy asks incredulously. '*Then* what happened?'

'Well, then the postman came into the house and lifted up her nightie and began petting her all over,' reported the parrot.

The man is horrified. 'Oh no!' he exclaims. 'Then what?'

'Then he lifted up the nightie, got down on his knees and began to kiss her all over, starting with her breasts and slowly going down . . .'

'Well,' demands the frantic guy, '*then what happened?*'

'Damned if I know,' says the parrot. 'I got a hard-on and fell off my perch!'

An old farmer's rooster was getting along in years so the farmer decided to get a new rooster for his hens. The old rooster saw the young one strutting around and realised that he was being replaced. He decided to do something about it.

He walked up to the new bird and said, 'So you're the new stud in town? Well, I'm not ready for the chopping block yet. To prove it, I challenge you to a race around that hen house over there. We'll run around it 10 times and whoever finishes first gets to have all the hens for himself.'

The young rooster was a proud sort, and he thought he was easily a match for the old guy.

'You're on,' he said, 'and since I'm so great, I'll even give you a head start of half a lap. I'll still win easily!'

So the two roosters went over to the henhouse and all the hens gathered to watch.

The race began and the hens started cheering the old rooster on. After the first lap, the old rooster was still in the lead. After the second lap, the old guy's lead had slipped a little, but he was still hanging in there. Unfortunately, the old rooster's lead continued to slip each time around, and by the fifth lap he was just barely in front of the young fella.

By then the farmer had heard the commotion. He thought there was a fox after his chickens so he ran into the house, got his shotgun and ran into the barnyard.

When he got there, he saw the two roosters running around the henhouse, with the old rooster still slightly in the lead.

He immediately took his shotgun, aimed, fired and blew the young rooster away.

As he walked away he said to himself, 'Damn, that's the third gay rooster I've bought this month.'

A police officer came upon a terrible car crash where two people had been killed. As he looked at the wreckage a little monkey came out of the brush and hopped around the crashed car. The officer looked down at the monkey and said, 'I wish you could talk.'

The monkey looked up at the officer and nodded his head.

'You can understand what I'm saying?' asked the officer.

Again, the monkey nodded.

'Well, did you see what happened?'

The monkey nodded. He pretended to have a can in his hand and turned it up to his mouth.

'They were drinking?' asked the officer.

The monkey nodded.

The monkey then pinched his fingers together and held them to his mouth, sucking deeply.

'They were smoking marijuana too?' asked the officer.

The monkey nodded. He made a sexual sign with his fingers.

'So they were playing around as well!?' asked the astounded officer.

Again, the monkey nodded.

'Now wait, you're saying your owners were drinking, smoking and playing around before they wrecked the car?'

The monkey nodded.

'What were you doing during all this?' asked the officer.

The monkey held up his hands on an imaginary steering wheel.

One day an out-of-work mime visits the zoo and attempts to earn some money as a street performer. Unfortunately, as soon as he starts to draw a crowd, a zookeeper grabs him and drags him into his office.

He thinks he is in trouble, but in fact, the zookeeper explains to the mime that the zoo's most popular attraction, a gorilla, has died suddenly and the keeper fears that attendance at the zoo will fall off. He offers the mime a job to dress up as the gorilla and play the role until they can get another one.

The mime accepts and the next morning he puts on a gorilla suit and enters the cage before the crowd arrives.

He discovers that it's a great job. He can sleep all he wants, play and make fun of people, and he draws bigger crowds than he ever did as a mime.

However, eventually the crowds get bored with him and he tires of just swinging around on tyres. He begins to notice that the people are paying more attention to the lion in the cage next to his. Not wanting to lose the attention of his audience, he climbs to the top of his cage, crawls across a partition, and dangles from the top to the lion's cage. Of course, this makes the lion furious, but the crowd loves it.

At the end of the day the zookeeper comes and gives the mime a raise for being such a good attraction. This goes on for some time. The mime keeps taunting the lion, the crowds grow larger, and his salary keeps going up.

Then one terrible day when he is dangling over the furious lion he slips and falls. The mime is terrified. The lion gathers itself and prepares to pounce. The mime is so scared that he begins to run round and round the cage with the lion close behind.

Finally, the mime starts screaming and yelling, 'Help, Help me!', but the lion is quick and pounces. The mime soon finds himself flat on his back looking up at the angry lion and the lion says, 'Shut up you idiot! Do you want to get us both fired?'

Harry gets a new job at the zoo. On his first morning he is given three tasks. The first is to weed the exotic fish pool. Harry wades in and starts to weed when suddenly a bloody great fish leaps out and bites him. Enraged, Harry beats the offending fish to death. He realises that his boss is not going to be pleased so, in a flash of inspiration, he decides to feed the dead fish to the lions to get rid of the evidence.

'Lions will eat anything,' he says to himself.

Harry's second job is to clear out the monkey house. He is shovelling away when a couple of chimps start throwing shit at him. Harry has a short temper, and finds himself beating the chimps with his spade and he kills them instantly.

Again, he finds himself with some dead bodies to dispose of, so he decides to feed the chimps to the lions.

'Lions will eat anything,' he says to himself.

Harry's last job is to collect honey from some South American bees. He begins to clean the hives out when suddenly the bees start swarming and stinging him repeatedly. Harry loses it and swipes the whole swarm of bees to death. He is unfazed at the carnage because he knows what to do.

'Why not? Lions will eat anything,' he says to himself.

Later that day a new lion arrives at the zoo. It wanders up to another lion and asks, 'What's the food like here?'

'Absolutely brilliant. Today I had fish and chimps with mushy bees.'

A travelling salesman was driving down a country road when he noticed a pig standing by the gate to a farm. Something was different about the pig and the salesman slowed down for a better look.

As he got closer he noticed that the pig had a wooden leg. It was intricately carved. Someone had taken a lot of time to make this leg for the pig.

The salesman decided to drive up to the farmhouse to find out more about the pig with the wooden leg. The farmer came out to meet him.

The salesman said, 'I couldn't help but notice your pig with the wooden leg. What happened to him?'

'That pig is a special pig to us,' replied the farmer. 'Yes sir, he's really a special pig all right.'

'What makes him such a special pig?'

'That pig saved our lives. Our house caught on fire and he came up on the porch and banged and banged on the door and grunted and made such a ruckus that he woke us up. He saved our lives. He sure is a special pig to us.'

THE ADULT ONLY JOKE BOOK III

'I see,' said the salesman. 'He sure is a special pig all right.
I can understand that now, but how did he get the wooden leg?'

'Now didn't I tell you that pig was a special pig? Anyone
knows that you don't eat a special pig like that all at once!'

A bloke received a mouse for his birthday and he loved it so
much that he never parted with it. This mouse sat on his
shoulder and went everywhere with him, to work, to parties,
even to the opera.

One day, a good friend of his died. He went to pay his
respects with his little friend on his shoulder. On his way home,
he suddenly realised that the mouse was gone!

He retraced all his moves for the day and realised that the last
place he had seen the mouse was at the viewing at the funeral
home. The mouse must have jumped off his shoulder into the
open coffin. When the lid was put on the coffin he would have
been trapped.

He raced back across town, but arrived too late. The body had
been removed and was already being transported to the
cemetery in the hearse.

The man collapsed, filled with grief. He couldn't believe that
he did not heed his mother's constant adage. 'Never,' she used to
say, 'lock a gift mouse in the hearse.'

A city slicker moves to the country and decides he's going to
take up farming. He heads to the local co-op and tells the
man, 'Give me 100 baby chickens.'

The co-op man complies.

A week later the man returns and says, 'Give me 200 baby
chickens.'

The co-op man complies.

Again, a week later the man returns. This time he says, 'Give
me 500 baby chickens.'

'Wow!' the co-op man replies, 'You must really be doing well!'

'Naw,' says the man with a sigh, 'I'm either planting them too deep or too far apart!'

An aspiring veterinarian put himself through veterinary school working nights as a taxidermist. Upon graduation, he decided he could combine his two vocations to better serve the needs of his patients and their owners, while doubling his practice and, therefore, his income.

He opened his own offices with a shingle on the door reading 'Dr Jones, Veterinary Medicine and Taxidermy – either way, you get your pet back!'

10 SIGNS THAT YOU'RE AT A BAD ZOO

1. The stripes on the zebra tend to peel away in the heat.
2. There is a sticker on the rear end of the elephant reading 'Property of Jim's Costume Hire.'
3. When no one else is looking, you swear that the monkeys are mocking you.
4. The bear exhibit is actually the guys from the football team doing a training camp.
5. The zookeeper always wants to take the rhino for a walk.
6. The lion in the lion cage closely resembles the one from The Lion King.
7. If you deposit 50c, the giraffe will magically appear and talk to you.
8. The gorilla keeps getting distracted, brushing his cigarette ash off his chest.
9. Ask the tour guide too many questions and you're suddenly dipped in some sort of sauce and placed in the tiger's den.
10. The tiger's name is Bruce.

BLONDES

An overweight blonde went to see her doctor for some advice. The doctor advised her to run 10km a day for 30 days. This, he promised, would help her lose 20kg.

The blonde followed the doctor's advice and, after 30 days, she was pleased to find that she had indeed lost the whole 20kg.

She phoned the doctor and thanked him for the wonderful advice which produced such effective results. At the end of the conversation, however, she asked one last question:

'How do I get back, since I am now 300km from home?'

Q: Santa Claus, the Easter Bunny, the Tooth Fairy, a smart blonde, and a dumb blonde are walking down the street when they spot a $100 bill on the ground. Who gets it?

A: Nobody. The first four don't exist and the dumb blonde thought it was a gum wrapper.

A blonde was fishing and it started to rain, so he moved under the bridge for shelter.

His mate saw him and called, 'Sam, are you afraid of the rain?'

'No . . . the fish come here for shelter.'

The blonde bricklayer was doing some work on the fireplace in Mr Cabot's expensive home. He was much impressed by the moose-head over the fireplace.

'It's a beautiful animal, Mr Cabot,' he said, 'the biggest I've ever seen.'

'Yes,' said Mr Cabot, 'that moose was a fighter among moose. I tracked him for over two days, and it took six men nearly 30 hours to get him back to our Jeep.'

Shaking his blonde curls in admiration, the bricklayer said, 'Wow, what a great hunter, and what a huge catch. Do you mind if I go into the next room and see the rest of him?'

Q: A blonde and a brunette jump off the Empire State Building. It takes the blonde three minutes longer to hit the ground than the brunette. Why?

A: Because she had to stop to ask for directions.

Judi the blonde runs crying into the office.

'What's wrong?' gasps her best friend Carol.

'It's my boyfriend,' gushes Judi. 'He was working on the engine under the hood of his car when the lid came down and cut off a finger!'

'My god,' shrieks Carol. 'Did it amputate his whole finger?'

'No, thank goodness,' sniffs Judi. 'But it was the one just next to it!'

A blonde walks into a pharmacy and asks the pharmacist for a bottom deodorant.

'Sorry, we don't sell bottom deodorant,' the pharmacist replies, struggling to keep from laughing.

'But I always buy it here,' the blonde says. 'I bought one last month.'

Thinking quickly, the pharmacist suggests, 'I don't know what you bought before, maybe you can bring in the empty container next time.'

'Sure,' the blonde replies. 'I'll bring it with me tomorrow.'

The next day, the blonde walks into the shop again and hands the pharmacist an almost-empty deodorant stick.

'This is just a normal deodorant,' the pharmacist tells her. 'You use it under your arms.'

'No, it is not,' the blonde answers. 'It says so here – "To apply, push up bottom".'

A blonde received a certificate for helicopter flying lessons for her birthday. One day she was bored and decided to give it a try.

When she arrived at the helipad, the instructor said, 'Well, there's only one helicopter here, and it only has one seat. If I show you how to do it, do you mind going up solo?'

'No problem, I can handle it,' replied the blonde.

He showed her the inner workings of the helicopter and sent her on her way, only asking that she radio in every 400ft, just to make sure everything was going smoothly.

At 400ft, she radioed in saying 'Wow! This is so much fun!'

At 800 ft she radioed in again saying, 'This is pretty easy, I could do this all day!'

The instructor waited and waited for her to radio in at 1200 ft, but he didn't hear from the blonde. Soon he heard a crash in the field next to the station. He ran out to find that the blonde crashed! Luckily she survived.

'What happened?' he exclaimed.

'Well, I was doing fine, but, I started to get cold, so I just turned off the big fan.'

Q: Why do blondes take the pill?
A: So they know which day of the week it is.

A policeman pulled a blonde over after she'd been driving the wrong way up a one-way street.

'Do you know where you were going?' he asks her.

'No, but wherever it is, it must be bad, because everyone else was leaving.'

TOP 10 BLONDE INVENTIONS

1. Waterproof towel.
2. Solar-powered torch.
3. Submarine screen door.
4. A book on how to read.
5. Inflatable dart board.
6. Dictionary index.
7. Ejector seat in a helicopter.
8. Powdered water.
9. Pedal-powered wheel chair.
10. Waterproof tea bags.

The blonde's attempt on Mount Everest was a valiant effort, but it failed. He ran out of scaffolding.

A blonde, a brunette, and a redhead are escaping from jail. The police are on their tails so the brunette climbs up a tree to hide.

A police officer walks up to the tree and yells, 'Who's there?'

'Tweet tweet,' replies the brunette.

All appears well so the police officer walks away.

The redhead has hidden up the next tree and as the officer walks past it he shouts, 'Who's there?'

The redhead, thinking quickly, says 'Meow'.

The officer goes on to the next tree, where the blonde is hiding.

'Who's there?' he calls.

'Moooo,' says the blonde.

Q: Why are blonde jokes so short?
A: So brunettes can remember them.

Q: How can you tell if a blonde has been using the computer?
A: The joystick is wet.

Q: What is the quickest way to get into a blonde's pants?
A: Pick them up off the floor.

Q: Why don't blondes play Frisbee?
A: It hurts their teeth.

Two blondes were travelling through the Dorset countryside when they saw a sign saying 'CLEAN REST ROOM AHEAD.' So they did.

A blonde was trying to sell her car, but she was having a lot of problems selling it as it had 300,000km on the clock. She was lamenting her problem one day when a brunette workmate pulled her aside.

'There is a possibility to make the car easier to sell, but it's not legal,' said the brunette.

'That doesn't matter,' replied the blonde. 'I just want to sell it.'

'OK,' said the brunette. 'Here's the address of a friend of mine. He owns a car repair shop. Tell him I sent you and he will turn the counter in your car back to 50,000km. That will make it easier to sell.'

'Great,' said the blonde. 'I'll give it a try.'

A few weeks later the brunette asked the blonde, 'Did you sell your car?'

'No,' replied the blonde. 'Why should I? It only has 50,000km on it.'

A blonde walks into an electronics store and says, 'I'd like to buy that television please.'

The salesperson replies, 'I'm sorry. We don't sell to blondes here.'

The blonde goes home and dyes her hair brown. She returns to the store a few days later and again asks to buy the TV.

'I told you, we don't sell to blondes. Please go home!' the salesperson tells her.

The blonde goes home, shaves her head and puts on a baseball cap. She waits a few days once again goes to the shop to buy the television.

'We just don't sell to blondes here. It's store policy. Please, give up. Go home!' the salesperson exclaims.

'Look I dyed my hair, and you still knew I was blonde. I shaved my head and wore a hat, but you still knew I was blonde! How do you do it?' she asks exasperated.

The salesperson points to the item she wants to buy. 'Well, first of all, that's a microwave.'

Two blonde blokes landed themselves a job at a sawmill. Just before morning tea one yelled: 'Help! I lost me finger!'

'Have you now?' said the first blonde. 'And how did you do that?'

'I just touched this big spinning thing here like thi- Darn! There goes another one!'

Three blondes are attempting to change a light bulb. Finally, one of them decides to call 000.

'Help!' she says. 'We need help. We are three blondes changing a light bulb.'

'Hm!' replies the operator. 'You put in a fresh bulb?'

'Yes.'

'The power in the house is on?'

'Of course.'

'And the switch is on?'

'Yes, yes.'

'And the bulb still won't light up?'

'No, it's working fine.'

'Then what's the problem?' asks the operator.

'We got dizzy spinning the ladder around and we all fell and hurt ourselves.'

Tired of the blonde-bashing, it all becomes too much for one blonde who decides to commit suicide by hanging herself from a tree in the park. A few days later a man walks past the tree with his dog and spots her hanging from the tree. He asks the blonde what she is doing.

'I'm hanging myself,' she replies.

'You're supposed to put the noose around your neck, not your waist,' says the onlooker.

'I tried that,' replies the blonde, 'but I couldn't breathe.'

Two blondes were walking down the street when they spotted a face-powder compact on the footpath. They picked it up to see who it belonged to so they could return it.

'This person looks familiar,' said the first blonde, opening it up.

The second one said, 'Let me see. Silly, that's me!'

Q: Why don't blondes eat bananas?
A: They can't find the zipper.

Q: How did the blonde try to kill the fish?
A: She tried to drown it.

Q: What's the difference between a blonde and a 747?
A: Not everyone has been in a 747.

A blonde was walking along when she looked up to see a bird flying overhead. Suddenly, the bird dropped a load when it was directly over her.

The blonde said, 'Good thing I had my mouth open, or that would've hit me right in the face!'

A cop was driving down a country road when he saw a car in a ditch. He pulled over to see if anyone was in the car.

A blonde popped her head out the window and said, 'Oh officer, thank god. I was in an accident!'

'Well I can see that! Are you OK?' replied the officer.

The blonde nodded.

'What happened?'

'It was so strange. I was driving down the road and from nowhere a tree jumped in front of me, so I swerved to the other side and there was another tree, so I swerved again, but another one was there, so one last time I swerved to the other side but the damn tree got me and sent me into this ditch!'

The officer started laughing hard.

'What's so funny?' the blonde asked.

'Miss, there are no trees on this road for miles. That was your car air freshener swinging back and forth!'

Q: What is a blonde's idea of safe sex?
A: Locking the car doors.

A blonde with two very red ears went to see her doctor. The doctor asked her what had happened.

'I was ironing a shirt and the phone rang,' she said. 'But instead of picking up the phone, I accidentally picked up the iron and stuck it to my ear.'

'Jeezus!' the doctor exclaimed in disbelief. 'So, what happened to your other ear?'

'My friend rang back.'

A blonde was down on her luck. In order to raise some money, she decided to kidnap a kid and hold him for ransom. She went to the playground, grabbed a kid and took him behind a tree.

Then she wrote a note.

'I have kidnapped your kid. Tomorrow morning, put $10,000 in a paper bag and put it under the gum tree next to the slide on the north side of the playground. Signed, Blonde.'

The blonde then taped the note to the kid's shirt and sent him home to show it to his parents. The next morning the blonde checked, and sure enough, a paper bag was sitting beneath the gum tree.

The blonde opened the bag and found the $10,000 with a note that said, 'How could you do this to a fellow blonde?'

Two blonde blokes walk into a pet shop and go to the bird section.

One says to the other, 'That's them!'

The clerk comes over and asks if he can help them.

'Yeah, we'll take four of them birds in that cage up there. Put them into a paper bag.'

The clerk does so and the two guys pay for the birds and leave the shop. They get into a van and drive until they are high up in the hills and stop at the top of a cliff with a 500ft drop.

'This looks like a good place, eh?' asks the first blonde.

'Oh, yeah, this looks good,' replies the second.

They flip a coin and the first blonde gets to go first. He takes two birds out of the bag, places them on his shoulders and jumps off the cliff.

The second blonde watches as his mate drops off the edge and a few seconds later he hears a *splat*!

He looks over the edge of the cliff and shakes his head. 'Blow that, this budgie jumping is too dangerous for me!' he says.

A young blonde was on holiday in north Queensland. She was desperate for a pair of genuine crocodile shoes but was reluctant to pay the high prices the local vendors were asking.

After becoming very frustrated with the 'no haggle' attitude of one of the shopkeepers, the blonde shouted, 'Maybe I'll just go out and catch my own crocodile so I can get a pair of shoes at a reasonable price!'

'By all means, be my guest. Maybe you'll be lucky and catch yourself a big one!' said the shopkeeper.

Determined, the blonde turned and headed for the mangroves, set on catching herself a crocodile.

Later in the day, the shopkeeper was driving home, when he spotted the young woman standing waist deep in the water, shotgun in hand. Just then, he saw a huge 4m croc swimming quickly toward her.

She took aim, killed the creature, and with a great deal of effort hauled it on to the bank. Lying nearby were several more of the dead creatures. The shopkeeper watched in amazement as the blonde flipped the crocodile on its back.

'Damn it, this one isn't wearing any shoes either!' she shouted in frustration.

A blonde, a brunette and a redhead are shipwrecked on a desert island together. One day they are walking along the beach when one sees a bottle lying on the ground. It turns out there's a genie inside, and as there are three wishes they get one each.

The brunette goes first and says: 'I miss my family; I wish I was home again.'

Poof! The brunette disappears.

The redhead takes her turn. She too wishes to be returned to her ancestral home, and her wish is granted.

The blonde stands alone on the beach and starts to cry.

'I wish my friends would come back,' she says.

Three blondes were all vying for the last available position on the local police force. The detective conducting the interview looked at the three of them and said, 'So you all want to be cops, eh?'

The blondes all nodded.

The detective got up, opened a filing cabinet and pulled out a folder. Sitting back down, he opened it up and withdrew a photograph.

'To be a detective, you have to be able to *detect*. You must be able to notice things such as distinguishing features and oddities such as scars, etc.'

He stuck the photo in the face of the first blonde and withdrew it after two seconds.

'Now,' he said, 'did you notice any distinguishing features about this man?'

'Yes, I did,' said the blonde immediately. 'He only has one eye!'

The detective shook his head and said, 'Of course he only has one eye in this picture! It's a *profile* of his face! You're dismissed!'

The first blonde hung her head and walked out of the office. The detective then turned to the second blonde, stuck the photo in her face for two seconds and pulled it back.

'What about you? Notice anything unusual or outstanding about this man?'

'Yep! He only has one ear!' replied the second blonde.

The detective put his head in his hand. 'Didn't you hear what I just said to the other lady? This is a *profile* of the man's face! Of course you can only see one ear! You're excused, too! You'd never make a good detective!'

The second blonde walked sheepishly out of the office and the detective turned his attention to the last blonde.

'This is probably a waste of time, but . . .'

He flashed the photo in her face for a couple of seconds.

'Alright. Did *you* notice anything distinguishing or unusual about this man?'

'Yes, I did. This man wears contact lenses.'

The detective frowned, took another look at the picture and began looking at some of the papers in the folder.

He looked up at the blonde with a puzzled expression. 'You're absolutely right! His bio says he wears contacts. How in the world could you tell that by looking at this picture?'

'Duh! He has only one eye and one ear, he certainly can't wear glasses.'

Heard the one about the three blondes that went ice fishing and didn't catch anything? By the time they cut a hole big enough for the boat to fit in, it was time to go home.

A friend of mine's a blonde and I asked her to take me to the airport. We were on the freeway and she looked up at a sign that said 'Airport Left'.

So she turned around and went home.

Q: How can you tell if a blonde is having a bad day?
A: Her tampon is behind her ear and she can't find her pen!

Two telephone company crews were putting up telephone poles. At the end of the day, the company foreman asked the first crew how many poles they had put in the ground.

'Fifteen,' said one of the workmen.

'Not bad, not bad at all,' said the foreman.

Turning to the blonde crew he asked the same question.

'Four,' said one of the blondes.

'Four?' the foreman yelled. 'The others did fifteen, and you only did four?'

'Yes, but look at how much of each pole they left sticking out of the ground.

Eleven people were clinging precariously to a wildly swinging rope suspended from a crumbling outcrop on Mount Everest. Ten were blonde, one was brunette.

For the group to survive one of them would have to sacrifice their life and let go of the rope. If that didn't happen the rope would break and everyone would perish.

For an agonising few moments no one volunteered. Finally the brunette gave a truly touching speech saying she would sacrifice herself to save the lives of the others.

And all the blondes applauded.

A blonde arrived for her first golf lesson and the pro asked her to take a swing at a ball to see how well she'd do.

The blonde did so and completely stuffed the shot.

The pro said, 'Your swing is good but you're gripping the club too hard. Grip the club gently as you would your husband's penis.'

The blonde took another shot and nailed the ball 350 metres straight down the fairway.

The pro said, 'That was excellent!! Let's try it again, only this time take the club out of your mouth.'

Two blondes were out hunting. It started getting dark and they realised that they were lost.

'I've heard that if you get lost in the bush you should shoot three shots into the air and then sit down and wait for someone to find you.' said the first blonde.

So they did. A few hours went by and no one came so they decided to shoot three more shots into the air, but still no one came. It was late now and they were going to try again when the second blonde said, 'Someone better hurry up and save us . . . we only have two arrows left.'

A blonde bloke finds a genie lamp and rubs it and out comes the genie.

'Master you have released me from the lamp and I grant you three wishes, what would you like?'

The blonde bloke scratches his head.

'A bottle of Guinness that never gets empty,' he says.

'Granted master,' retorts the genie and produces the bottle.

The blonde bloke is delighted and gets drunk on this one magic Guinness bottle for weeks. Then he remembers that he has two other wishes.

He rubs the lamp again and the genie appears.

'Yes master, you have two more wishes, what would you like?'

'You know that magic, never-ending Guinness bottle?' he asks the genie. 'Well, for my final two wishes, I'd like another two of them.'

Two blondes opened a swimming pool during a drought. They put up a sign at the gate.

'Due to a water shortage, only lanes one and four will be open. Thank you.'

Three girls are walking in a magical forest. Suddenly, a witch comes out of the woods.

'Each of you has to say one good thing about herself,' says the witch. 'If you lie, I will make you disappear!'

The first girl, a brunette, says, 'I think I am a very kind and thoughtful person'.

'Poof!' and she disappears.

The second girl, a redhead, says, 'I think I am very sexy'.

'Poof!' she also disappears.

The third girl, a blonde, says, 'Well, I think –'

'Poof!' and she is gone.

A man was surf fishing along the beach when he found a bottle. He looked around but didn't see anyone so he opened it. A genie appeared and thanked the man for letting him out.

'I am so grateful to get out of that bottle that I will grant you any wish,' said the genie, 'but I can only grant one.'

The man thought for a while and finally said, 'I have always wanted to go to Hawaii and fish along the beautiful beaches. I've never been able to go because I can't fly. Planes are much too frightening for me. On a boat, I see all that water and I become very claustrophobic. So I wish for a road to be built from here to Hawaii.'

The genie thought for a few minutes and said, 'No, I don't think I can do that. Just think of all the work involved. Consider all the piling needed to hold up a highway and how deep they would have to go to reach the bottom of the ocean. Imagine the amount of pavement needed. No, that really is just too much to ask. Isn't there something else you desire?'

The man thought for a few minutes.

'Ok. There is one other thing I have always wanted. I would like to be able to understand my beautiful blonde wife. What makes her laugh and cry, why is she temperamental, why is she so difficult to get along with, when does she want attention and when doesn't she? Basically, what makes my beautiful, blonde wife tick.'

'So,' replied the genie, 'do you want two lanes or four?'

A blonde goes into a drug store to buy some condoms because her friend told her that she should learn about safe sex. She walks up to the pharmacist and asks: 'How much for a box of rubbers?'

'They're $6 for a box of three,' he replies. 'Plus 60c for the tax.'

'Oh,' replies the blonde, 'I always wondered how they kept them on.'

A woman hired a contractor to repaint the interior of her house. The woman walked the man through the second floor of her home and told him what colours she wanted for each room. As they walked through the first room, the woman said, 'I think I would like this room in a cream colour.'

The contractor wrote on his clipboard, walked to the window, opened it and yelled out, 'Green side up!' He then closed the window and continued following the woman to the next room.

The woman looked confused, but proceeded with her tour. 'In this room, I was thinking of an off-blue.' Again, the contractor wrote this down, went to the window, opened it and yelled out, 'Green side up!'

This baffled the woman, but she was hesitant to say anything. In the next room, the woman said she would like it painted in a light rose colour. And once more, the contractor opened the window and yelled, 'Green side up!'

Struck with curiosity, the woman mustered up the nerve to ask, 'Why do you keep yelling "Green side up" out my window every time I tell you the colour I would like the room?'

'Because across the street I have a crew of blondes laying instant lawn.'

It was a really hot day and a blonde decided she would buy a drink. She went to a vending machine and when she put her money in, a can of drink came out. So she kept putting money in.

She was there for so long that a line formed behind her. Finally, a guy in line said, 'Will you hurry up? We're all hot and thirsty!'

'No way,' replied the blonde. 'I'm still winning!'

Q: How many blondes does it take to milk a cow?
A: Eleven. One to hold the udders, and 10 to lift the cow up and down.

A bloke walks into a pub with a crocodile on a leash and puts it up on the bar. He turns to the amazed drinkers.

'Here's the deal,' he says. 'I'll open this crocodile's mouth and place my genitals inside. Then the croc will close his mouth for one minute. He'll then open his mouth and I'll remove my wedding tackle unscathed. In return for witnessing this spectacle, each of you will buy me a drink.'

After a few moments' silence the crowd murmurs approval.

The man stands up on the bar, drops his trousers, and places his privates in the crocodile's mouth. The croc closes his mouth as the crowd gasps. After a minute, the man grabs a beer bottle and raps the crocodile hard on the top of its head. The croc opens his mouth and the man removes his genitals – unscathed as promised.

The crowd cheers and the first of his free drinks is delivered. The man calls for silence and makes another offer. 'I'll pay anyone $1000 who's willing to give it a try'.

A hush falls over the crowd. After a while, a hand goes up at the back. It's a blonde.

'I'll try,' she says. 'But only if you promise not to hit me on the head with that beer bottle.'

While out one morning in the park, a jogger found a brand new tennis ball, and, seeing no-one around that it might belong to, he slipped it into the pocket of his shorts.

Later, on his way home, he stopped at the pedestrian crossing, waiting for the lights to change. A blonde girl standing next to him eyed the large bulge in his shorts.

'What's that?' she asked, her eyes gleaming with lust.

'Tennis ball,' came the breathless reply.

'Oh,' said the blonde girl sympathetically, 'that must be painful. I had tennis elbow once.'

Three women are about to be executed – a redhead, a brunette, and a blonde. The guard brings the redhead forward and the executioner asks if she has any last requests. She says no, and the executioner shouts, 'Ready! Aim –'

Suddenly the redhead yells, 'Earthquake!'

Everyone is startled and they all throw themselves on the ground for safety. When they look up the redhead has escaped.

The guard brings the brunette forward and the executioner asks if she has any last requests. She says no, and the executioner shouts, 'Ready! Aim –'

Suddenly the brunette yells, 'Tornado!'

Again, everyone is startled and dives for cover. When they look up, the brunette has escaped.

By now the blonde has it all worked out. The guard brings her forward and the executioner asks if she has any last requests. She says no, and the executioner shouts, 'Ready! Aim –'

And the blonde yells, 'Fire!'

Boyfriend: Why do you never scream my name when you have an orgasm?

Blonde: Because you are never there.

Q: What nursery rhyme do blondes know meticulously off by heart?

A: Hump-me, dump-me . . .

Q: Why did the blonde have lipstick on her steering wheel?

A: She was trying to blow the horn.

A man watched out his window as the blonde next door went outside to check her mailbox. She had no mail, so she went back inside her house.

Two minutes later, the same blonde went outside for the second time to check her mailbox, and still, she had no mail. The man was confused.

One minute later, the blonde came out for a third time and again she had no mail.

This time, her neighbour went over to her and said, 'The mailman won't be here for another three hours, why do you keep on checking your mail?'

'Oh, because my computer keeps on saying, 'You've got mail'.

A blonde had two horses. She couldn't tell her two horses apart so she decided to ask her neighbour for some advice.

'Maybe you should nick the ears of one horse,' said her neighbour, 'and then you could tell them apart.'

So the blonde went home and did that. The next day the blonde went to check up on her horses. However she still could not tell them apart, because the other horse also had a nicked ear. She went back over to her neighbour's.

'My other horse has a nicked ear, too.' she said, 'Do you have any other ideas as to how to tell them apart? They are both girls.'

'Hmmmm.' said her neighbour, 'cut one's tail shorter than the other.'

So the blonde went home and did that. The next day, though, when she looked at them, both horses had the same length of tail.

As a last resort the neighbour suggested that she should consider measuring the horses. Maybe one stood taller than the other one.

The blonde did this and excitedly rushed home and phoned her neighbour. 'You were right!' she said. 'The black horse is bigger than the white one!'

D erek drove his brand new Mercedes to his favourite bar, and put it in the car park at the back. He went inside, where the bar was being looked after by Beverley, the regular waitress.

Beverley was a pretty blonde, and as Derek walked into the bar, she greeted him happily. He bought a drink, and went and sat at a table.

A few minutes later, Beverley ran up to him yelling, 'Derek! Derek! I was putting the rubbish out the back and I just saw someone driving off with your new Mercedes!'

'Dear God! Did you try to stop him?'

'No,' she said, 'I did better than that! I got the licence plate number!'

CATS

MIRACLE CAT DIET

Here is the new Miracle Cat Diet! It will also work on humans. Just follow this diet for one week and you'll find that you look and feel better.

Good Luck!

Day One

Breakfast: Open can of expensive gourmet cat food. Any flavour as long as it cost more the 75c per can – and place ½ cup on your plate. Eat one bite of food; look around the room disdainfully. Knock the rest on the floor. Stare at the wall for awhile before stalking off into the other room.

Lunch: Four blades of grass and one lizard tail. Throw it back up on the cleanest carpet in your house.

Dinner: Catch a moth and play with it until it is almost dead. Eat one wing. Leave the rest to die.

Bedtime snack: Steal one green bean from your partner's plate. Bat it around the floor until it goes under the refrigerator. Steal one small piece of chicken and eat half of it. Leave the other half on the sofa. Throw out the remaining gourmet cat food from the can you opened this morning.

Day Two

Breakfast: Pick up the remaining chicken bite from the sofa. Knock it onto the carpet and bat it under the television set. Chew on the corner of the newspaper as your partner tries to read it.

Lunch: Break into the fresh French bread that you bought for your dinner party on Saturday. Lick the top of it all over. Take one bite out of the middle of the loaf.

Afternoon snack: Catch a large beetle and bring it into the house. Play toss and catch with it until it is mushy and half dead. Allow it to escape under the bed.

Dinner: Open a fresh can of dark-coloured gourmet cat food – tuna or beef works well. Eat it voraciously. Walk from your kitchen to the edge of the living room rug. Throw up on the rug. Step into it as you leave. Track footprints across the entire room.

Day Three

Breakfast: Drink part of the milk from your partner's cereal bowl when no one is looking. Splatter part of it on the closest polished aluminium appliance you can find.

Lunch: Catch a small bird and bring it into the house. Play with it on top of your down-filled comforter. Make sure the bird is seriously injured but not dead before you abandon it for someone else to deal with.

Dinner: Beg and cry until you are given some ice cream or milk in a bowl of your own. Take three licks and then turn the bowl over on the floor.

Final Day

Breakfast:	Eat six bugs, any type, making sure to leave a collection of legs, wings and antennae on the bathroom floor. Drink lots of water. Throw up the bugs and all of the water on your partner's pillow.
Lunch:	Remove the chicken skin from last night's chicken takeaway leftovers that your partner put in the rubbish bin. Drag the skin across the floor several times. Chew it in a corner and then abandon it.
Dinner:	Open another can of expensive gourmet cat food. Select a flavour that is especially runny, like chicken and giblets in gravy. Lick off all the gravy and leave the actual meat to dry and get hard.

WHAT IS YOUR MOGGY SAYING TO YOU?

Miaow	Feed me.
Meeow	Pet me.
Mrooww	I love you.
Miioo-oo-oo	I am in love and must meet my betrothed outside beneath the hedge. Don't wait up.
Mrow	I feel like making noise.
Rrrow-mawww	Please, the time has come to clean the kitty litter.
Rrrow-miawww	I have remedied the kitty litter untidiness by shovelling the contents as far out of the box as practical.
Miaowmiaow	Play with me.
Miaowmioaw	Have you noticed the shortage of available cat toys in this room?

Mioawmioaw	Since I can find nothing better to play with, I shall see what happens when I sharpen my claws on this handy piece of furniture.
Raowwwww	I think I shall now spend time licking the most private parts of my anatomy.
Mrowwwww	I am now recalling, with sorrow, that some of my private parts did not return with me from that visit to the vet.
Roww-maww-roww	I am so glad to see that you have returned home with both arms full of groceries. I will now rub myself against your legs and attempt to trip you as you walk towards the kitchen.
Gakk-ak-ak	My digestive passages seem to have formed a hairball. Wherever could this have come from? I shall leave it here upon carpet.
Mow	Snuggling is a good idea.
Moww	Shedding is pretty good too.
Mowww!	I was enjoying snuggling and shedding in the warm clean laundry until you removed me so unkindly.
Miaow! Miaow!	I have discovered that, although one may be able to wedge one's body through the gap behind the stove and into that little drawer filled with pots and pans, the reverse path is slightly more difficult to navigate.
Mraakk!	Oh, small bird! Please come over here.
SsssRoww!	I believe that I have found a woodchuck or similar animal.
Mmmrowmmm	It is certain that the best tasting fish is one you have caught yourself.
Mmmmmmm	If I sit in the sunshine for another hour or so, I think I shall be satisfied.

Mreoaw	Please ask room service to send up another can of tuna fish.
Mreeeow	Do you serve catnip with that?
Mroow	I have forced my body into a tiny space in order to look cute. How am I doing?
Miaooww! Mriaow!	Since you are using the can opener, I am certain that you understand the value of a well-fed and pampered cat. Please continue.

10 THOUGHTS ABOUT CATS

1. Dogs believe they are human. Cats believe they are God.
2. Do not meddle in the affairs of cats, for they are subtle and will piss on your computer.
3. There is no snooze button on a cat who wants breakfast.
4. Thousands of years ago, cats were worshipped as gods. Cats have never forgotten this.
5. Cats are smarter than dogs. You can't get eight cats to pull a sled through snow.
6. From a cat's point of view, all things belong to cats.
7. Cats operate on the principle that it never does any harm to ask for what you want.
8. Managing senior programmers is like herding cats.
9. Dogs come when they're called; cats take a message and get back to you later.
10. Cats aren't clean, they're just covered with cat spit.

LAWS OF FELINE PHYSICS

Law of Cat Inertia

A cat at rest will tend to remain at rest, unless acted upon by some outside force – such as the opening of cat food, or a nearby scurrying mouse.

Law of Cat Motion

A cat will move in a straight line, unless there is a really good reason to change direction.

Law of Cat Magnetism

All blue blazers and black sweaters attract cat hair in direct proportion to the darkness of the fabric.

Law of Cat Thermodynamics

Heat flows from a warmer to a cooler body, except in the case of a cat, in which case all heat flows to the cat.

Law of Cat Stretching

A cat will stretch to a distance proportional to the length of the nap just taken.

Law of Cat Sleeping

All cats must sleep with people whenever possible, in a position as uncomfortable for the people involved, and as comfortable for the cat, as possible.

Law of Cat Elongation

A cat can make her body long enough to reach any counter top that has anything remotely interesting on it.

Law of Cat Obstruction

A cat must lie on the floor in a position to obstruct the maximum amount of human foot traffic.

Law of Cat Acceleration

A cat will accelerate at a constant rate, until he gets good and ready to stop.

Law of Dinner Table Attendance

Cats must attend all meals when anything good is served.

Law of Rug Configuration

No rug may remain in its naturally flat state for very long.

Law of Obedience Resistance

A cat's resistance varies in proportion to a human's desire for her to do something.

First Law of Energy Conservation

Cats know that energy can neither be created nor destroyed and will, therefore, use as little energy as possible.

Second Law of Energy Conservation

Cats also know that energy can only be stored by a lot of napping.

Law of Refrigerator Observation

If a cat watches a refrigerator long enough, someone will come along and take out something good to eat.

Law of Electric Blanket Attraction

Turn on an electric blanket and a cat will jump into bed at the speed of light.

Law of Random Comfort Seeking

A cat will always seek, and usually take over, the most comfortable spot in any given room.

Law of Bag or Box Occupancy

All bags and boxes in a given room must contain a cat within the earliest possible nanosecond.

Law of Cat Embarrassment

A cat's irritation rises in direct proportion to her embarrassment multiplied by the amount of human laughter.

Law of Milk Consumption

A cat will drink his weight in milk squared, just to show you he can.

Law of Furniture Replacement

A cat's desire to scratch furniture is directly proportional to the cost of the furniture.

Law of Cat Landing

A cat will always land in the softest place possible; often the mid-section of an unsuspecting, reclining human.

Law of Fluid Displacement

Acat immersed in milk will displace her own volume, minus the amount of milk consumed.

Law of Cat Disinterest

Acat's interest level will vary in inverse proportion to the amount of effort a human expends in trying to interest him.

Law of Pill Rejection

Any pill given to a cat has the potential energy to reach escape velocity.

Law of Cat Composition

A cat is composed of matter + anti-matter + it doesn't matter.

EASY INSTRUCTIONS ON HOW TO GIVE YOUR CAT A PILL

1. Pick up the cat and cradle it in the crook of your left arm, as if holding a baby.
2. Position right forefinger and thumb on either side of cat's mouth and gently apply pressure to the cheeks while holding the pill in your right hand.
3. As the cat opens its mouth, pop pill into mouth.
4. Allow cat to close mouth and swallow.
5. Retrieve pill from floor and cat from behind the sofa.
6. Cradle cat in left arm and repeat the process.
7. Retrieve cat from bedroom, and throw the soggy pill away.
8. Take a new pill from foil wrap, cradle cat in left arm, holding rear paws tightly with left hand.

9. Force jaws open and push pill to back of mouth with right forefinger.

10. Hold mouth shut for a count of 10.

11. Retrieve pill from the goldfish bowl and cat from top of wardrobe.

12. Call spouse from garden.

13. Kneel on floor with cat wedged firmly between knees, holding front and rear paws.

14. Ignore low growls emitted by cat.

15. Get spouse to hold cat's head firmly with one hand while forcing wooden ruler into mouth.

16. Drop pill down ruler and rub cat's throat vigorously.

17. Retrieve cat from curtain rail; get another pill from foil wrap.

18. Make a note to buy new ruler and repair curtains.

19. Carefully sweep shattered figurines from hearth and set aside for repair later.

20. Wrap cat in a large towel and get spouse to lie on cat with its head just visible from below spouse's armpit.

21. Put pill in the end of a drinking straw, force cat's mouth open with a pencil and blow down the drinking straw.

22. Check the label to ensure pill is not harmful to humans and drink a glass of water to take the taste away.

23. Apply a band-aid to spouse's forearm and remove blood from carpet with cold water and soap.

24. Retrieve cat from neighbour's shed.

25. Get another pill.

26. Place cat in a cupboard and close the door onto cat's neck, leaving head showing.

27. Force mouth open with a dessert spoon.

28. Flick pill down throat with elastic band.

29. Fetch a screwdriver from garage and put the cupboard door back on its hinges.

30. Apply a cold compress to cheek and check records for the date of your last tetanus shot.

31. Throw T-shirt away and fetch a new one from the bedroom.
32. Ring the fire brigade to retrieve cat from the tree across the road.
33. Apologise to the neighbour who crashed into a fence while swerving to avoid cat.
34. Take the last pill from foil wrap.
35. Tie the cat's front paws to the rear paws with garden twine and bind tightly to the leg of the dining table.
36. Find heavy duty pruning gloves in shed.
37. Force cat's mouth open with a small spanner.
38. Push pill into mouth followed by a large piece of fillet steak.
39. Hold cat's head vertically and pour 500ml of water down throat to wash pill down.
40. Get spouse to drive you to emergency room; sit quietly while the doctor stitches your fingers and forearm and removes pill remnants from your right eye.
41. Stop by a furniture shop on the way home to order a new table.
42. Arrange for the vet to make a house call.

COPS

A policeman, who's a disagreeable sort, stops a local farmer on a minor traffic infringement and berates the poor man this way and that, dressing him down most unfairly. After the lecture, which the farmer takes well, the constable starts writing the man up.

As he's writing, he begins to swat at flies circling his head.

'The circle flies botherin' you, are they?' asks the farmer.

'Why do you call 'em circle flies, old man?'

'We call 'em that on the farm 'cause we find 'em flying around and around the horses' behinds,' says the farmer.

'Are you calling me a horse's arse?' snarls the cop.

'Oh, saints, no, I wouldn't think of such a thing.'

The cop goes back to writing.

'Kinda hard to fool the flies, though.'

A cop pulls a guy over for speeding and the guy's defence is, 'I was just going with the flow of traffic.'

'Ever go fishing?' asks the cop.

'Yeah.'

'Ever catch all the fish?'

SEVEN THINGS TO DO IN A DRIVING TEST

1. Rev the car really high, turn to the examiner, and say with an evil look, 'Buckle up!'
2. Turn the radio on. When the examiner goes to turn it off slap his/her hand.
3. After the examiner gets in the car, pop the hood, get out and check the oil.

4. Fill your car with beer bottles.
5. In the middle of driving, put your arm around the examiner.
6. Swear at everybody on the road.
7. When you stop at a light, start revving the engine while looking back and forth between the person next to you and the light.

THINGS NOT TO SAY TO A POLICE OFFICER

- I can't reach my licence unless you hold my beer.
- Aren't you the guy from the Village People?
- Hey, you must've been doing about 190kph to keep up with me. Good job!
- I thought you had to be in relatively good physical condition to be a police officer.
- Yes, I know there are no other cars around. That's how far ahead of me they are.
- Gee that's terrific. The last officer only gave me a warning, too!
- You're not going to check the boot, are you?
- Sorry, officer. I didn't realise my radar detector wasn't turned on.
- Listen, pal, I pay your salary!
- Want to race to the station, Sparky?
- On the way to the station let's get a six pack.
- You'll never get those cuffs on me . . . you big pussy!
- Come on write the friggin' ticket, the bar closes in 20 minutes!
- How long is this going to take? Your wife is expecting me.
- Hey big boy, is that your nightstick or are you just glad to see me?
- You know, I was going to be a cop too, but I decided to finish year seven instead.
- So, uh, are you on the take, or what?
- Do you know why you pulled me over? Good, at least one of us does.
- So are you still a little crabby because your mother didn't let you play with a gun when you were little?

Two prisoners escaped from custody. One was seven feet tall, the other four feet.

Police searched high and low for them.

Q: Did you hear about the criminal acrobat?
A: He turned himself in.

Policeman: You're not allowed to fish here.
Boy: I'm not fishing. I'm giving my pet worm a bath.

Policeman: You need a permit to catch fish.
Boy: I'm doing fine just using worms.

Did you hear the one about the police who arrested two kids, one for stealing a battery and one for playing with fireworks?

They charged one and let the other one off.

Q: How do prisoners call home?
A: With cell phones.

Q: What do traffic policemen put on their sandwiches?
A: Traffic jam.

Q: What were the gangster's final words?
A: 'What is that violin doing in my violin case?'

All the toilet seats have been stolen from the Police Station.
The cops have nothing to go on!

The police complimented me on my driving today. They left a note on my windscreen that said 'Parking Fine.'

Q: Why was the baby pencil crying?
A: His mum was doing a long sentence.

Woman: Officer, officer, someone's stolen my wig.
WPoliceman: Don't worry, we'll comb the area.

Traffic Cop: Can you please blow into this bag.
TMotorist: Why, are your chips too hot?

Twenty puppies were stolen from a pet shop. Police are warning people to look out for anyone selling hot dogs.

A squad car driver was covering a quiet beat out in the sticks, when he was amazed to find a former police lieutenant covering the same beat.

He stopped the car and asked, 'Why, Smithson, this wouldn't be your new beat way out here in the sticks, would it?'

'That it is,' Smithson replied grimly, 'ever since I arrested Judge O'Shea on his way to the masquerade ball.'

'You mean you pinched his honour?'

'How was I to know that his convict suit was only a costume?'

'Well, that's life. There's a lesson in here somewhere.'

'That there is,' replied Smithson. 'Never book a judge by his cover.'

A farmer was involved in a terrible road accident with a large truck. He ended up in court fighting for a big compensation claim.

'I understand you're claiming damages for the injuries you're supposed to have suffered?' said the counsel for the insurance company.

'Yes, that's right,' replied the farmer.

'You claim you were injured in the accident, yet I have a signed police statement that says when the attending police officer asked you how you were feeling, you replied, "I've never felt better in my life." Is that the case?'

'Yeah, but –'

'A simple yes or no will suffice.'

'Yes,' replied the farmer quietly.

Then it was the turn of the farmer's counsel to ask the questions.

'Please tell the court the exact circumstance of events following the accident when you made your statement of health,' his lawyer said.

'Certainly,' replied the farmer. 'After the accident my horse was thrashing around with a broken leg and my poor old dog was howling in pain. This cop comes along, takes one look at my horse and shoots him dead. Then he goes over to my dog, looks at him and shoots him dead too. Then he comes straight over to me, with his gun still smoking, and asks me how I was feeling. Now, mate, what the hell would you have said to him?'

Three convicts were on the way to prison. They were each allowed to take one item with them to help them occupy their time while incarcerated.

On the bus, one turned to another and said, 'So, what did you bring?'

The second convict pulled out a box of paints. 'I'm going to use my time to study art. What did you bring?'

The first convict pulled out a deck of cards.

'I brought cards. I won't be bored. I can play poker, solitaire, gin and any number of other games.'

The third convict sat quietly aside, grinning to himself. The other two noticed and asked, 'Why are you so smug? What did you bring?'

The guy pulled out a box of tampons.

'What can you do with those?'

The third prisoner pointed to the box and replied, 'Well according to the box, I can go horseback riding, swimming and roller-skating.'

A young skinhead started a job on a farm. The boss sent him to the back paddocks to do some fencing work, but come evening, he was half an hour late.

The boss got on the CB radio to check if he was all right.

'I've got a problem, boss. I'm stuck 'ere. I've hit a pig!'

'Ah well, these things happen sometimes,' the boss said. 'Just drag the carcass off the road so nobody else hits it in the dark.'

'But he's not dead, boss. He's gotten tangled up on the bull-bar, and I've tried to untangle him, but he's kicking and squealing, and he's real big boss. I'm afraid he's going to hurt me!'

'Never mind,' said the boss. 'There's a .303 under the tarp in the back. Get that out and shoot him. Then drag the carcass off the road and come on home.'

'OK, boss.'

Another half an hour went by, but there was still not a peep from the kid. The boss got back on the CB. 'What's the problem, son?'

'Well, I did what you said boss, but I'm still stuck.'

'What's up? Did you drag the pig off the road like I said?'

'Yeah boss, but his motorcycle is still jammed under the truck.'

A highway patrolman waited outside a popular bar, hoping for a bust. At closing time everyone came out and he spotted his potential quarry. The man was so obviously inebriated that he could barely walk. He stumbled around the parking lot for a few minutes, looking for his car. After trying his keys on five other cars, he finally found his own vehicle.

He sat in the car a good 10 minutes, as the other patrons left. He turned his lights on, then off, wipers on, then off. He then started to pull forward into the grass, then he stopped.

Finally, when he was the last car, he pulled out onto the road and started to drive away. The patrolman, waiting for this, turned on his lights and pulled the man over. He administered the breathalyser test, and to his great surprise, the man blew a 0.00.

The patrolman was dumbfounded. 'This equipment must be broken!' he exclaimed.

'I doubt it,' said the man. 'Tonight I'm the designated decoy!'

A man in his 40s bought a new BMW and went out on the interstate for a nice evening drive. The top was down, the breeze was blowing through what was left of his hair, and he decided to open her up.

As the needle jumped up to 140kph, he suddenly saw flashing red and blue lights behind him.

'There's no way they can catch a BMW,' he thought to himself and opened her up further.

The needle hit 150, 160 . . . then the reality of the situation hit him.

'What the hell am I doing?' he thought and pulled over.

The cop came up to him, took his licence without a word, and examined it and the car. 'It's been a long day,' said the cop, 'this is the end of my shift, and it's Friday the 13th. I don't feel like more paperwork, so if you can give me an excuse for your driving that I haven't heard before, you can go.'

The guy thinks for a second and says, 'Last week my wife ran off with a cop. I was afraid you were trying to give her back.'

'Have a nice weekend,' said the officer.

COUNTRY FOLK

On a drive in the country, a city slicker noticed a farmer lifting a pig up to an apple tree and holding the pig there as it ate one apple after another.

'Maybe I don't know what I'm talking about,' said the city slicker, 'but if you just shook the tree so the apples fell to the ground, wouldn't it save a lot of time?'

'Time?' said the farmer. 'What does time matter to a pig?'

Billy-Bob and Ray were talking one afternoon. Billy-Bob tells Ray, 'Ya know, I reckon I'm 'bout ready for a holiday. Only this year I'm gonna do it a little different. The last few years, I took your advice about where to go. Three years ago you said to go to Hawaii. I went to Hawaii and Earline got pregnant. Then two years ago, you told me to go to the Bahamas, and Earline got pregnant again. Last year you suggested Tahiti and darned if Earline didn't get pregnant again.'

'So, what you gonna do this year that's different?' asks Ray.

'This year I'm taking Earline with me.'

The first grade class gathered around the teacher for a game of 'Guess the Animal'. The first picture the teacher held up was of a cat.

'OK, boys and girls,' she said brightly, 'can anyone tell me what this is?'

'I know, I know, it's a cat!' yelled a little boy.

'Very good, Eddie. Now, who knows what this animal is called?'

'That's a dog!' piped up the same little boy.

'Right, again. And what about this animal?' she asked, holding up a picture of a deer.

Silence fell over the class. After a minute or two, the teacher said, 'I'll give you a hint, children. It's something you're mother calls your father.'

'I know, I know,' screamed Eddie. 'It's a horny bastard!'

Two farmers were driving their tractor down the middle of a country road. A car comes around the corner breaks hard to avoid them, skids, tumbles twice and lands in a field.

Jimmy says to Seamus, 'It's just as well we got out of that field.'

Three dead bodies turn up at the mortuary, all with very big smiles on their faces. The coroner calls the police to tell them the causes of death.

'First body: Frenchman, 60, died of heart failure while making love to his mistress. Hence the enormous smile,' says the Coroner.

'Second body: Scotsman, 25, won a thousand dollars on the lottery, spent it all on whisky. Died of alcohol poisoning, hence the smile.'

'What of the third body?' asks the inspector.

'Ah, this is the most unusual one: Billy-Bob, the country lad from Oklahoma, 30, struck by lightning.'

'Why is he smiling then?'

'Thought he was having his picture taken.'

10 WAYS TO TELL IF YOUR CHURCH IS A COUNTRY CHURCH

1. The collection plates are hub-caps from a '56 Chevy.
2. High notes on the organ set the dogs on the floor to howling.
3. The choir robes were donated by Billy-Bob's BBQ, in fact they're aprons embroidered with his logo.

4. Opening day of duck season is recognised as an official church holiday.
5. In a congregation of 500 members, there are only seven last names in the church directory.
6. There is a special cake sale to raise funds for a new church septic tank.
7. Upon learning that Jesus fed the 5000, the men want to know whether the two fish were snapper or bream, and what bait was used to catch 'em.
8. The finance committee refuses to provide funds for the purchase of a chandelier because none of the members knows how to play one.
9. Baptism is referred to as 'branding'.
10. The baptismal is a galvanised wash tub.

10 WAYS TO TELL IF YOU'RE A STAR WARS FAN FROM THE COUNTRY

1. Your Jedi robe is in jungle camouflage.
2. You have used your light sabre to open a bottle of VB.
3. You have a cousin who bears a strong resemblance to Chewbacca.
4. You can easily describe the taste of barbecued Ewok.
5. You have a land-speeder up on blocks in the front yard.
6. You wear your Darth Vader helmet when driving the tractor.
7. Wookies are offended by your BO.
8. You were the only person drinking Jack Daniels during the cantina scene.
9. Although you had to kill him, you kinda thought that Jabba the Hutt had a pretty good handle on how to treat his women.
10. When watching TV, you've used The Force to get yourself another beer so you didn't have to wait for a commercial break.

LETTER TO A SON

Dear son,

I'm writing this real slow because I know you can't read fast. Your pop read that all accidents happen within 20km of home so we have moved. He now has a lovely new job with 700 men under him – he cuts grass at the cemetery. There was a washing machine at the new house, but it's not working too good. Last week I put in 12 shirts, pulled the chain and I haven't seen them since.

We can't send you the new address as the last family that lived here took the numbers with them so they wouldn't have to change their address.

We have some good news and some bad news. Your sister, Billy-Mae, had a baby yester morn. Don't know if it's a boy or girl so we don't know if you're an aunt or uncle.

Sadly, three of your friends went off the bridge last week in a car accident. One was driving, and the other two were in the back. The driver lived, as he rolled down the window and swam to safety. The other two drowned – they couldn't get the tailgate down.

Please write back. If you don't get this letter, let me know and I will send you another one.

Love, Ma

PS I was going to send you some money, but I'd already sealed the envelope.

TIPS FOR COUNTRY BUMPKINS WHO MOVE TO THE CITY

- Never take a beer to a job interview.
- Always identify people in your yard before shooting at them.
- It's considered tacky to take an esky to church.

- When decanting wine, make sure that you tilt the paper cup and pour slowly from the cask so as not to 'bruise' the fruit of the vine.
- A centrepiece for the table should never be anything prepared by a taxidermist.
- Do not allow the dog to eat at the table, no matter how good his manners are.
- While ears need to be cleaned regularly, this is a job that should be done in private using one's own truck keys.
- Dirt or grease under the fingernails is a social no-no, as they tend to detract from a woman's jewellery and alter the taste of her finger foods.
- When dating (outside the family) establish with your date's parents what time she is expected back. Some will say 10pm; others might say Monday. If the latter is the answer, it is the man's responsibility to get her to school on time.
- When at the theatre, crying babies should be taken to the lobby and picked up immediately after the movie has ended.
- Livestock, usually, is a poor choice for a wedding gift.
- Unless you are the groom, kissing the bride at a wedding for more than 5 seconds may get you shot.
- Though uncomfortable, say yes to socks and shoes for special occasions such as weddings.
- When approaching an intersection, the vehicle with the largest tyres always has the right of way.
- Never tow another car using pantyhose and duct tape.

SOUTHERN TERRORIST ADVISORY ATLANTA

The governors of Alabama, South Carolina, Arkansas, Georgia and Mississippi announced today that they have made a disturbing discovery in their states. Apparently, a small number of Al Qaeda terrorists have become romantically involved with local redneck girls.

The result is not pretty and they now have the sad task of reporting the creation of a new sector of the human race: Islamabubbas.

So far, only a smattering of actual births have been reported, but Pat Robertson's Christian Coalition is hard at work trying to isolate and seal them off. To date, the Coalition has identified the following children:

Mohammed Billy Bob Abba Bubba
Mohammed Jethro Bin Thinkin Boudit
Mohammed Forrest Gumpa Bubba
Mohammed Rubba Dub Dubba Bubba
Bobbie Joe Bubba Amgood Atat
Betty Jean Hasbeena Badgurl
Linda Sue Bin There Dundat

Not surprisingly, the Coalition believes they all seem to have sprung from one couple: Mohammed Whoozyadaddy and Yomamma Bin Lovin On De Couch Again.

Bubba, Earl and Jeb were stumbling home late one night and found themselves on the road that led past the old graveyard.

'Come have a look over here,' says Bubba, 'It's Zeb Jones' grave, God bless his soul, he lived to the ripe old age of 87.'

'That's nothing,' says Earl, 'here's one named Butch Smith. It says here that he was 95 when he died.'

Just then, Jeb yells out, 'But here's a fella that died when he was 145 years old!'

'What was his name?' asks Bubba.

Jeb lights a match to see what else is written on the stone marker and exclaims, 'Miles, from Georgia.'

A nationwide search is held for the country's best poet. There is pretty stiff competition but eventually it comes down to two finalists – one a Yale graduate, the other a country lad.

The final contest is for them to write a poem in two minutes containing the word Timbuktu.

The Yale graduate recites his poem first.

Slowly across the desert sand
Trekked a lonely caravan.
Men on camels two by two
Destination Timbuktu.

The audience goes wild. They think the country lad doesn't stand a chance. Nevertheless, he stands up and recites his poem.

Me and Tim ahunting went
Met three whores in a pop-up tent
They were three and we were two
So I bucked one and Timbuktu.

IT FOR COUNTRY FOLK

Analogue:	Makes a stove hotter
Byte:	What them damn flies do
Bits:	The marks the damn flies leave
Chat:	What our wimmin folk do
Chip:	Munchies for TV
Click:	What ma truck starter does
Client:	Them damn Yankees I take fishing
Crash:	What we do with our trucks
Dot matrix:	Old Ben's wife
Download:	Getting the wood off the truck
Enter:	Yankee talk for C'mon in ya'll
Flame:	What I light the stove with

Floppy disc:	From carrying too much wood
Floppy drive:	Driving with a flat tyre
Format:	My pick-up truck needs two formats
Hard drive:	Getting home in the winter time
Internet:	Where we want them fish to land
IP address:	We call it the outhouse
Java:	Cuppa hot coffee
Joy stick:	A beer tap
Keyboard:	Where I hangs ma keys
Laptop:	Where the kitty sleeps
Links:	Where golfers go
Log-on:	Making a wood stove hotter
Log-off:	Don't put on no more wood
Main frame:	What holds up the barn roof
Megabyte:	A bite from a large dog
Megahertz:	A log falling on ma toe
Microchip:	Small pieces in the munchie bag
Modem:	What I did to the hay fields
Monitor:	Keeping an eye on the stove
Mouse pad:	Hippy talk for a mouse's home
Mouse:	What eats the grain in the barn
MUD:	My front yard after it rains
Network:	Them TV stations
Newbie:	My daughter's little boy
Obsolete:	Any PC we own
Port:	Fancy northern wine
Program:	What we get at a ball game
Prompt:	What the mail ain't in the winter time
RAM:	The thing that splits the log
Remote:	My mother-in-law
Scanner:	What we do with our wimmin folk
Screen:	What we put in during fly season
Server:	The bartender or waitress
Site:	My yard, home or town

Software:	Them plastic knives and forks
Spam:	What we eat Tuesdays and Fridays
State of the art:	A PC we can't afford
URL:	Outside the city
Usenet:	To take them fish out of the water
Web:	What them damn spiders make
Windows:	What we shut when it's cold

YOU KNOW YOU'RE A COUNTRY BUMPKIN IF:

- You think a stock tip is advice about grooming your hogs
- 'He needed killing' is a valid defence
- You have an 'Elvis' jelly mould
- Your wife owns a homemade fur coat
- You and your dog use the same tree
- You vacuum your bed rather than change the sheet
- Your idea of talking during sex is, 'Ain't no cars coming, baby'
- Your dog and your wallet are both on chains
- A 'Say No to Crack' sign reminds you to pull up your pants
- Your PC keyboard only goes up to number six
- Your wife keeps a spit cup on the ironing board
- Your diploma says, 'From the Trucking Institute'
- You think Dom Perignon is a mafia leader
- You've been too drunk to fish
- Your idea of a seven-course meal is a bucket of KFC and a six pack
- You say, 'It's so dry, the trees are bribing the dogs'
- You got your wife's phone number from a wall in a bar's restroom
- Jack Daniels is on your list of most admired people
- You go Christmas shopping for your mother, sister and wife – and you only need one gift
- You borrowed your dad's tractor for your first date
- E-I-E-I-O is how you spell farm

- On your job application, under 'sex', you put 'as often as possible'
- You can tell your age by the number of rings in your bathtub
- Your beer can collection is considered a tourist attraction in your town
- Going to your bathroom at night requires shoes and a torch
- You painted your car with house paint
- You get lost in thought and find yourself in unfamiliar territory
- You think genitalia is an Italian airline
- You have more buckles than pants
- One of your kids was born on a pool table
- You think safe sex is a padded headboard
- Your house doesn't have curtains but your truck does
- You think 'loading the dishwasher' means taking your wife out and getting her drunk
- Your coffee table used to be a cable spool
- Your stereo speakers used to belong to the drive-in
- Your Halloween pumpkin has more teeth than your wife
- You think duel airbags refers to your wife and your mother-in-law
- You think there's nothing wrong with incest as long as you keep it in the family

DEFINITIONS

NEW PARENT'S DICTIONARY

Adult:	A person who has stopped at both ends and is now growing in the middle.
Amnesia:	Condition that enables a woman who has gone through labour to have sex again.
Bottle feeding:	An opportunity for daddy to get up at 2am too.
Cannibal:	Someone who is fed up with people.
Chickens:	The only animals you eat before they are born and after they are dead.
Committee:	A body that keeps minutes and wastes hours.
Drooling:	How teething babies wash their chins.
Dumb waiter:	One who asks if the kids would care to order dessert.
Dust:	Mud with the juice squeezed out.
Egotist:	Someone who is usually me-deep in conversation.
Family Planning:	The art of spacing your children the proper distance apart to keep you from falling into financial disaster.
Feedback:	The inevitable result when a baby doesn't appreciate the strained carrots.
Full name:	What you call your child when you're mad at him.
Gossip:	A person who will never tell a lie if the truth will do more damage.

Grandparents:	The people who think your children are wonderful even though they're sure you're not raising them right.
Hair stylist:	A place where women curl up and dye.
Hearsay:	What toddlers do when anyone mutters a dirty word.
Impregnable:	A woman whose memory of labour is still vivid.
Independent:	How we want our children to be as long as they do everything we say.
Look out!	What it's too late for your child to do by the time you scream it.
Music:	A complex organisation of sounds that is set down by the composer, incorrectly interpreted by the conductor, who is ignored by the musicians, the result of which goes unnoticed by the audience.
Owwww!:	The first word spoken by children with older siblings.
Prenatal:	When your life was still somewhat your own.
Prepared childbirth:	A contradiction in terms.
Puddle:	A small body of water that draws other small bodies wearing dry shoes.
Show off:	A child who is more talented than yours.
Sterilise:	What you do to your first baby's pacifier by boiling it and to your last baby's pacifier by blowing on it.
Storeroom:	The distance required between the supermarket aisles so that children in shopping carts can't quite reach anything.
String quartet:	A good violinist, a bad violinist, an ex-violinist, and someone who hates

	violinists, all getting together to complain about composers.
Temper tantrums:	What you should keep to a minimum so as to not upset the children.
Thunderstorms:	A chance to see how many family members can fit into one bed.
Top bunk:	Where you should never put a child wearing Superman jammies.
Two-minute warning:	When the baby's face turns red and she begins to make those familiar grunting noises.
Verbal:	Able to whine in words.
Weaker sex:	The kind you have after the kids have worn you out.
Whodunit:	None of the kids that live in your house.
Whoops:	An exclamation that translates roughly into 'get a sponge'.

FOREVER PICKING YOUR NOSE

Autopick:	The kind you do in a car, when no one's looking. Also can mean automatic pick, the one you do when you're not even thinking about it, at work, while talking to a co-worker or during a meeting.
Camouflaged pick:	When, in the presence of other people, you wrap your forefinger in a tissue, then thrust it in deep and hold back the smile.
Deep salvage pick:	Reminiscent of the deep sea exploration to find the Titanic, you probe deep into your nasal passages.
Depression pick:	When you are sad, and the only way to fill the void is to pick so hard and fast

	that the agony overcomes your feeling of remorse and depression.
Extra pick:	When you have been digging for nuggets hour upon hour and suddenly you hit the jackpot! Excitement only equalled by winning the lottery.
Fake nose scratch:	When you pretend you've got an itch but you're really trolling the nostril edge for stray boogers.
Kiddie pick:	When you're by yourself and you uninhibitedly twist your forefinger into your nostril with childlike joy and freedom. And the best part is, there's no time limit!
Making a meal out of it:	You do it so furiously, and for so long, you're probably entitled to dessert.
Pick a lot:	What we would call abnormal amounts of picking. Anything in the three digit realm we consider a bit too much for a 24-hour timeframe.
Pick and flick:	Snot now becomes a weapon against your sister and others in range around you.
Pick and save:	When you have to pick it quickly, just when someone looks away, and then you pocket the snot so they don't catch on to what you did.
Pick and stick:	You wanted it to be a 'pick and flick', but it stubbornly clings to your fingertip.
Pick your brains:	Done in private, this is the one where your finger goes in so far, it passes the septum.

Pipe-cleaner pick:	The kind where you remove a piece of snot so big, it improves your breathing by 90%.
Surprise pickings:	When a sneeze or laugh causes snot to come hurling out of your nose, and you have to gracefully clean it off your shirt.
Utensil pick:	When fingers, and even your thumb, just aren't enough to get the job done to your satisfaction.

GUIDE TO PERSONAL ADVERTISEMENTS

Independent thinker	Crazy.
High-spirited	Crazy, hyperactive, and throws things.
Free-spirited	Really crazy and irresponsible.
Ample	Large.
Huggable	Larger.
Zaftig	Really large.
Large and sassy	Fat and loudmouthed.
Slender	Skinny.
Svelte	Anorexic.
Petite	Short.
Dynamic	Pushy.
Assertive	Pushy with a mean streak.
Excited about life's journey	No concept of reality.
Moody	Manic-depressive.
Soulful	Manic-depressive and quiet.
Poetic	Manic-depressive and boring.
Unpredictable	Manic-depressive and off medication.
Looking for Mr/Ms Right	Looking for Mr/Ms Rich.
Very human	Quasimodo.
Uninhibited	Lacking basic social skills.

Irreverent	Mean and lacking basic social skills.
Aging child	Self-centred adult.
Freedom-loving	Undependable.
Young at heart	Over 40.
Youthful	Over 50 and in major denial. Should get rid of ponytail.
Chatty	Never shuts up.
Humorous	Watches too much TV and never shuts up.
Claims a sense of humour	Hasn't got one.
Financially secure	Has a job.
Affectionate	Horny.
Romantic	Horny.
Passionate	Really horny.

OFFICE SPEAK

404:	Someone who's clueless. From the internet error message '404 not found', meaning that the requested document could not be located.
Adminisphere:	The rarefied organisational layers beginning just above the rank and file. Decisions that fall from the adminisphere are often profoundly inappropriate or irrelevant to the problems they were designed to solve.
Alpha geek:	The most knowledgeable, technically proficient person in an office or work group.
Assmosis:	The process by which some people seem to absorb success and

	advancement by kissing up to the boss rather than working hard.
Blamestorming:	Sitting around in a group, discussing why a deadline was missed or a project failed, and who was responsible.
Chainsaw consultant:	An outside expert brought in to reduce the employee headcount, leaving the top brass with clean hands.
Chips and salsa:	Chips? Hardware. Salsa? Software, as in 'Well, first we gotta work out if the problem's in your chips or your salsa'.
CLM:	Career Limiting Move. Used among microserfs to describe ill-advised activity.
Cube farm:	An office filled with cubicles.
Dilberted:	To be exploited and oppressed by your boss. Derived from the experiences of Dilbert, the geek-in-hell comic strip character.
Flight risk:	Used to describe employees who are suspected of planning to leave a company or department soon.
Generica:	Features of the landscape that are exactly the same no matter where one is, such as fast food joints, strip malls, subdivisions.
Going postal:	Euphemism for being totally stressed out, for losing it. Makes reference to the unfortunate track record of postal employees who have snapped and gone on shooting rampages.
Good job:	A get-out-of-debt job. A well-paying job people taken in order to pay off debts,

one that they will quit as soon as they are solvent again.

Idea hamsters:	People who always seem to have their idea generators running.
Irritainment:	Entertainment and media spectacles that are annoying but you find yourself unable to stop watching them. The OJ trials were a prime example. Bill Clinton's shameful video Grand Jury testimony is another.
Microserf:	The lowest rank of workers in the new digital industries.
Mouse potato:	The online, wired generation's answer to the couch potato.
Ohnosecond:	That minuscule fraction of time in which you realise that you've just made a big mistake.
Percussive maintenance:	The fine art of whacking the heck out of an electronic device to get it to work again.
Prairie dogging:	When someone yells or drops something loudly, and people's heads pop up over the walls to see what's going on.
Salmon day:	The experience of spending an entire day swimming upstream only to get screwed and die in the end.
Seagull manager:	A manager, who flies in, makes a lot of noise, craps on everything, and then leaves.
Sitcom:	Single Income, Two Children, Oppressive Mortgage. What yuppies turn into when they have children and

	one of them stops working to stay home with the kids.
Squirt the bird:	To transmit a signal to a satellite.
Starter marriage:	A short-lived first marriage that ends in divorce with no kids, no property and no regrets.
Stress puppy:	A person who seems to thrive on being stressed out and whiney.
Swiped-out:	An ATM or credit card that has been rendered useless because the magnetic strip is worn away from extensive use.
Tourists:	People who take training courses just to get a holiday from their jobs, as in 'We had three serious students in the class; the rest were just tourists'.
Treeware:	Hacker slang for documentation or other printed material.
Uninstalled:	Euphemism for being fired.
Vulcan nerve pinch:	The taxing hand position required to reach all the appropriate keys for certain commands.
Xerox subsidy:	Euphemism for swiping free photocopies from one's workplace.

BUMPER STICKERS

- A day without sunshine is like, night.
- Always be sincere. Even when you don't mean it.
- Baby in boot.
- Bad cop – no donut.
- Be nice to your kids. They'll choose your nursing home.
- Boycott shampoo! Demand real poo.
- Constipated people don't give a crap.

- Dead people are cool.
- Death is hereditary.
- Diarrhoea is inherited. It runs in your jeans.
- Don't follow me, I'm lost.
- Dyslexics of the world, untie!
- Ever stop to think, and forget to start again?
- Go ahead and honk. I'm reloading.
- Happiness is seeing your mother-in-law's face on the back of a milk carton.
- Help. Daddy farted, and we can't get out!
- How many roads must a man travel down before he admits he is lost?
- How much deeper would the ocean be if sponges didn't live there?
- Humpty Dumpty didn't fall . . . he was pushed.
- I love cats. They taste just like chicken.
- I love kids, but I can't eat a whole one.
- I read Playboy for the articles and watch porn for the music.
- I tried to snort coke once, but the ice cubes got stuck in my nose.
- I used to be indecisive; now I'm not sure.
- I'm not a complete idiot. Some pieces are missing.
- If a couple divorce in Kentucky, are they still brother and sister?
- If carrots are so good for the eyes, how come I see so many dead rabbits on the highway?
- If God intended man to smoke, he would have set us on fire.
- If the music is too loud, you're too old.
- If you can read this, my wife fell off.
- Man who walks through airport turnstile sideways is going to Bangkok.
- Moody bitch seeks nice guy for love-hate relationship.
- Some day your prince will come. Mine got lost, took a wrong turn and is too stubborn to ask for directions.
- Sometimes I wake up grumpy. Other times I let him sleep.

- Support wildlife. Throw a party.
- The light at the end of the tunnel is an oncoming train.
- This truck has been in 15 accidents . . . and hasn't lost one yet.
- What if the whole world farted at the same time?
- When blondes have more fun, do they know it?
- Where there's a whip, there's a way.
- Why be difficult? Be impossible.
- Why is the alphabet in that order? Is it because of that song?
- You are the object of my erection.
- Your lucky number is 32345543423225. Watch for it everywhere.

WHAT DO WE CALL . . .

A woman who can balance a bottle of beer on her head?
Beatrix.

S omeone who is born on the first day of the month?
Bill.

S omeone who is stranger than fiction?
Ruth.

T wins?
Kate and Duplicate. And their brothers, Pete and Repeat.

A woman who gambles?
Betty.

A man with beef, gravy and vegetables on his head?
Stu.

A German barber?
Herr Dresser.

A man sitting in a tree?
A Woody.

A man with strong spectacles?
A Seymour.

A woman who climbs up walls?
A Ivy.

A person who lives in Paris?
A A parasite.

A man who is always there when you need him?
A Andy.

A n eight-sided cat?
A An octopus.

A man with a rug on his head?
A Matt.

A woman with one foot on each side of a river?
A Bridget.

A man floating in the sea?
A Bob.

A deer with no eyes?
A No idea.

A deer with no eyes and no legs?
A Still no idea.

A mountain that blows its stack?
A volcano.

A person with no arms and legs, at the bottom of the ocean?
Sandy.

A monkey who is king of the jungle?
Henry the Ape.

S omething to put on your horse when you want to ride at night?
Satellite.

A dog that constantly strays?
Rover.

A woman with a frog on her head?
Lily.

A thirsty physician?
Dry dock.

A man with a car's numberplate on his head?
Reg.

A man with a speedometer on his head?
Miles.

A man with a computer on his head?
Mac.

A man with a duck on his head?
Donald.

A man with money on his head?
Bill.

A girl with two toilets on her head?
Lu-lu.

A woman with a ball of wool on her head?
Barbara black sheep.

An astronaut's favourite meal?
Launch.

A girl who gets up early?
Dawn.

A man with a tissue paper head?
Russell.

A scientist whose career is in ruins?
An archaeologist.

A man who lifts up cars in a garage?
Jack.

A woman who keeps horses?
Gi Gi.

A dog that is always rushing about?
A dachshund.

Superheroes who have been run over?
Flatman and Ribbon.

The man who designed King Arthur's round table?
Sir Cumference.

A woman who was eaten by her cannibal husband?
Henrietta.

An ancient Egyptian with no teeth?
Gummy mummy.

A man with a wooden head?
Edward.

A very sweet girl?
Candy.

A girl who is very fragile?
Crystal.

A man who thinks about dying all the time?
Will.

A man who works at the airport?
Ron Way.

A man who sells cars for a living?
Morris.

Morris' son?
Morris Minor.

A boat-keeper's wife?
Maude.

A man who drives trucks for a living?
Laurie.

A lion with a toothache?
Rory.

A crime boss with a fish down his trousers?
The Cod Father.

A girl who lives at the beach?
Sandy.

A school teacher?
Mark.

A groundsman?
Pete.

A florist?
Daisy.

A market gardener?
Mr Bean.

A friendly fellow?
Buddy.

A big hairy man who looks like a bear?
Teddy.

A soundman?
Mike.

A racing-car driver?
Max.

A solicitor?
Sue.

A n artist?
Art.

A rabbit keeper?
Warren.

A fisherman?
Rod.

A man who sells pies at the football?
Alf Time.

A perfume shop owner?
Frank in Scents.

A man who writes long novels?
Warrren Peace.

A fish that tunes pianos?
A piano tuna.

A girl who likes to cook outside?
Barbie.

A hotel porter?
Carrie.

An explorer who liked eating biscuits?
Captain Cookie.

A girl who is always falling over?
Miss Hap.

The woman who fell off the white cliffs?
Eileen Dover.

A band for old men?
Pop Group.

YOU'RE DEFINITELY AN 80'S CHILD IF:

- You can remember what Michael Jackson looked like before his nose fell off.
- You wore a banana clip or one of those slap on wrist bands at some point during your youth.
- You wore French rolls on the bottom of your splatter painted jeans.
- You had slouch socks, and puff painted your own shirt at least once.
- You know the profound meaning of 'Wax on, wax off.'
- You can name at least half of the members of the elite 'Brat Pack'.
- You have seen at least 10 episodes of *Fraggle Rock.*
- You know that another name for a keyboard is a 'synthesiser'.
- You hold a special place in your heart for *Back to the Future.*
- You fell victim to 80's fashion: spandex pants and big hair, crimped and combed over to the side.
- You owned an extensive collection of Cabbage Patch Kids and Trolls.
- You wore fluorescent clothing.
- You could break dance.

- Or wished you could.
- You remember when Atari was a state-of-the-art video game system. That is, ping pong.
- You remember MC Hammer.
- You own cassettes.
- You believed that in the year 2000 we'd all be living on the moon.
- You own any of the Care-Bear glasses from Pizza Hut.
- *Poltergeist* freaked you out.
- You carried your lunch to school in a gremlins lunchbox.
- You have pondered why Smurfette was the only female smurf.
- You wanted to have an alien like Alf living in your house.
- You wore biker shorts underneath a short skirt and felt stylish.
- You wore tights under shorts and felt stylish.
- You had a Swatch watch.
- You spent countless hours trying to perfect the Care-Bear stare.
- You had Wonder Woman underwear.
- You wanted to be the Hulk for Halloween.
- You thought that Transformers were more than meets the eye.
- Partying 'like it's 1999' seemed soooo far away!

DEEP END

PHRASES YOU MAY NEED IF TRAVELLING IN ASIA

Are you harbouring a fugitive?:	Hu Yu Hai Ding?
See me A.SAP:	Kum Hia Nao
Stupid Man:	Dum Gai
Small Horse:	Tai Ni Po Ni
Your price is too high!:	No Bai Dam Thing!
Did you go to the beach?:	Wai Yu So Tan
I bumped into a coffee table:	Ai Bang Mai Ni
I think you need a facelift:	Chin Tu Fat
It's very dark in here:	Wai So Dim?
Has your flight been delayed?:	Hao Long Wei Ting?
That was an unauthorised execution:	Lin Ching
I thought you were on a diet?:	Wai Yu Mun Ching?
This is a tow away zone:	No Pah King
Do you know lyrics to the Macarena?:	Wai Yu Sing Dum Song?
You are not very bright:	Yu So Dum
I got this for free:	Ai No Pei
I am not guilty:	Wai Hang Mi?
Please, stay a while longer:	Wai Go Nao?
Meeting was scheduled for next week:	Wai You Kum Nao
They have arrived:	Hia Dei Kum
Stay out of sight:	Lei Lo
He's cleaning his automobile:	Wa Shing Ka
He is a large man:	Wun Fat Gai

10 THINGS TO DO AT K-MART

1. Set all the alarm clocks to go off at 10-minute intervals throughout the day.
2. Leave cryptic messages on the typewriters.
3. Re-dress the mannequins as you see fit.
4. Walk up to an employee and tell him in an official tone, 'I think we've got a Code Three in Homewares', and see what happens.
5. While walking through the clothing department, ask yourself loud enough for all to hear, 'Who buys this crap anyway?'
6. Ride a display bicycle through the store; claim you are taking it for a test drive.
7. Move 'Caution: Wet Floor' signs to carpeted areas.
8. Make up nonsense products and ask employees if there are any in stock. (eg Shnerples).
9. 'Re-alphabetise' the CDs.
10. When an announcement comes over the loudspeaker, drop to your knees and scream, 'No, no, it's those voices again'.

WAYS TO REALLY ANNOY PEOPLE

- Learn Morse code, and have conversations with friends in public consisting entirely of 'Beeeep Bip Bip Beeep Bip . . .'
- Push all the flat Lego pieces together really tightly.
- Leave the photocopier set to reduce 200%, extra dark, A3 paper, 98 copies.
- Sniffle incessantly.
- Forget the punch line to a long joke, but assure the listener it was a 'real hoot.'
- Do not add any inflection to the end of your sentences, producing awkward silences with the impression that you'll be saying more at any moment.
- Holler random numbers while someone is counting.

- Staple papers in the middle of the page.
- Produce a rental video consisting entirely of copyright warnings.
- Write the surprise ending to a novel on its first page.
- Honk and wave to strangers.
- ONLY TYPE IN UPPERCASE.
- only type in lowercase.
- dont use any punctuation either
- Repeat the following conversation a dozen times:
  'Do you hear that?'
  'What?'
  'Never mind, it's gone now.'
- Stand over someone's shoulder, mumbling, as they read.
- Lie obviously about trivial things such as the time of day.
- Never make eye contact.
- Never break eye contact.

DIET FOR STRESS

BREAKFAST:

½ grapefruit
1 slice whole wheat toast
300ml skim milk

LUNCH:

250g lean grilled chicken breast
1 cup steamed spinach
1 cup herb tea
1 biscuit

MID-AFTERNOON SNACK:

The rest of the biscuits in the pack
1 litre ice cream, nuts, cherries and whipped cream
1 jar hot fudge sauce

DINNER:

2 loaves of garlic bread
4 cans or 1 large bottle of coke
1 large sausage, mushroom and cheese pizza
3 snickers bars

LATE EVENING SUPPER:

Entire frozen Sara Lee cheesecake (eaten directly from freezer)
12 Choc Wedges

RULES FOR THIS DIET

- If you eat something and no one sees you eat it, it has no calories.
- If you drink a diet soft drink with a chocolate bar, the calories in the chocolate bar are cancelled out by the diet soft drink.
- When you eat with someone else, calories don't count if you do not eat more than they do.
- Food used for medicinal purposes never counts, such as hot chocolate, brandy, toast and Sara Lee cheesecake.
- If you fatten up everyone else around you, then you look thinner.
- Movie-related foods do not have additional calories because they are part of the entertainment package and not part of one's personal fuel. Examples include maltesers, buttered popcorn, jaffas, kool mints and choc-tops.
- Biscuit pieces contain no calories. (The process of breaking causes calorie leakage.)
- Things licked off knives and spoons have no calories if you are in the process of preparing something.
- Foods that have the same colour have the same number of calories. Examples include spinach and pistachio ice cream; mushrooms and mashed potatoes.
- Chocolate is a universal colour and may be substituted for any other food colour.
- Anything consumed while standing has no calories. This is due to gravity and the density of the caloric mass.
- Anything consumed from someone else's plate has no calories since the calories rightfully belong to the other person and will cling to his/her plate. (We all know how calories like to cling!)
- Remember that 'stressed' spelt backwards is 'desserts'.

DOCTOR, DOCTOR

'**D**oc, I can't stop singing the green, green grass of home.'
'That sounds like Tom Jones syndrome.'
'Is it common?'
'It's not unusual.'

A guy walks into the psychiatrist wearing only cling-film for shorts.
The shrink says, 'Well, I can clearly see you're nuts.'

A small town doctor was famous in the area for always catching large fish. One day while he was on one of his frequent fishing trips he got a call that a woman at a neighbouring farm was giving birth. He rushed to her aid and delivered a healthy baby boy. The farmer had nothing to weigh the baby with so the doctor used his fishing scales.
According to them, the baby weighed 20kg.

'**D**oc, I've got a cricket ball stuck up my backside.'
'How's that?'
'Don't you start.'

'**D**octor, I can't pronounce my F's and Th's.'
'Well you can't say fairer than that then.'

Bloke goes to the doctors with a lettuce leaf sticking out of his arse.
'Hmmmm, that's strange,' says the doctor.
Bloke replies, 'That's just the tip of the iceberg'.

Doctor: I haven't seen you in a long time.
DPatient: I know, I've been ill.

Patient: I've hurt my arm in several places.
PDoctor: Well don't go there any more.

Dentist: Say Aahh.
DPatient: Why?
Dentist: My dog's died.

A guy goes in to see a psychiatrist.
'Doc, I don't seem to be able to make any friends, so I need help from you, you fat bastard!'

A guy is going on an ocean cruise, and he tells his doctor that he's worried about getting seasick.

'Just eat 2kg of stewed tomatoes before you leave the dock,' says the doctor.

'Will that keep me from getting sick, Doc?'

'No, but it'll look real pretty in the water.'

An epileptic from an interment camp
Was seduced on her couch by a tramp
But the first time he squeezed her
She had a grand seizure
And broke both his balls and a lamp

A man came to hospital after a serious accident.
'Doctor, doctor, I can't feel my legs!' he shouted.

'I know you can't, I've cut your arms off.'

Man goes to the doc, with a strawberry growing out of his head.

'I'll give you some cream to put on it,' says the doctor.

Patient: It hurts every time I raise my arm. What shall I do?
Doctor: Keep your arms by your side.

Patient: Doctor, doctor, I have a head like a turnip, three
ears, two noses and a mouth. What am I?
Doctor: Ugly.

Health Inspector: You've got too many flies in here.
Butcher: Is that so? How many should I have?

Dentist: Strewth! That is the biggest cavity that I've ever
seen, that I've ever seen, I've ever seen.
Patient: You don't have to repeat it.
Dentist: I didn't. That was the echo.

Dentist: Why are you screaming? I haven't started drilling yet.
Patient: You're standing on my toe.

Patient: Doctor, doctor, if I give up wine, women and song,
will I live longer?
Doctor: No, but it will seem longer.

Patient: Doctor, doctor, how was my check up?
Doctor: Perfect. You'll live to be 80.
Patient: But I am 80.
Doctor: In that case, it's been nice knowing you.

Q: Why do surgeons wear masks?
A: So that if they make a mistake no-one will know who did it.

Patient: What causes baldness?
Doctor: Lack of hair.

Patient: Doctor, doctor, an Alsatian bit me on the finger.
Doctor: Which one?
Patient: I don't know. All Alsatians look the same to me.

David, a keen fisherman, had driven by a lake many times and had seen a lot of anglers pulling in plenty of fish, so he decided to give his luck a try. On his first day of fishing he had no luck at all but another fisherman near him was scooping in one fish after another. He had to know the secret.

'Excuse me sir, but would you mind telling me what sort of bait you are using?' he asked.

The other man looked around a bit embarrassed. 'Well, I am a surgeon, and quite by accident I found that human tonsils work very well.'

David thanked the surgeon and left. The next day, he returned to the lake, but still had no luck with his ordinary bait. He noticed there was another man reeling in fish after fish.

'Excuse me,' asked David, 'but could you suggest a bait that I could try?'

'Well, I can, but I am not sure it will do you any good. I'm a surgeon and I'm using a bit of human appendix.'

It seemed that the fish in this lake would require a little more effort than normal, but David was willing to give the lake one more try. On the third day, David still had no luck. There was yet another man near him bringing in fish left and right. David wanted to confirm what he already knew.

'Excuse me sir, but are you a doctor?'

'No,' replied the man. 'I'm a Rabbi.'

KEEP AWAY FROM BARS

The World Health Organization (WHO) has just issued an urgent warning about BARS (Beer and Alcohol Requirement

Syndrome). A newly identified problem, this disease has spread rapidly throughout the world and affects people of many different ages. Believed to have started in Ireland in 1500 BC, the disease seems to affect people who congregate in pubs and taverns, or who just congregate.

It is not known how the disease is transmitted but approximately three billion people worldwide are affected, with thousands of new cases appearing every day. Early symptoms of the disease include an uncontrollable urge to consume a beer or alcoholic beverage at 6pm. This urge is most keenly felt on Fridays.

More advanced symptoms of the disease include talking loudly, singing off-key, aggression, heightened sexual attraction and confidence (even towards fuglies), uncalled-for laughter, uncontrollable dancing and unprovoked arguing.

In the final stages of the disease, victims are often cross-eyed, and speak incoherently. Vomiting, loss of memory, loss of balance, loss of clothing and loss of virginity can also occur. Sometimes death ensues, usually accompanied by the victim shouting, 'Hey Fred, bet you can't do this!' or 'Wanna see how fast it goes?' or 'Come on! You're all a pack of weak pricks'.

'Doctor, doctor, I swallowed a whole cantaloupe.'
'You're just feeling melon-choly.'

'Doctor, doctor, I think I'm a clock.'
'You're winding me up.'

'Doctor, doctor, my hands are killing me.'
'Take them off your throat.'

'**D**octor, doctor, how long have I got?'
'10.'
'10 what? 10 months? 10 weeks?'
'10, 9, 8, 7 . . .'

'**D**octor, doctor, have you got something for a migraine?'
'Take this hammer and hit yourself on the head.'

DOGS

HOW MANY DOGS DOES IT TAKE TO CHANGE A LIGHT BULB?

Australian shepherd:	First, I'll put all the light bulbs in a little circle.
Basset hound:	Zzzzzzzzzzzzz . . .
Border collie:	Just one. Then I'll replace any wiring that's not up to code.
Boxer:	Who needs light? I can still play with my squeaky toys in the dark.
Chihuahua:	Yo quiero Taco Bulb?
Cocker spaniel:	Why change it? I can still pee on the carpet in the dark.
Dachshund:	You know I can't reach that stupid lamp!
Doberman:	While it's out, I'll just take a nap on the couch.
Golden retriever:	The sun is shining, the day is young, we've got our whole lives ahead of us, and you're inside worrying about a stupid burned-out bulb?
Greyhound:	It isn't moving. Who cares?
Jack Russell terrier:	I'll just pop it in while I'm bouncing off the walls.
Labrador:	Oh, me, me! Pleeease let me change the light bulb! Can I? Huh? Huh?
Malamute:	Let the border collie do it. You can feed me while he's busy.

Mastiff:	Screw it yourself! I'm not afraid of the dark.
Old English sheepdog:	Light bulb? That thing I just ate was a light bulb?
Pointer:	I see it, there it is, there it is, right there!
Poodle:	I'll just blow in the border collie's ear and he'll do it. By the time he finishes rewiring the house, my nails will be dry.
Rottweiler:	Make me!
Westie:	Dogs do not change light bulbs – people change light bulbs. I am not one of them so the question is, how long before I can expect my light again?

CROSS BREED DOGS

Bloodhound x labrador	=	Blabador, a dog that barks incessantly.
Bull terrier x shi'tzu	=	Bullshitz, a gregarious but unreliable breed.
Cocker spaniel x rottweiler	=	Cockrot, the perfect puppy for that philandering ex-husband.
Collie x malamute	=	Commute, a dog that travels to work.
Deerhound x terrier	=	Derriere, a dog that's true to the end.
Great pyrenees x dachshund	=	Pyradachs, a puzzling breed.
Irish water spaniel x English springer spaniel	=	Irish springer, a dog fresh and clean as a whistle.
Kerry blue terrier x skye terrier	=	Blue skye, a dog for visionaries.
Labrador retriever x curly coated retriever	=	Lab coat retriever, the choice of research scientists.

Malamute x pointer	=	Moot point, favourites of lawyers but . . . it doesn't seem to matter.
Newfoundland x basset hound	=	Newfound asset hound, a dog for financial advisors.
Pekingese x Lhasa apso	=	Peekasso, an abstract dog.
Pointer x setter	=	Poinsetter, a traditional Christmas pet.
Terrier x bulldog	=	Terribull, a dog that makes awful mistakes.

DOG DEFINITIONS

Bath: This is a process by which the humans drench the floor, walls and themselves. You can help by shaking vigorously and frequently.

Bicycles: Two-wheeled exercise machines, invented for dogs to control body fat. To get maximum aerobic benefit, you must hide behind a bush and dash out, bark loudly and run alongside for a few yards; the person then swerves and falls into the bushes, and you prance away.

Bump: The best way to get your human's attention when they are drinking a fresh cup of coffee or tea.

Deafness: This is a malady which affects dogs when their person wants them in and they want to stay out. Symptoms include staring blankly at the person, then running in the opposite direction, or lying down.

Dog Bed: Any soft, clean surface, such as the white bedspread, or the newly upholstered couch in the living room.

Drool: Is what you do when your person has food and you don't. Sit as close as you can to your person, look sad and let the drool fall to the floor, or better yet, on their laps.

Leash: A strap that attaches to your collar, enabling you to lead your person where you want him/her to go.

Love: Is a feeling of intense affection, given freely and without restriction. The best way you can show your love is to wag your tail. If you're lucky, a human will love you in return. If not, you can always sniff their crotches.

Rubbish Bin: A container that the neighbours put out once a week to test your ingenuity. You must stand on your hind legs and try to push the lid off with your nose. If you do it right you are rewarded with margarine wrappers, empty shampoo bottles and mouldy crusts of bread.

Sniff: A social custom to use when you greet other dogs. Place your nose as close as you can to the other dog's rear end and inhale deeply, repeat several times, or until your person makes you stop. This can also be done to human's crotches.

Sofas: Are to dogs like napkins are to people. After eating it is polite to run up and down the front of the sofa and wipe your whiskers clean.

10 RULES OF DOG PROPERTY

1. If I like it, it's mine.
2. If it's in my mouth, it's mine.
3. If I can take it from you, it's mine.
4. If I had it a little while ago, it's mine.
5. If I'm chewing something up, all the pieces are mine.
6. If its mine, it must never appear to be yours in any way.
7. If it just looks like mine, it's mine.

8. If I saw it first, it's mine.
9. If you are playing with something and you put it down, it automatically becomes mine.
10. If it's broken, it's yours.

Outside of a dog, a man's best friend is a book. Inside of a dog, it's too dark to read.

DOGS & MEN

Why Dogs Are Better Than Men
- Dogs miss you when you're gone.
- Dogs do not play games with you – except Frisbee (and they never laugh at how you throw).
- Dogs don't feel threatened by your intelligence.
- You can train a dog.
- Dogs are easy to buy for.
- You are never suspicious of your dog's dreams.
- Dogs understand what no means.
- Dogs understand if some of their friends can't come inside.
- Middle-aged dogs don't feel the need to abandon you for a younger owner.
- Dogs admit it when they're lost.
- Dogs aren't threatened if you earn more than they do.

How Dogs & Men Are Alike
- Both take up too much space on the bed.
- Both have irrational fears about vacuum cleaning.
- Both mark their territory.
- Both are bad at asking you questions.
- Both have an inordinate fascination with women's crotches.
- Neither does any dishes.

- Both pass gas shamelessly.
- Neither of them notice when you get your hair cut.
- Both are suspicious of the postman.
- Neither knows how to talk on the telephone.
- Neither understands what you see in cats.

How Men Are Better Than Dogs
- Men only have two feet that track in mud.
- Men don't have to play with every man they see when you take them around the block.
- Men don't shed as much, and if they do, they hide it.
- It's fun to dry off a wet man!

DOGS VS CATS

What Is a Dog?
1. Dogs lie around all day, sprawled on the most comfortable piece of furniture.
2. They can hear a package of food opening half a block away, but don't hear you when you're in the same room.
3. They can look dumb and lovable all at the same time.
4. When you want to play, they want to play.
5. When you want to be alone, they want to play.
6. They are great at begging.
7. They do disgusting things with their mouths and then try to give you a kiss.

Conclusion: Dogs are tiny men in little fur coats.

What Is a Cat?
1. Cats do what they want, and they rarely listen to you.
2. They're totally unpredictable and moody.
3. They whine when they are not happy.

4. When you want to play, they want to be alone.
5. When you want to be alone, they want to play.
6. They expect you to cater to their every whim.
7. They drive you nuts and cost an arm and a leg.

Conclusion: Cats are tiny women in little fur coats.

DOMESTIC TIPS

LIFESTYLE ADVICE

A TEASPOON placed in a glass on the back seat of your car makes a handy audible gauge for road bump severity.

AVOID being wheel-clamped by jacking your car up, removing the wheels and locking them safely in the boot until you return.

AVOID cutting yourself while slicing vegetables by getting someone else to hold them while you chop away.

AVOID parking tickets by leaving your windscreen wipers turned to 'fast wipe' whenever you leave your car parked illegally.

DON'T INVITE drug addicts round for a meal on Boxing Day. They may find the offer of cold turkey embarrassing or offensive.

EXPENSIVE hair gels are a con. Marmalade is a much cheaper alternative, but beware of bees in the summer.

INCREASE the life of your carpets by rolling them up and keeping them in the garage.

KEEP the seat next to you on the train vacant by smiling and nodding at people as they walk up the aisle.

NO TIME for a bath? Simply wrap yourself in masking tape and remove the dirt by peeling it off.

OLD contact lenses make ideal portholes for small model boats.

OLD telephone directories make ideal personal address books. Simply cross out the names and address of people you don't know.

PUTTING just the right amount of gin in your goldfish bowl makes the fish's eyes bulge and causes them to swim in an amusing manner.

SAVE electricity by turning off all the lights in your house and walking around wearing a miner's hat.

SAVE on booze by drinking cold tea instead of whisky.

SAVE petrol by pushing your car to your destination. Invariably passers-by will think you've broken down and help.

TO CHECK if the light goes off when the refrigerator door is closed drill a hole, two centimetres in diameter, in your refrigerator door so that you can peek through it.

WHEN reading a book, try tearing out the pages as you read them. This saves the expense of buying a bookmark, and the paper can later be used for shopping lists.

WHEN shopping, take your dustbin to the supermarket with you so that you can see which items you have recently run out of.

HANDY HINTS AROUND THE HOME

Smell gas? Locate the suspected leak by striking an ordinary match in every room in the house until a loud explosion reveals the source of the escaping gas.

To stop nose bleeds, simply place your head between your knees until your heart stops.

When you leave the house simply plug the phone into your video recorder. Not only will it record the caller's voice, but you will also get a picture of them speaking, probably.

Transform your garage into a drive-thru restaurant by sitting in your car, lowering your window and demanding that your wife brings you a cup of tea, on roller skates.

Pretend to be Welsh by putting coal dust behind your ears, talking gibberish and singing all the time.

If a small child is choking on an ice cube, don't panic. Simply pour a jug of boiling water down its throat and hey presto! The blockage is almost instantly removed.

Save electricity on freezing winter nights by simply unplugging your fridge and placing the contents of it on your doorstep.

Help the local police by popping into the mortuary every day to see if you can identify any of the bodies.

Fill a shredded wheat with pink soap and, hey presto – an inexpensive Steelo soap pad.

Save money on expensive earrings by sticking Mentos or sugared almonds to your ear with Blu-Tack.

Can't afford contact lenses? Simply cut out small circles of cling wrap and press them into your eyes.

Fumes from burning settees can be lethal, so before sitting down always look around and plan your escape route in the event of a fire.

Edge your lawn into the shape of a pair of trousers then mow it in lines so it looks like a huge pair of green corduroy trousers. Pockets can simply be added by planting small flower beds.

Townies: whenever you see country folk driving into town in their green Range Rovers to go shopping, jump up and down screaming 'Get off my land!' Then shoot their dog.

Save money on expensive personalised car number plates by simply changing your name to match the existing plate.

Avoid embarrassment after tripping in the street by repeating the same movement several times to make it look like a normal part of your behaviour.

Hey vegetarians: make your veggie burgers go further by adding a 200g of mince to them.

Stop flies landing on your dinner by placing a pile of poo on the dinner table. The flies will be so busy munching on the faeces they will leave you to enjoy your meal.

Avoid the morning-after hangover – simply stay drunk past noon.

Brighten up dull Monday mornings at work by concealing a bottle of vodka in your jacket pocket and taking swigs from it at regular intervals throughout the day.

Are you sick and tired of using the same jokes over and over? Why not send them in to be recycled. You'll be saving lots of hot air that would have otherwise effected global warming.

Housewives: When nipping out to the shops, remember to carry a stiff broom in the boot of your car. Use it to sweep the broken glass to the side of the road every time you have a minor accident.

Bomb disposal experts' wives: Keep hubby on his toes by packing his lunchbox with plasticine and an old alarm clock.

Bus drivers: Pretend you are an airline pilot by wedging your accelerator pedal down with a heavy book, securing the steering wheel with some old rope, and then strolling back along the bus chatting casually to the passengers.

X-Files fans: Create the effect of being abducted by aliens by drinking two bottles of vodka. You'll invariably wake up in a strange place the following morning, having had your memory mysteriously 'erased'.

Increase blind people's electricity bills by switching all their lights on when their guide dog isn't looking.

International Master Criminals: Tell your guards to shoot James Bond in the head at the first opportunity. Under no circumstances give him a guided tour of your base, tell him your plans for the destruction of the world, or leave him in the custody of attractive women in bikinis.

EDUCATION

At school Phil was told by a classmate that most adults are hiding at least one dark secret, and that this makes it very easy to blackmail them by simply saying to them, 'I know the whole truth'. Phil decides to go home and try it out. He walks in and is immediately greeted by his mother. Straight away, he looks at her and says, 'I know the whole truth'.

His mother quickly hands him $20 and says, 'Just don't tell your father'. Quite pleased, the boy waits for his father to get home from work and says, 'I know the whole truth'. The father promptly hands him $40 and says, 'Please don't say a word to your mother'.

Ecstatic at how easy this is Phil decides to try it on another adult. On his way to school the next day he sees the postman. The boy greets him by saying, 'I know the whole truth'. The mailman immediately drops the mail, opens his arms, and says, 'Then come give your daddy a great big hug!'.

A mathematician named Hall
Has a hexahedronical ball
And the cube of its weight,
Times his pecker's, plus eight
Is his phone number – give him a call.

A little boy returning home from his first day at school said to his mother, 'Mum, what's sex?'.

His mother, who believed in all the most modern educational theories, gave him a detailed explanation, covering all aspects of the tricky subject.

When she had finished, the little lad produced an enrolment form which he had brought home from school and said, 'Yes, but how am I going to get all that into this one little square?'.

A progressive professor named Tinners
Held a class every evening for sinners.
   They were graded and spaced
   So the really debased
   Would not be held back by beginners.

YOU KNOW YOU ARE NO LONGER A STUDENT WHEN:

- Your potted plants stay alive.
- Shagging in a single bed seems absurd.
- You keep more food than beer in the fridge.
- You haven't seen a daytime soap opera in over a year.
- 8am is not ridiculously early.
- You hear your favourite song in the elevator at work.
- You carry an umbrella.
- Your friends marry instead of hook-up, and divorce instead of break-up.
- You go from 12 weeks of holiday a year to four.
- You go to parties that the police don't raid.
- Adults feel comfortable telling jokes about sex in front of you.
- You refer to college students as kids.
- You drink wine, scotch and martinis instead of beer, bourbon, and rum.

The children were lined up in the cafeteria of a Catholic elementary school for lunch. At the head of the table was a large pile of apples. A nun had made a note and posted it on the apple tray, 'Take only one. God is watching.'

At the other end of the table was a large pile of chocolate-chip cookies. A child had written a note, 'Take all you want. God is watching the apples.'

A nerd was walking on campus one day when his nerd friend rode up on an incredible shiny new bicycle. The first nerd was stunned and asked, 'Where did you get such a nice bike?'

'Well, yesterday I was walking home minding my own business when a beautiful woman rode up to me on this bike. She threw the bike to the ground, took off all her clothes and said, "Take what you want!".'

The first nerd nodded approvingly and said, 'Good choice. The clothes probably wouldn't have fitted.'

There once was an old man of Esser,
Whose knowledge grew lesser and lesser,
It at last grew so small,
He knew nothing at all,
And now he's a college professor.

A professor stood before his philosophy class. Wordlessly, he picked up an empty jar and filled it with golf balls. He asked the students if the jar was full. They agreed that it was.

The professor then poured pebbles into the jar, shaking the jar lightly so they rolled into the spaces between the golf balls. He asked the students again if the jar was full. They agreed it was.

Next the professor poured sand into the jar. The sand filled up the smaller gaps. He asked once more if the jar was full. The students responded with a unanimous 'yes'.

The professor then produced two cans of beer from under the table and poured the entire contents into the jar, filling the empty spaces in the sand. The students laughed.

'Now,' said the professor, as the laughter subsided, 'This jar represents your life. The golf balls are the important things, your family, your health, your friends and your favourite passions – things that would mean something even if you lost everything else. The pebbles are things that matter a little less, like your job, your house, your car. The sand is everything else – the small stuff. Yet these things are the ones that we tend to fixate on.

'If you put the sand into the jar first,' he continued, 'there is no room for the pebbles or the golf balls. The same goes for life. If you spend all your time and energy on the small stuff, you will never have room for the things that are important to you. Pay attention to the things that are critical to your happiness. Play with your children. Take your partner out to dinner. There will always be time to clean the house and mow the lawn. Take care of the golf balls first, the things that really matter. The rest is just sand.'

One of the students raised her hand and inquired what the beer represented.

The professor smiled. 'It just goes to show you that no matter how full your life may seem, there's always room for a couple of beers.'

A confused driving student one night
Made a left by mistake at the light
Then she turned left twice more
With intent to be sure
For she knew that three wrongs make a right.

DICTIONARY OF DEFINITIONS OF TERMS COMMONLY USED IN MATH LECTURES

Briefly:	I'm running out of time, so I'll just write and talk faster.
Check for yourself:	This is the boring part of the proof, so you can do it on your own time.
Clearly:	I don't want to write down all the in-between steps.

Hint:	The hardest of several possible ways to do a proof.
It's easily shown:	Even you should be able to prove this.
Let's talk it through:	I don't want to write it on the board in case I make a mistake.
Obviously:	I hope you weren't sleeping when we discussed this earlier, because I refuse to repeat it.
Proof omitted:	Trust me, it's true.
Recall:	I shouldn't have to tell you this, but for those of you who erase your memory tapes after every test.
Similarly:	At least one line of the proof of this case is the same as the previous equation.
Trivial:	If I have to show you how to do this, you're in the wrong class.

An advanced society has worked out how to package knowledge in pill form. A student, needing some help, goes to the pharmacy and asks what knowledge pills are available.

'Here's a pill for English literature,' says the pharmacist.

The student takes the pill and swallows it and has new knowledge about English literature.

'What else do you have?' asks the student.

'Well, I have pills for art history, biology, and world history.'

The student swallows these pills and has new knowledge about the subjects. 'Do you have a pill for maths?'

'Wait just a moment', says the pharmacist. He goes into the storeroom and brings back a huge pill and drops it on the counter.

'I have to take that huge pill for maths?' asks the student.

'Well, maths always was a little hard to swallow.'

TOP 5 EXCUSES FOR NOT DOING MATHS HOMEWORK:

1. I accidentally divided by zero and my paper burst into flames.
2. It is Isaac Newton's birthday.
3. I have a solar powered calculator and it was cloudy.
4. I took time out to snack on a donut and a cup of coffee.
5. I didn't have to do homework at the last six schools I was at.

THE DEVOLUTION OF MATHS TEACHING

1960   A peasant sells a bag of potatoes for $10. His costs amount to four-fifths of his selling price. What is his profit?

1970   A farmer sells a bag of potatoes for $10. His costs amount to four-fifths of his selling price, that is, $8. What is his profit?

1980   A farmer exchanges a set P of potatoes with set M of money. The cardinality of the set M is equal to 10, and each element of M is worth $1. Draw 10 big dots representing the elements of M. The set C of production costs is composed of two big dots less than the set M. Represent C as a subset of M and give the answer to the question. What is the cardinality of the set of profits?

1990   A farmer sells a bag of potatoes for $10. His production costs are $8, and his profit is $2. Underline the word 'potatoes' and discuss with your classmates.

2000   A farmer sells a bag of potatoes for $10. His or her production costs are 0.8 of his or her revenue. On your calculator, graph revenue vs costs. Run the POTATO program to determine the profit. Discuss the result with students in your group. Write a brief essay that analyses this example in the real world of economics.

Algebraic symbols are used when you do not know what you are talking about.

IF YOU ARE GOING TO FAIL YOUR EXAM, YOU MIGHT AS WELL ENJOY IT

- Bring a pillow. Fall asleep (or pretend to) until the last 15 minutes. Wake up, and say 'Oh Jeez, better get cracking!'
- Talk the entire way through the exam. Read questions aloud, debate your answers with yourself out loud. If asked to stop, yell out, 'I'm so sure you can hear me thinking.'
- Arrive wearing a black cloak. After about 30 minutes, put on a white mask and start yelling, 'I'm here, the phantom of the opera,' until they drag you away.
- After you get the exam, call the instructor over, point to a question, and ask for the answer.
- Try to get people in the room to do the Mexican Wave.
- Get a copy of the exam paper and run down the hall screaming, 'Dr Evil, Dr Evil, I've got the secret documents!'
- If it's a maths or science exam, answer in essay form. If it's long answer or essay form, answer with numbers and symbols.
- Make paper aeroplanes out of the exam paper. Aim them at the instructor's left nostril.
- Walk in, get the exam, sit down. About five minutes into it, loudly say to the instructor, 'I don't understand any of this!'
- Bring a Game Boy and play with the volume at maximum level.
- Come down with a bad case of Tourette's syndrome during the exam. The louder you make the 'involuntary' sounds, the better.
- On the answer sheet find a new and interesting way to refuse to answer every question. For example, 'I refuse to answer this question on the grounds that it conflicts with my religious beliefs.'

- Fifteen minutes into the exam, stand up, rip up all the papers into very small pieces, and throw them into the air. Then calmly ask for another copy of the exam.
- Twenty minutes into it, throw your papers down violently, scream out 'Screw this!' and walk out triumphantly.
- Every five minutes, stand up, collect all your things, move to another seat, and continue with the exam.
- Turn in the exam approximately 30 minutes into it. As you walk out say loudly, 'Too easy!'

EMPLOYMENT

Tom has a problem with getting up late in the morning and is always late for work. His boss is mad at him and threatens to fire him if he doesn't do something about it. So Tom goes to his doctor, who gives him a pill and tells him to take it before he goes to bed.

Tom sleeps well and, in fact, beats the alarm in the morning. He has a leisurely breakfast and drives cheerfully to work.

'Boss,' he says, 'the pill actually worked! I'm here early today.'

'That's true,' says the boss, 'But where were you all of yesterday?'

It has been said that physicists stand on one another's shoulders. If this is the case, then programmers stand on one another's toes, and software engineers dig each other's graves.

There was an announcer named Herschel
Whose habits became controversial,
Because when out wooing
Whatever he was doing
At 10 he'd insert a commercial

The highest moment in the life of a mathematician is that time after he has proved the result, but before anyone has found the mistake.

There are just three types of accountants: those who can count and those who can't.

An accountant is someone who knows the cost of everything and the value of nothing.

An Auditor is one who arrives after the battle is lost and bayonets the wounded.

Q: How do you save a drowning accountant?
A: Take your foot off his head.

Q: Why did the Auditor cross the road?
A: Because he did it last year!

Q: Why did God create economists?
A: So accountants would have someone to laugh at!

Q: What is the difference between a tragedy and a catastrophe?
A: A tragedy is a ship-full of accountants going down in a storm. A catastrophe is when they can all swim!

Q: Who was the world's first accountant?
A: Adam. He turned a leaf and made an entry!

FASHIONABLE ACADEMIC MATHEMATICAL SPEAK TO REPLACE PLAIN ENGLISH

Arithmetic:	Number theory.
Clever scheme:	Algorithm.
Concave:	Non-convex.
Consequently:	Ipso facto.
Constant:	Invariant.
Count:	Enumerate.
Distance:	Metric measure.
Empty:	Vacuous.
Mistake:	Non sequitur.

Nothing:	Initialise to zero.
Obvious:	Has an easy-to-understand, but hard-to-find solution.
One:	Unity.
Path:	Trajectory.
Several:	A plurality.
Similar:	Homologous.
Starting place:	Get a handle.
Therefore:	Ergo.
Think:	Hypothesise.
Tip-top point:	Apex.
Trivial:	Has two easy-to-understand, but hard-to-find solutions.
Truth:	Tautology.
Vanishes:	Tends to zero.

Three guys are sitting at a table eating dinner. The first guy says, 'I have to go to the bathroom,' and he comes back with his hand by his ear.

'Why is your hand by your ear?' asks the second guy.

'I'm receiving a phone call,' he says, sitting down.

'I have to go to the bathroom,' says the second guy.

When he comes back he's looking at his hand and the third guy asks, 'Why are you looking at your hand?'

'I'm receiving a text message.'

The last guy says 'I have to go to the bathroom.'

When he comes out there's toilet paper coming out of his pants.

'Why do you have toilet paper coming out of your pants?' asks the first guy.

'I'm receiving a fax.'

There was a young architect named Yorick
Who could, when feeling euphoric,

Display for selection
Three kinds of erection:
Corinthian, Ionic and Doric!

Q: Why does the government jail people for theft?
A: It doesn't want any competition.

Q: Why was the sailor buried at sea?
A: Because he was dead.

When Picasso was tender in years
He considered some other careers
When he read a reportage
Of an imminent shortage
Of models with eyes in their ears.

One day a farmer called up an engineer, a physicist and a mathematician and asked them to fence off the largest possible area with the least amount of fence.

The engineer made the fence in a circle and proclaimed that he had the most efficient design.

The physicist made a long, straight line and proclaimed, 'We can assume the length is infinite.' He pointed out that fencing off half of the earth was certainly the most efficient way to do it.

The mathematician built a tiny fence around himself and said 'I declare myself to be on the outside.'

A chemist, a physicist and a mathematician are stranded on an island when a can of food washes ashore. The chemist and the physicist come up with many ingenious ways to open the can. Suddenly the mathematician gets a bright idea.

'Let's just assume we have a can opener.'

A biologist, a physicist and a mathematician were sitting in a street café watching the crowd. Across the street they saw a man and a woman entering a building. Ten minutes later they reappeared with a third person.

'They have multiplied,' said the biologist.

'Oh no, it's an error in measurement,' the physicist sighed.

'If exactly one person enters the building now, it will be empty again,' the mathematician concluded.

An engineer, a physicist and a mathematician are staying in a hotel. The engineer wakes up and smells smoke. He goes out into the hallway and sees a fire, so he fills a rubbish bin from his room with water and douses the fire. He goes back to bed.

Later, the physicist wakes up and smells smoke. He opens his door and sees a fire in the hallway. He walks down the hall to a fire extinguisher and after calculating the flame velocity, distance, extinguisher pressure and trajectory, puts out the fire with the minimum amount of energy needed.

Later, the mathematician wakes up and smells smoke. He goes to the hall, sees the fire and the fire extinguisher. He thinks for a moment and then exclaims, 'Ah, a solution exists!' and then goes back to bed.

A mortician who practiced in Fife
Made love to the corpse of his wife.
'How could I know, Judge?
She was cold, did not budge
Just the same as she'd acted in life.'

A mathematician, a physicist and an engineer went to the races and laid their bets on the horses. Things didn't go too well.

They were commiserating in the bar after the race, and the engineer says, 'I don't understand why I lost all my money.

I measured all the horses and calculated their strength and mechanical advantage and worked out how fast they could run –'

The physicist interrupted him, 'But you didn't take individual variations into account. I did a statistical analysis of their previous performances and bet on the horses with the highest probability of winning.'

'If you're so hot why are you broke?' asked the engineer.

Before the argument can grow, the mathematician takes out his pipe and they get a glimpse of his well-fattened wallet. Obviously here was a man who knew something about horses. They both demanded to know his secret.

'Well,' he said, 'first I assumed all the horses were identical and spherical . . .'

Johnny's warehouse job was a bore.
Packing boxes all day was a chore.
   For this job he had yearned
   But it's one he'd have spurned
If the 'ware' hadn't sounded like 'whore'.

An engineer, an accountant, a chemist and a bureaucrat were bragging about how smart their dogs were. To settle the argument they agreed to put their dogs through their paces.

The engineer called to his dog, 'T-square, do your stuff.'

The dog took out paper and pen and drew a circle, a square and a triangle. Everyone was suitably impressed.

The accountant called, 'Taxation, do your stuff.'

The pooch went to the kitchen, got a dozen cookies and made four stacks of three. The others nodded their surprise.

So the chemist called, 'Beaker, do your stuff.'

The dog went to the fridge for a bottle of milk, got a 250ml glass and poured exactly 200ml without spilling a drop. Everyone agreed that was great.

Finally it was the bureaucrat's turn, 'Coffee-Break, do your stuff!'

Coffee-Break ate the cookies, drank the milk, chewed the paper, said he injured his mouth doing so, filed a claim for unsafe working conditions, put in for worker's compensation and took extended sick leave.

A salesman from KFC approached the pope with a brilliant offer. For a million dollars all the pope would have to do is change the Lord's Prayer from 'Give us this day our daily bread' to 'Give us this day our daily chicken.' While the salesman tried hard to convince the pope that it was an inconsequential change, His Holiness refused the offer.

Two weeks later, the salesman returned to the pope. He reiterated his offer but this time promised 10 million dollars. The pope considered it for a little longer this time, but again refused the man's generous offer.

Another week later, the man returned and offered the pope 20 million dollars to change the Lord's Prayer. After some deliberation the pope reluctantly accepted. The following day, the pope met with his council.

'I have some good news and some bad news,' he said. 'The good news is, that we have just received a cheque for 20 million dollars.'

'What is the bad news, Your Holiness?'

'The bad news is we have lost the Wonder Bread account.'

There once was a midwife of Gaul
Who had almost no business at all.
She cried, 'Hell and damnation!
There's no procreation,
God made the French penis too small.'

Biologists think they are biochemists. Biochemists think they are physical chemists. Physical chemists think they are physicists. Physicists think they are gods. And God thinks he is a mathematician.

Medicine makes people ill, mathematics make them sad and theology makes them sinful.
- Martin Luther

A mathematician is a blind man in a dark room looking for a black cat that isn't there.
- Charles Darwin

A geneticist living in Delft
Scientifically played with himself,
And when he was done
He labelled it 'son',
And filed it away on a shelf.

A salmon fisherman was out in the ocean fishing when his boat sank. He was lucky enough to make it to a deserted island where he had to survive on what he could find. When a coastguard eventually rescued him, he noticed there was a fire pit with the feathers of a protected bird scattered around it.

'You know, it's illegal to kill a California condor, I'm afraid I'm going to have to arrest you,' he said.

The fisherman protested for some time saying that he killed it because he was going to starve. He wailed and cried and the coastguard eventually took pity on him and let him off.

'Out of curiosity,' the coastguard asked, 'what did it taste like?'

'Well, it was kind of a mix between a snowy owl and a bald headed eagle.'

A bobby of Nottingham Junction
Whose organ had long ceased to function
Deceived his good wife
For the rest of her life
With the aid of his constable's truncheon.

A guy walks into a post office one day to see a middle-aged, balding man standing at the counter methodically placing 'love' stamps on bright pink envelopes with hearts all over them. He watches as the man takes out a perfume bottle and sprays scent all over them.

The guy's curiosity gets the better of him, and he asks the man what he is doing.

'I'm sending out 1000 Valentine cards signed, "Guess who?"'

'But why?'

'I'm a divorce lawyer.'

I n the prime of her career, a world-famous painter started to lose her eyesight. Fearful that she might lose her career, she went to see the best eye surgeon in the world. After several weeks of delicate surgery and therapy, her eyesight was restored.

The painter was so grateful that she decided to show her gratitude by repainting the doctor's office. Part of her mural included a gigantic eye on one wall. When she had finished her work, she held a press conference to unveil the mural.

During the press conference, one reporter noticed the eye on the wall.

'What was your first reaction upon seeing your newly painted office, especially that large eye on the wall?' he asked the doctor.

'My first thought was "Thank God I'm not a gynaecologist."'

A young naval officer was being put through his paces by an old sea captain.

'What would you do if a sudden storm sprang up on the starboard?' asked the captain.

'Throw out an anchor, sir.'

'What would you do if another storm sprang up aft?'

'Throw out another anchor, sir.'

'And if another terrific storm sprang up forward, what would you do then?'

'Throw out another anchor, sir.'

'Hold on,' said the captain. 'Where are you getting all those anchors from?'

'From the same place you're getting your storms, sir.'

The population of a country is 20 million. Of that, 10 million are retired, leaving 10 million to do the work. But there are three million in school, which leave seven million to do the work. Of this there are two million employed by the federal government. And since we know they don't do a bloody thing, this leaves five million to do the work. One million are in the armed forces (ie, let's soak up more tax dollars while we play Doom), which leaves four million to do the work. Take from the total the three and a half million people who work for state and local governments and that leaves 500,000 to do the work.

There are 188,000 in hospitals, so that leaves 312,000 to do the work. There are 300,000 unemployed, so that leaves 12,000 to do the work. There are 11,998 people in prisons. That leaves just two people to do the work. You and me.

And you're sitting there reading jokes. No wonder I'm tired; I'm the doing all of the work myself!

Two bone-weary public servants were working their little hearts and souls out. Their department was just too busy for staff to be able take flexitime. But there had to be a way.

One of the two public servants suddenly lifted his head. 'I know how to get some time off work,' the man whispered.

'How?' hissed the blonde at the next workstation.

Instead of answering, the man quickly looked around. No sign of his supervisor. He jumped up on his desk, kicked out a couple of ceiling tiles and hoisted himself up. 'Look!' he hissed, then swinging his legs over a metal pipe, hung upside down.

Within seconds, the supervisor emerged from the department head's office at the far end of the floor. He saw the worker hanging from the ceiling, and asked him what on earth he thought he was doing.

'I'm a light bulb' answered the public servant.

'I think you need some time off,' barked his supervisor. 'Get out of here – that's an order – and I don't want to see you back here for at least another two days! You understand me?'

'Yes sir,' the public servant answered meekly, then jumped down, logged off his computer and left. The blonde was hot on his heels.

'Where do you think you're going?' the boss asked.

'Home,' she said lightly. 'I can't work in the dark.'

A quick witted astronaut, Dwight,
Was asked 'bout his upcoming flight,
'Did you have worry one
Bout landing on the sun?'
'Heck no, we're landing at night!'

A lost balloonist lands in a random field and asks a man out walking his dog, 'Where am I?'

'You are three feet in front of me in the middle of a field,' replies the man.

'You must be an accountant!'

'How did you know that?'

'Easy. What you just told me is 100% accurate but absolutely useless!'

ETHNICITY

An American decided to write a book about famous churches around the world. He bought a plane ticket and took a trip to Orlando, thinking that he would start by working his way across the USA from south to north. On his first day he was inside a church to take photographs when he noticed a golden telephone mounted on the wall with a sign saying '$10,000 per call'. The man, intrigued, asked a priest what the telephone was used for.

'That is a direct line to heaven. For $10,000 you can talk to God.'

The man thanked the priest and went along his way. Next stop was Atlanta. There, at a very large cathedral, he saw the same golden telephone with the same sign under it. He asked a nearby nun about it.

'That is a direct line to heaven. For $10,000 you can talk to God.'

He thanked the nun and then travelled to Indianapolis, Washington DC, Philadelphia, Boston and New York. In every church he saw the same golden telephone with the same '$10,000 per call' sign under it.

The American, upon leaving Vermont, decided to travel to Australia to see if Australians had the same phone. He arrived in Australia, and again, in the first church he entered, there was the same golden telephone, but this time the sign under it read '40c per call.' The American was surprised so he asked the priest about the sign.

'Father, I've travelled all over America and I've seen this same golden telephone in many churches. I'm told that it is a direct line to heaven, but in the US the price was $10,000 per call. Why is it so cheap here?'

The priest smiled and answered, 'You're in Australia now, son – it's a local call.'

Q: What do you say to a Kiwi bloke with a be-yooooood-i-ful woman on his arm?
A: Hey, nice tattoo.

Q: How do Kiwis practice safe sex?
A: They paint an X on the back of the sheep that kick.

Amarried couple on holiday in Pakistan went to a marketplace. In the far corner of the market was a dimly lit stall, with a wizened old man sitting out the front of it. As they walked past he implored them to come into his shop to see his special sandals.

'These sandals,' he said, 'have magic powers. They make the wearer wild about sex like a great desert camel.'

The wife was intrigued, but the husband, who believed himself to be the world's greatest lover, was disbelieving.

'I tell you it is true,' said the old Pakistani man. 'Try them on for yourself!'

Reluctantly the man tried on the sandals. As soon as his feet slipped into the shoes he got a wild look in his eyes – a look his wife hadn't seen in many years. Frenzied by his raw sexual power the husband rushed the Pakistani man, threw him on a table and started tearing at the guy's pants.

'You have them on the wrong feet! You have them on the wrong feet!' screamed the Pakistani.

Gallagher opened the morning newspaper and was dumbfounded to read in the obituary column that he had died. He quickly phoned his best friend Finney.

'Did you see the paper?' asked Gallagher. 'They say I died!'

'Yes, I saw it!' replied Finney. 'Where are you callin' from?'

Q: How do you fit 40 Cubans into a telephone booth?
A: Tell them that it floats.

The security forces got all of the Saddam look-alikes together and told them that they have some good news and some bad news. The good news was that Saddam survived the bombings, so they all still had jobs.

One of the look-alikes asked, 'What's the bad news?'

'He lost an arm and an eye.'

A group of bureaucrats from the European Union are out on a chartered luxury liner through the Pacific. A storm blows up, the cruiser starts to sink, and everyone abandons ship. By a quirk of fate, the only survivors are two men and one woman from each of the EU countries. They stagger onto the shore of a beautiful desert island. After three months, things have changed.

One Italian man has killed the other Italian man in a fight over the Italian woman.

The two Frenchmen and the French woman are enjoying a threesome, but complain bitterly about the multitude of foreigners on their island.

The two Englishmen are waiting patiently for someone to introduce them to the English woman.

The German men have a strict, weekly alternating sex-schedule; the woman gets weekends off.

The Dutch men are fully prepared, in general, to share the woman. However, they are still debating how to ensure that both will have an exactly equal share, how to reduce supervision cost, and how to guarantee the woman equal rights. They are writing to the Hague.

The Luxemburg men are still recovering from the shock of seeing half the population of Luxembourg stranded on the island. But they will soon start collecting seashells on the beach.

The Finnish men took one look at the endless ocean, one look at the Finnish woman, and started swimming.

They were soon overtaken by the Portuguese men.

The Danish trio embarked on a search for people to join them in an orgy. They gladly accepted the participation of the Finnish woman, and are still vainly trying to persuade the Portuguese woman.

The Spanish men are protecting the virginity of the Spanish woman and are constantly and suspiciously spying on one another. Meanwhile, she dances flamenco.

The Austrian men initiated a yodelling contest for the woman. The loser immediately started learning flamenco, as well as Portuguese, Finnish and Danish.

The Greek men are sleeping with each other and the Greek woman is cleaning and cooking for them.

The Swedish woman keeps on bitching about female exploitation while the men are sunbathing and waiting for her to tell them what to do.

The Irish began by setting up a distillery for which they expect to receive a substantial EU subsidy. They don't recall if sex is in the picture, because it gets sort of foggy after the first few rounds of coconut whisky. But they're happy that, at least, the English aren't getting any.

Q: How many Irishmen does it take to replace a light bulb?
A: 30, two to hold the light bulb and 28 to drink till the room starts spinning.

Barty was trapped in a bog and seemed a goner when Big Mick O'Reilly wandered by.

'Help!' Barty shouted, 'Oi'm sinkin'!'

'Don't worry,' assured Mick. 'Next to the Strong Muldoon, Oi'm the strongest man in Erin, and Oi'll pull ye right out o' there.'

Mick leaned out and grabbed Barty's hand and pulled and pulled to no avail.

After two more unsuccessful attempts, Mick said to Barty, 'Shure, an' Oi can't do it. The Strong Muldoon could do it alone, mebbe, but Oi'll have to get some help.'

'Mick! Mick! D'ye think it will help if Oi pull me feet out of the stirrups?

A German, an American and a Mexican are travelling in the Amazon. They are captured by an irate tribe who decides to punish them for straying on their tribal lands.

The head of the tribe says to the German, 'What do you want on your back for your whipping?'

'I will take oil!' says the German.

So they put oil on his back, and a large Amazonian whips him 10 times resulting in enormous welts on his back.

The Amazons haul the German away, and say to the Mexican, 'What do you want on your back?'

'I will take nothing!' says the Mexican, and he stands up straight and takes his 10 lashings without a single flinch.

'What will you take on your back?' the Amazons ask the American.

'I'll take the Mexican.'

An Irishman walks into a pub and asks for three pints of Guinness. The bartender brings him three pints. The man takes alternate sips of each one until they're gone. He then orders three more.

'Sir, you don't have to order three at a time. I can keep an eye on it and when you get low I'll bring you a fresh cold one,' says the bartender.

'You don't understand,' says the Irishman. I have two brothers, one in Australia and one in the States. We made a vow to each other that every Saturday night we'd still drink together.

So right now, my brothers have three Guinness stouts too, and we're drinking together.'

The bartender thought that was a wonderful tradition. And so every week the man came in and ordered three beers. Then one week he came in and ordered only two. He drank them and then ordered two more.

'I know your tradition and I'd just like to say that I'm sorry that one of your brothers died.' said the bartender.

'Oh, me brothers are fine. I just quit drinking.'

A guy goes into the store and says to the clerk, I would like some Polish sausage.

'Are you Polish?' asks the clerk.

'Well, yes I am. But if I had asked for Italian sausage would you ask me if I was Italian? Or if I had asked for German sausage, would you ask me if I was German? Or if I had asked for a taco would you ask if I was Mexican?'

'Well, no.'

'Then, why do you ask me if I'm Polish just because I ask for Polish sausage?'

'Because this is a hardware store.'

Q: Why do Greeks wear thick gold chains?
A: So they know where to stop shaving.

Q: What do you call a hot chick in Lebanon?
A: A tourist.

Q: Why did the punk cross the road?
A: To smash the chicken.

Q: Why did fifty punks cross the road?
A: Because the chicken was smashing the punk.

Q: What do you call an Arab hairdresser?
A: Ali Barber.

Q: What do you call a Lebanese baby?
A: Kebub.

Q: How do you make a Lebanese baby shut up?
A: Shush Kebub.

Two Norwegian anglers were being swept rapidly out to sea, clinging to the keel of their upturned boat, faces lashed by hail and sleet, bodies soaked by spray and icy waves.

Gunnar yelled to Leif, 'Turned out to be a rotten day, didn't it?'

Leif considered this point for a few seconds, then yelled back, 'Ja Gunnar. Good job we decided not to go mountaineering.'

An Australian, a Kiwi and South African are in a bar one night having a beer. All of a sudden the South African drinks his beer, throws his glass in the air, pulls out a gun and shoots the glass to pieces.

'In Seth Efrika our glasses are so cheap that we don't need to drink from the same one twice,' he says.

The Kiwi, obviously impressed by this, drinks his beer, throws his glass into the air, pulls out his gun and shoots the glass to pieces.

'Wull mate, in Niw Zulland we have so much sand to make the glasses that we don't need to drink out of the same glass twice either,' he says.

The Australian, cool as a koala, picks up his beer and drinks it, throws his glass into the air, pulls out his gun and shoots the South African and the Kiwi.

He turns to the astonished barman and says, 'In Australia we have so many bloody South Africans and friggin' Kiwis that we don't need to drink with the same ones twice.'

Liam had left Dublin to go up to Belfast for a bit of skydiving. Late Sunday evening he was found in tree by a farmer.

'What happened,' said the farmer.

'My parachute didn't open.'

'Well, if you had of asked the locals before you jumped, they would have told you nothing opens here on a Sunday.'

Q: What do you call three hairy southern European types in the sauna?

A: Gorillas in the mist.

Q: Why didn't the Italian Olympic boxing team compete at Sydney 2000?

A: They found out you have to fight one on one.

O'Toole had been working in the lumber yard for twenty years and all that time he'd been stealing the wood and selling it. At last his conscience began to bother him and he went to confession to repent.

'Father, it's 15 years since my last confession, and I've been stealing wood from the lumber yard all those years,' he told the priest.

'I understand my son. Can you make a Novena?'

'Father, if you have the plans, I've got the lumber.'

Q: Why did a group of Columbians run away from a computer lab?

A: Because the computer said 'You have performed an illegal operation and will be shutdown.'

PROOF THAT JESUS WAS JEWISH:

1. He went into his father's business.
2. He lived at home until the age of 33.

3. He was sure his mother was a virgin, and his mother was sure he was God.

PROOF THAT JESUS WAS PUERTO RICAN:

1. His first name was Jesus.
2. He was bilingual.
3. He was always being harassed by the authorities.

PROOF THAT JESUS WAS A CALIFORNIAN:

1. He never cut his hair.
2. He walked around barefoot.
3. He invented a new religion.

PROOF THAT JESUS WAS BLACK:

1. He called everybody brother.
2. He liked Gospel.
3. He couldn't get a fair trial.

Father Murphy walks into a pub in Donegal and says to the first man he meets, 'Do you want to go to heaven?'

'I do Father,' said the man.

'Then stand over there against the wall.'

Then the priest asked a second man, 'Do you want to got to heaven?'

'Certainly, Father,' the man replied.

'Stand over there against the wall.'

Then Father Murphy walked up to O'Toole and said, 'Do you want to go to heaven?'

O'Toole said, 'No, I don't Father.'

'I don't believe this. You mean to tell me that when you die you don't want to go to heaven?'

'Oh, when I die, yes. I thought you were getting a group together to go right now.'

The good Father was warning his listeners about the suddenness of death.

'Before another day is ended,' he thundered, 'somebody in this parish will die.'

Seated in the front row was a little old Irishman who laughed out loud at this statement.

Very angry, the priest said to the jovial old man, 'What's so funny?'

'Well,' spoke up the oldster, 'I'm not a member of this parish.'

Brothers Mike and Seamus O'Malley are the two richest men in town and complete shites, both of 'em. They swindle the church out of its property, foreclose on the orphanage and cheat widows out of their last penny. One day Seamus up and dies and Mike pays a visit to the priest.

'Father,' he says, 'my good name will be upheld in this town. You'll be givin' the eulogy for me brother and in that eulogy you are going to say "Seamus O'Malley was truly a saint".'

'I won't do such a thing,' says the priest. 'T would be a lie!'

'I know you will,' says Mike. 'I hold the mortgage on the parish school and if you don't say those words, I'll foreclose.'

The priest is over a barrel. 'And if I pledge to say those words,' he says, 'then you'll sign the note over free and clear?'

'Done,' cackles Mike and he signs over the note. Next morning at the funeral, the priest begins the eulogy.

'Seamus O'Malley was a mean-spirited, spiteful, penurious, lying, cheating, arrogant and hateful excuse for a human being,' he says. 'But compared to his brother, Mike, Seamus O'Malley was truly a saint.'

Two English ladies were discussing their holiday plans on a London street corner near an Irish lady.

'We're planning a lovely holiday in Devon this year,' said one.

'Oh you oughtn't to do that,' said the other, 'there are Irish there! It would be awful.'

'Dear me!' said the first lady. 'Well where are you going?'

'Salisbury,' she replied.

'But Salisbury is simply crawling with Irish!' the first objected.

At this point the Irish lady could no longer hold her tongue. 'Why don't ye go t' hell,' she suggested. 'There be no Irish there!'

Irish they were, and drunk for sure, and they sat in the corner of Mulligan's newly refurbished bar. Across the wall opposite was a huge mirror, 4m long and stretching from floor to ceiling. Glancing around the room Pat suddenly spotted their reflection in the mirror.

'Mick, Mick,' he whispered. 'Don't look now but there's two fellas over there the image of us!'

'In the name of God,' said Mick, spotting the reflection. 'They're wearing identical clothes and everything.'

'That does it,' said Pat. 'I'm going to buy them a drink.'

But as Pat started to rise from his seat, Mick said, 'Sit down Pat. One of them's coming over.'

'Well, Mrs O'Connor, so you want a divorce?' the solicitor asked his client. 'Tell me about it. Do you have a grudge?'

'Oh, no,' replied Mrs O'Connor. 'Sure now, we have a carport.'

The solicitor tried again. 'Well, does the man beat you up?'

'No, no,' said Mrs O'Connor, looking puzzled. 'Oi'm always first out of bed.'

Still hopeful, the solicitor tried once again. 'What I'm trying to find out are what grounds you have.'

'Bless ye, son. We live in a flat - not even a window box, let alone grounds.'

'Mrs O'Connor, you need a reason that the court can consider. What is the reason for you seeking this divorce?'

'Ah, well now. Sure it's because the man can't hold an intelligent conversation.'

POLITICALLY CORRECT SPEAK TO PROTECT MINORITIES:

Aquatically challenged:	drowning.
Biologically challenged:	dead.
Caucasian culturally-disadvantaged:	white trash.
Certified astrological consultant:	crackpot.
Certified crystal therapist:	crackpot.
Certified past-life regression hypnotist:	crackpot.
Chronologically-gifted:	old.
Co-dependent:	finger-pointer.
Creatively re-dyed:	blonde.
Differently-brained:	stupid.
Differently-organised:	messy.
Energy-efficient:	off.
Environmentally-correct human:	dead.
Facially-challenged:	ugly.
Factually-unencumbered:	ignorant.
Financially inept:	poor.
Folically independent:	bald.
Genetically discriminating:	racist.
Gravitationally-challenged:	fat.
Horizontally-challenged:	thin.
Horizontally-gifted:	fat.
In denial:	unaware that forgetting something obviously proves it happened.

In recovery: drunk/junkie.
Intellectually-impaired: stupid.
Life-impaired: dead.
Metabolically-challenged: dead.
Monetarily-challenged: poor.
Morally -challenged: a crook.
Morally-handicapped: someone who has no other reason
                                                to park in a handicapped zone.

Motivationally-challenged: lazy.
Musically-delayed: tone deaf.
Nasally-disadvantaged: large nose.
Nasally-gifted: really big nose.
Outdoor urban-dwellers: homeless.
Person living with entropy: dead.
Petroleum transfer
technician: gas station attendant.
Sanitation engineer: garbage man.
Sexually-focused,
chronologically-gifted
individual: dirty old man.
Socially-challenged: nerd.
Spatially-perplexed: drunk.
Uniquely-coordinated: clumsy.
Vertically-challenged: short.
Visually-challenged: blind.

AN IRISHMAN IS A MAN WHO:

- May not believe there is a God, but is darn sure of the
  infallibility of the pope.
- Won't eat meat on Friday, but will drink Jameson for breakfast.
- Has such great respect for the truth, he uses it only in
  emergencies.
- Sees things not as they are, but the way they never will be.

- Cries at sad movies, but cheers in battle.
- Hates the English, but reserves his cruelty for countrymen.
- Gets more Irish the further he gets from Ireland.
- Believes in civil rights, but not in his neighbourhood.
- Believes to forgive is divine, therefore doesn't do it himself.
- Loves religion for its own sake, but also because it makes it so inconvenient for his neighbours.
- Scorns money, but worships those who have it.
- Considers any Irishman who achieves success to be a traitor.

Mick and Paddy were walking home after a night on the beer when a severed head rolled along the ground.

Mick picked it up and said to Paddy, 'Shit, that looks like Sean!'

'No Sean was taller than that,' said Paddy.

Paddy and Seamus were giving a motorcycle a ride on a brisk autumn day. After a wee bit Paddy, who was sitting behind Seamus, began to holler 'Seamus, Seamus, the wind is cutting me chest out!'

'Well, Paddy me lad,' said Seamus, 'why don't you take your jacket off and turn it from front to back. That'll block the wind for you.'

So Paddy took Seamus' advice and turned his jacket from front to back. After a bit, Seamus turned to talk to Paddy and was horrified to see that Paddy wasn't there. Immediately he turned the bike around and retraced their route. After a short time he came to a turn and saw some farmers standing around Paddy who was sitting on the ground.

'Tanks be to heaven, is he alright?' Seamus asked.

'Well,' said one of the farmers, 'he was alright when we found him here but since we turned his head the right way around he hasn't said a word!'

PRESS RELEASE FROM THE OFFICE OF THE PRIME MINISTER, NEW ZEALAND

Following the successful disbanding of the armed forces the prime minister of New Zealand, Helen Clark, has unveiled a bold new plan to totally disband the entire nation. In a statement to the world's press Prime Minister Clark unveiled her 'Great Step Nowhere' plan.

Launching the plan, Clark suggested that reports that their armed forces had been forced to say 'bang, bang' during war exercises had been the final nail in the coffin for the once-almost-proud nation.

'For years now we've been doing nothing of value,' she said. 'All our really profitable industries have gone overseas. Music, kiwi fruit, Russell Crowe. After that, it's basically just a bunch of sheep and a once-proud rugby team. Even the Cricketers are poor by world standards.'

Clark went on to outline the timetable for disbanding the nation following the sale of the navy's two dinghies and after the army gives its shotgun back to the British.

In a sometimes emotional presentation, Ms Clark outlined the difficulties facing the former country.

'Every nation has its problems but, as the leader, you can always look at some other loser nation and say, "They're worse off than us". We finally realised that we could no longer do that.'

The killer blow came last Monday when the New Zealand treasury tabled a report that found that Aussie wicket-keeper Adam Gilchrist's new contract with the Australian Cricket Board had him earning more than the entire New Zealand GDP.

'When that hit us we realised that the ship of state was pretty much gunwale deep in sediment and it was time to turn off the bilge pumps and move to a real country,' a treasury spokesman said.

All industry and businesses are expected to have left the islands by the end of June and all Government responsibilities will cease on the first of July. Any farmers wishing to remain will do so on a purely subsistence basis with the possibility of a feudal system developing by the end of September.

The All Blacks will maintain a training facility near Otago until the end of August after which time New Zealand, in all its forms and pursuits, will cease to exist.

When asked how the loss of the entire nation of New Zealand will affect the region, a World Bank spokesman called for an atlas.

Recently, Germany conducted some scientific exploration involving their best scientists. Core drilling samples of earth were taken to a depth of 50m and during the examinations, small pieces of copper were discovered. After running many arduous tests on these samples, the German government announced that ancient Germans, 25,000 years ago, had a nationwide telephone network.

Naturally, the British government was not that easily impressed. They ordered their own scientists to take British core samples at a depth of 100m. From these samples, they found small pieces of glass and soon announced that the ancient Brits, 35,000 years ago, already had a nationwide optical-fibre network.

Irish scientists were outraged. Immediately after this announcement, they ordered their scientist to take samples in Ireland at a depth of 200m, but found absolutely nothing. They concluded that the ancient Irish, 55,000 years ago, were an even more advanced civilisation, as they already had a mobile telephone network in place.

An Irish blessing: May you be in heaven half an hour before the devil knows you are dead.

Q: What is Irish diplomacy?
A: It's the ability to tell a man to go to hell so that he will look forward to making the trip.

When the Irish say that St Patrick chased the snakes out of Ireland, what they don't tell you is that he was the only one who saw any snakes!

FAMILIES

A three-year-old went with his father to see a new litter of kittens. Upon returning home, he breathlessly informed his mother that there were two boy kittens and two girl kittens.

'How did you know?' his mother asked.

'Daddy picked them up and looked underneath,' the child explained. 'I think it was printed on the bottom.'

One night I was chatting with Mum about how she had changed as a mother from the first child to the last. She told me she had mellowed a lot over the years.

'When your oldest sister coughed or sneezed, I called the ambulance,' she said. 'When your youngest brother swallowed 20c, I just told him it was coming out of his allowance.'

A woman in the hospital has just had twins, a boy and a girl. She had a caesarean and is in the recovery room just coming out of the anaesthetic.

The nurse comes into the room and says, 'Your brother has taken the liberty to name the children.'

'Oh no. He probably gave them stupid names.'

'Well, the girl's name is Denise.'

'That's not bad, I like it. What about the boy?'

'The boy's name is De-nephew.'

Neighbour: What are you up to there, Tim?
Tommy: My goldfish died and I've just buried him.
Neighbour: That's an awfully big hole for a goldfish, isn't it?
Tommy: That's because he's inside your stupid cat.

A big-game hunter went on safari with his wife and mother-in-law. One evening, while still deep in the jungle, his wife awoke to find her mother gone. Rushing to her husband, she insisted that he help her find her mother.

The hunter picked up his rifle, took a swig of whisky, and started to look for her. In a clearing not far from the camp, they came upon a chilling sight: the mother-in-law was backed up against a thick, impenetrable bush and a large male lion stood facing her.

The wife cried, 'What are we going to do?'

'Nothing,' said the husband.

'The lion got himself into this mess. Let him get himself out of it.'

A woman gets on a bus with her baby. The bus driver says: 'That's the ugliest baby that I've ever seen. Ugh!'

The woman goes to the rear of the bus and sits down, fuming. She says to a man next to her: 'The driver just insulted me!'

'You go right up there and tell him off – go ahead, I'll hold your monkey for you.'

Little Josh comes home from first grade and tells his father that they learned about the history of Valentine's Day.

'Since Valentine's Day is for a Christian saint and we're Jewish,' he asks, 'will God get mad at me for giving someone a valentine?'

His father thinks a bit, then says, 'No, I don't think God would get mad. Who do you want to give a valentine to?'

'Osama bin Laden.'

'Why Osama bin Laden?'

'Well, I thought that if a little American Jewish boy could have enough love to give Osama a valentine, he might start to think that maybe we're not all bad and maybe start loving people a little bit. And if other kids saw what I did and sent valentines to Osama, he'd love everyone a lot more. And then he'd start going all over the place to tell everyone how much he loved them and how he didn't hate anyone anymore.'

His father's heart swells and he looks at his boy with new-found pride. 'Josh, that's the most wonderful thing I've ever heard.'

'I know,' Josh says, 'and once that gets him out in the open, the marines could blow the shit out of him.'

A young woman was taking an afternoon nap. When she woke up, she told her husband, 'I just dreamed that you gave me a pearl necklace for Valentine's day. What do you think it means?'

'You'll find out tonight,' he said.

That evening, the man came home with a small package and gave it to his wife. Delighted, she opened it. It was a book entitled *The Meaning of Dreams*.

Two cannibals are eating their dinner and one cannibal says to the other, 'I don't like my mother-in-law much.'

'Well, just eat your chips then.'

Husband: Shall we try a new position tonight?
Wife: Sure. You stand by the ironing board and I'll sit on the couch and drink beer and fart.

A newlywed farmer and his wife were visited by her mother, who immediately demanded an inspection of their home. The farmer had tried to be friendly to his new mother-in-law, hoping that theirs would be a non-antagonistic relationship. All to no avail. She nagged them at every opportunity, demanding changes, offering unwanted advice, and generally making life unbearable to the farmer and his new bride.

During a forced inspection of the barn, the farmer's mule suddenly reared up and kicked the mother-in-law in the head, killing her instantly. It was a shock to all, no matter what were their feelings toward her demanding ways.

At the funeral service a few days later, the farmer stood near the casket and greeted folks as they walked by. The pastor noticed that whenever a woman whispered something to the farmer, he would nod his head yes and say something. Whenever a man walked by and whispered to the farmer, however, he would shake his head no, and mumble a reply. Very curious about this bizarre behaviour, the pastor asked the farmer what was going on.

The farmer replied, 'The women say, "What a terrible tragedy" and I nod my head and say "Yes, it was." The men ask, "Can I borrow that mule?" and I shake my head and say, "I can't lend it to you. It's all booked up for a year."

A father and son went fishing one summer day. While they were out in their boat, the boy suddenly became curious about the world around him.

He asked his father, 'Dad, how does this boat float?'

'Don't rightly know son.'

'Dad, how do fish breathe underwater?'

'Don't rightly know son.'

'Dad, why is the sky blue?'

'Don't rightly know son.'

Finally, the boy asked his father, 'Dad, do you mind my asking you all of these questions?'

'Of course not, son. If you don't ask questions, you never learn nothin'.'

Q: Is it possible to kill a mother-in-law with newspaper?
A: Yes, but only if you wrap an iron in it.

Little Johnny: Mum, when I was on the bus with daddy this morning, he told me to give up my seat to a lady.

Mum: Well, you've done the right thing.

Little Johnny: But Mum, I was sitting on daddy's lap.

A little girl goes to visit Santa at the mall. When it is her turn she sits on his lap and Santa says 'Have you been good?'

The little girl replies, 'Yes, Santa, very good.'

'What would you like for Christmas?'

'I want Barbie and GI Joe.'

'GI Joe? Doesn't Barbie come with Ken?'

'No Santa,' says the little girl, 'Barbie fakes it with Ken. But she comes with GI Joe.'

A fisherman's wife was sitting on the bank of a river when the ranger came along and said, 'Excuse me madam but I need to speak to your husband. Can you tell me where he is?'

Pointing to a clump of reeds, she replied, 'Go over there and look for the pole with a worm on both ends.'

Sally: Mummy why can't I go swimming in the sea?

Mum: Because there are sharks in the sea.

Sally: But mummy, daddy is swimming in the sea.

Mum: That's different. He's insured.

Q: How much fishing tackle can a man accumulate before his wife throws him out?

A: I don't know the answer but I think I'm nearly there.

Standing at the edge of the lake, a man saw a woman flailing about in the deep water. Unable to swim, the man screamed for help. A trout fisherman ran up.

The man said, 'My wife is drowning and I can't swim. Please save her. I'll give you $100.'

The fisherman dived into the water. In 10 powerful strokes,

he reached the woman, put his arm around her, and swam back to shore.

Depositing her at the feet of the man, the fisherman said, 'OK, where's my $100?'

'Look, when I saw her going down for the third time, I thought it was my wife. But this is my mother-in-law.'

The fisherman reached into his pocket and said, 'Just my luck. How much do I owe you?'

Teacher: How was your holiday, Penny?

Penny: Great. My brother and I spent the whole time on the beach, burying each other in the sand.

Teacher: That sounds like fun.

Penny: Yep, daddy says we can go back next year and find him.

A little kid gets onto a city bus and sits right behind the driver. He starts yelling, 'If my dad was a bull and my mum a cow I'd be a little bull.'

The driver starts getting mad at the noisy kid, who continues with, 'If my dad was an elephant and my mum an elephant I would be a little elephant.'

The kid goes on with several animals until the bus driver gets angry and yells at the kid, 'What if your dad was gay and your mum was a prostitute?'

The kid smiles and says, 'I would be a bus driver!'

A six-year-old boy called his mother from his friend Charlie's house and confessed he had broken a lamp when he threw a football in their living room.

'But, Mum,' he said, brightening, 'you don't have to worry about buying another one. Charlie's mother said it was irreplaceable.'

Bill and Linda decided that the only way to pull off a Sunday afternoon quickie with their 10-year-old son in the apartment was to send him out on the balcony and order him to report on all the neighbourhood activities.

The boy began his commentary as his parents put their plan into operation.

'There's a car being towed from the parking lot,' he said. 'An ambulance just drove by.'

A few moments passed.

'Looks like the Andersons have company,' he called out. 'Matt's riding a new bike and the Coopers are having sex.'

Mum and dad stop short.

'How do you know that?' the startled father asked.

'Their kid is standing out on the balcony too,' his son replied.

A father watched his daughter playing in the garden. He smiled as he reflected on how sweet and innocent his little girl was. Suddenly she just stopped and stared at the ground. He went over to her and noticed she was looking at two spiders mating.

'Daddy, what are those two spiders doing?' she asked.

'They're mating,' her father replied.

'What do you call the spider on top, daddy?'

'That's a daddy longlegs.'

'So, the other one is a mummy longlegs?'

'No,' her father replied. 'Both of them are daddy longlegs.'

The little girl thought for a moment, then took her foot and stomped them flat.

'That might be OK in Sydney, but we're not having any of that shit here in Melbourne.'

ARE YOU READY TO HAVE A BABY?

Car test: Forget the roller. It's the station wagon for you.
                   Buy a chocolate ice cream cone and put it in

the glove compartment. Leave it there. Get a pencil. Stick it into the cassette player. Take a family size tub of deep fried chips. Mash them into the back seat. Run a garden rake along both sets of doors. Now, after 300,000km and a second engine, try to trade it in.

Dressing test:	Obtain one giant, unhappy, live squid. Stuff it into a small net bag, at all times making sure that all the arms stay inside.
Eee-aaarrggh test:	Smear honey, peanut butter and soy sauce on the sofa and curtains. Place a fish stick and a hermit crab behind the couch and leave them there for the entire summer.
Feeding test:	Obtain a large plastic milk jug. Half fill with water. Suspend from the ceiling with a cord. Start the jug swinging. Try to insert spoonfuls of soggy cereal into the mouth of the jug, while pretending to be a helicopter. Now dump part of the contents of the jug over your head and the rest on the floor.
Ingenuity test:	Take a toilet paper roll. Turn it into an Easter candle. Use only sticky tape and a piece of foil. Take an egg carton. Using a pair of scissors and pot of paint, turn it into a happy rhino. Take a milk carton, an empty box of cocoa puffs and a ping-pong ball, and make an exact replica of the Eiffel Tower.
Land-mine test:	Get a giant box of Lego. Get your partner to spread them all over the house. Put on a blindfold. Endeavour to walk to the kitchen. Do not scream because this would wake a child at night.
Night test:	Prepare by obtaining a small cloth bag and fill it with 3-5kg of sand. Soak it thoroughly in

water. At 3pm, begin to waltz and hum with the bag. Continue until 9pm. Lay down your bag and set your alarm for 10pm. Get up, pick up your bag, and sing every song you have ever heard. Make up about a dozen more and sing these too until 4am. Set alarm for 5am. Get up and make breakfast. Keep this up for 5 years. Look happy.

Physical test (Men): Go to the nearest chemist. Set your wallet on the counter. Ask the shop assistant to help herself. Now proceed to the nearest supermarket. Go to the office and arrange for your pay check to be directly deposited to the store. Purchase a race guide. Go home and read it quietly for the last time.

Physical test (Women): Take a large beanbag chair and attach it to the front of your clothes. Leave it there for nine months. Now remove 10 of the beans. Try not to notice your closet full of clothes. You won't be wearing them for a while.

Shopping test: Borrow one or two small animals, such as goats, ferrets or Tasmanian devils, and take them with you as you shop. Always keep them in sight and pay for anything they eat or damage.

Warn-off assignment: Find a couple who already have a small child. Lecture them on how they can improve their method of bringing their child up, including patience, discipline, table manners and toilet training. Enjoy this experience. It will be the last time you will have all the answers.

DAD & SON WRITE

Dear Dad,

$chool i$ really great. I am making lot$ of friend$ and $tudying very hard. With all my $tuff, I $imply can't think of anything I need, $o if you would like, you can ju$t $end me a card, a$ I would love to hear from you.
Love,
Your $on.

Dear Son,

I kNOw that astroNOmy, ecoNOmics, and oceaNOgraphy are eNOugh to keep even an hoNOur student busy. Do NOt forget that the pursuit of kNOwledge is a NOble task, and you can never study eNOugh.
Love,
Dad

FISHING

Fishing - the worst day of fishing beats the best day of work.

An Irish fisherman's last wish was to be buried at sea, which was most unfortunate for his three friends, who died digging the grave

Fishing - One jerk on one end of the line waiting for a jerk on the other end!

There was an old sailor from Wales,
An expert at pissing in gales.
He could piss in a jar
From the top-gallant spar
Without even wetting the sails.

MacAndrews was visiting his cousin, O'Bannon. One day he decided to do a bit of fishing, when his cousin walked by.
'What are ye doing?' asked O'Bannon.
'Fishin',' said MacAndrews.
'Caught anything?'
'Ach, nae a bite.'
'What are ye usin' fer bait?'
'Worms.'
'Let me see it,' said O'Bannon.
MacAndrews lifted the line from the water and handed it to his cousin. O'Bannon took out his flask of poteen and dipped the worm in it. He handed it back to MacAndrews, who cast his

line once more. As soon as the worm hit the water, his rod bent over double, the line screaming out.

'Have ye got a bite?' asked O'Bannon.

'No!' shouted MacAndrews, fighting with the rod, 'The worm's got a salmon by the throat!'

Mrs Pete Monaghan came into the newsroom to pay for her husband's obituary. She was told by the kindly newsman that it was a dollar a word and he remembered Pete and wasn't it too bad about him passing away. She thanked him for his kind words and bemoaned the fact that she only had two dollars. But she wrote out the obituary, 'Pete died.'

The newsman said he thought old Pete deserved more and he'd give her three more words at no charge. Mrs Pete Monaghan thanked him profusely and rewrote the obituary: 'Pete died. Boat for sale'

At 3am, the manager of the local fisherman's club receives a phone call at home from a man who sounds quite drunk.

The man asked the manager, 'What time does the club open?'

'Noon,' said the manager and hung up.

An hour later the phone rang again and the same voice asked, 'What time does the club open?'

Again, the manager said, 'Noon' and hung up.

At 6.30am the phone rings and the same voice asks, 'Wenja shay the club opens at?'

'I told you before, it opens at noon. And if you don't sober up, you won't be allowed to get in.'

'Ah don' wanna get in, I wanna get out.'

If a fishing inspector and an insurance agent were both drowning and you could only save one of them, would you go to lunch or would you continue reading your paper?

A wealthy fisherman needed a brain transplant. His doctor told him he only had two brains on hand. One was of a college professor and cost $10,000. The other was of a fisherman and cost $500,000.

'You're kidding me Doc, $500,000 for a brain? That's awfully expensive.'

'Ah', said the doctor, 'but it's never been used.'

Very early one morning, there was a soft knock on the door and a whispered, 'Wanna go fishing, Ned?'

'Little early, isn't it Billy Joe?'

'What, for fishing?'

'No, for stupid questions.'

Two old mates are on a fishing trip in the northwest of Western Australia. One morning one of them keels over and dies but the other decides to keep fishing as the fish are still biting.

After he finishes he cleans his catch and puts his mate in the back of his 4WD. He drives for 36 hours, then decides he'd better tell the cops about his mate so he pulls into Carnarvon and tells the sergeant.

The sergeant listens to his story and says, 'Gee's he must be on the nose by now!'

'Nah I gilled and gutted him. He should be right for another 24 hours.'

Paddy Flaherty loves to fish and then go to the pub. He comes home drunk every evening toward 10pm. The missus has never been too happy about it. So one night she hides in the cemetery and decides to scare the shit out of him.

As poor Pat wanders by, up from behind a tombstone she jumps in a red devil costume screaming, 'Paddy Sean Flaherty, sure an ye don't give up your drinkin' and it's to hell I'll take ye.'

Pat, undaunted, staggers back and demands, 'Who the hell are you?'

'I'm the divil ye damned old fool'.

'Damned glad to meet you sir, I'm married to yer sister.'

You'll never hear a fisherman's wife say, 'Shouldn't you be down at the bar with your friends?'

Bob and Earl were two fishermen who lived for their sport. They fished at every opportunity and watched all the fishing shows on television. They pored over every magazine article on fishing and discussed tactics on how to win the major fishing competitions. They even agreed that whoever died first would try to come back and tell the other if there was fishing in heaven.

One summer night, Bob passed away in his sleep after coming in from a big day out fishing. He had had a good day and so he died happy. A few nights later, his buddy Earl awoke to the sound of Bob's voice coming from beyond.

'Bob, is that you?' Earl exclaimed. 'This is unbelievable! So tell me, is there fishing in heaven?'

'Well, I have some good news and some bad news for you. Which do you want to hear first?'

'Tell me the good news first.'

'The good news is that yes, there is fishing in heaven.'

'Oh, that is wonderful! So what could possibly be the bad news?'

'You're coming out fishing with me tomorrow night.'

First angler: I tell you, it was so long. I never saw another fish like it.

Second angler: I believe you.

I spent most of my life fishing, the rest I wasted.

I got a new rod and reel for my wife. Best trade I ever made.

——————

Q: How can a fisherman tell if his wife is dead?
A: The sex is the same, but the dishes pile up.

A drunken fisherman was seen crawling down some railroad tracks. Asked if there was a problem, he replied, 'Yeah, can you help me off this ladder.'

Some fishermen catch their best fish by the tale.

Fishing is the second-greatest thrill known to man. Catching a fish is the first.

Q: Why didn't Noah fish from his Ark?
A: Because he only had two worms.

A Maine fisherman died in poverty and many locals donated to a fund for his funeral. The owner of a home at the local lake was asked to contribute a dollar.

'A dollar,' she said, 'only a dollar to bury a fisherman? Here's a check, go bury a thousand of them.'

Ben, a local fisherman, went into his favourite bar and ordered six double vodkas.

Bob, the bartender said, 'Wow, you must have had a bad day.'

'Yeah', said Ben, 'I just found out my older brother is gay.'

The next day Ben showed up and again ordered six doubles.

Bob said, 'What, more problems?'

'Damn right, I just found out that my younger brother is gay.'

The third day, the same routine again – six doubles.

'What the hell, doesn't anyone in your family like women?' asked Bob.

'Yeah,' said Ben, 'I just found out my wife does.'

Give a man a fish and he'll eat for a day. Teach him how to fish and he will sit in a boat and drink beer all day.

A drunken fisherman stumbled upon a traditional baptismal service at the river where he fished. He walked out in the water to where the minister stood.

The minister turned to the drunk and said, 'Mister, are you ready to find Jesus?'

'Yes, reverend, I sure am.'

The minister then dunks the fellow under the water, pulls him up asking, 'Have you found Jesus?'

'No.'

So the preacher dunks him a bit longer, pulls him up and again asks, 'Did you find Jesus?'

'No.'

The minister is disgusted. He pushes the man under the water for about 30 seconds, pulls him up and asks in a harsh voice, 'Now, my good man, have you found Jesus yet?'

The old fisherman wipes his eyes, spits out some water and says to the minister, 'No. Are you sure this is where he fell in?'

Q: What is the richest fish in the world?
A: A goldfish.

A minister, chaplain of the local fisherman's club, had the members and their families gathered in his church for services.

In a loud voice he proclaimed, 'If I had all the beer in the world, I'd pour it in the river.'

With an even louder voice he said, 'If I had all the wine the world, I'd pour it in the river.'

He went on and in a booming voice said, 'If I had all the whisky in the world, I'd pour it in the river.'

At the conclusion of his sermon, the choir leader said, 'For our closing hymn, let us sing Number 47: Shall we Gather by the River.'

A man is out in his rowboat when suddenly a passing speed boat raises huge waves and the man's oars fall overboard. He is stranded out in the middle of the lake! After about two hours, he sees another row boat going by with a man and two women in it.

The first man yells, 'Hey buddy, can I borrow one of your oars?'

The other man yells back, 'They're not whores, they're my sisters.'

A pastor, a priest and a rabbi were out for a day of fishing. They had just pulled away from the dock when the rabbi said, 'Stop the boat, I forgot the coffee.'

The pastor, who was driving the boat, offered to turn around and go back to the dock. The rabbi indicated that there was no need to do this and quickly jumped out of the boat and ran across the water to shore and then to his car to fetch the coffee. The priest said that he would go too to help with the carrying. He climbed over the side, and skipped across the water behind the rabbi. Then they came back across the water with the picnic things and got back in the boat.

The pastor, not wanting to be shown up by the rabbi and the priest, made an excuse that he needed to go to the toilet and confidently jumped out of the boat attempting to run across the water like the rabbi and the priest. Instead, he sank quickly to the bottom of the lake. The priest looked at the rabbi, shook his head and said, 'We should have shown him where the rocks were.'

An elderly fisherman was at home, dying in bed, when he smelled his favourite aroma – chocolate chip cookies baking. He wanted one last cookie before he died, so he crawled to the kitchen, reached up to the cookie sheet on the table and grasped a warm, moist chip. His wife hit his hand with a spatula and yelled, 'Leave them alone. They're for the funeral.'

This fisherman goes to the river to check an illegal fish trap that he owns. He looks around to make sure there are no fishing inspectors about and pulls the fish trap out to check it. An inspector steps out of the bushes.

'Ahha!' he says.

The fisherman spins around and yells 'Shiiiit! Oh god. Noooo! Please don't hurt me!'

'Settle down, I'm not going to hurt you. I'm the fishing inspector'

'Thank God for that,' says the fisherman, 'I thought you were the bugger who owned this fish trap'.

Two fishermen were talking about the good old days.

'When I was a kid there were so many fish here I could always catch a few,' says the first one.

'When I was a kid we used a horse and cart and got enough fish to sell at the market.'

'How did you do that?'

'Well, we had this good old horse and we used to back the cart down into the water and put treacle on his tail. The flies got stuck in the treacle and when the fish jumped out of the water for the flies that good old horse just kicked them into the cart. We had a load of fish in no time.'

A taxidermist was driving through the country when he thought he would stop at a local bar and have a beer. The locals didn't like outsiders in their bar and when he entered he was greeted with dirty stares and low mumbles. He went to the bartender and asked for a beer.

'What do you do?' asked the barman.

'I'm a taxidermist.'

'Taxidermist? What is that?'

'Well, I mount animals, birds, and fish.'

The bartender turned to the other men in the bar and said, 'It's OK boys he's one of us'.

A young man and an old man were fishing on a pier. 'Last night I caught a fish that was over a metre long,' said the young man.

'Oh yeah, well I was here a couple of nights ago and I hooked something huge. After a 30-minute fight I finally got it up. It was an old lantern and, you won't believe this, but the thing was still lit,' said the old man.

'You must be lying. I find that too hard to believe.'

'I'll tell you what, you knock a couple of foot off your trout and I'll blow out my lantern.'

DICTIONARY OF FISHING TERMS

Angler:	An obsessed individual who owns a house that is falling down due to neglect; a truck, best described as 'rust-oleum' in colour; and a pristine boat that he wipes down with a chamois methodically before and after each trip.
Catch and release:	A conservation motion that happens most often right before the local ranger pulls over a boat that has caught over its limit.
Hook:	A curved piece of metal used to catch fish, or a clever advertisement to entice a fisherman to spend his live savings on a new rod and reel, or the punch administered by said fisherman's

wife after he spends their life savings on said rod and reel.

Knot:	An insecure connection between your hook and fishing line, or a permanent tangle on your spinning reel which forces you to go out and buy a bigger, better, much more expensive rig.
Landing net:	A net used to help drag a large wiggling fish, or an inebriated fishing buddy, on board.
Line:	Something you give your co-workers when they ask on Monday how your fishing went over the weekend.
Live bait:	The biggest fish you'll handle all day.
Lure:	An object that is semi-enticing to fish, but will drive an angler into such a frenzy that he will charge his credit card to the limit before exiting the tackle shop.
Quiet water:	Your surroundings after you stop cursing your bad luck and fall asleep at the reel.
Reel:	A weighted object that causes a rod to sink quickly when dropped overboard.
Rod:	An attractively painted length of fibreglass that keeps an angler from ever getting too close to a fish.
School:	A grouping in which fish are taught to avoid your $29.99 lures and hold out for burley instead.
Sinker:	A weight attached to a lure to get it to the bottom; or the nickname of your boat.
Skunk:	One who returns to the boat ramp many, many hours after his buddies have gone home so that there are no witnesses to his catch or lack thereof.
Tackle box:	A box shaped like your comprehensive first aid kit, but containing many sharp objects, so that

when you reach in the wrong box blindly to get a band-aid, you soon find that you need more than one.

Tackle: What your last catch did to you as you reeled him in, just before he wrestled free and jumped back overboard.

Test: The amount of strength a fishing line affords an angler when fighting fish in a specific weight range, or a measure of your creativity in blaming that darn line for once again losing the fish.

Thumb: A temporary hook holder.

Trawling: What you do after you've lost a $500 rod and reel set-up overboard.

Treble hook: Triples the odds of catching a fish. Quadruples the odds of getting the hook caught in your thumb (see Thumb).

I was glad when one fish got away. There just wasn't room in the boat for both of us!

Q: Which fish can perform operations?
A: A Sturgeon!

THE RULES OF FISHING

1. The least experienced fisherman always catches the biggest fish.
2. The worse your line is tangled, the better is the fishing around you.
3. Fishing will do a lot for a man but it won't make him truthful.

Q: What is the difference between a fish and a piano?
A: You can't tuna fish.

Vicar: I didn't see you in church last Sunday, Nigel. I hear
         you were out playing football instead?
Nigel: That's not true, vicar. And I've got the fish to prove it!

One day while driving home from his fishing trip in the pouring
rain, a man got a flat tyre outside a monastery. A monk came
out and invited him inside to have dinner and spend the night.
The motorist accepted. That night he had a wonderful dinner of
fish and chips. He decided to compliment the chef.

Entering the kitchen, he asked the cook, 'Are you the fish friar?'

'No,' the man replied, 'I'm the chip monk.'

A man phones home from his office and tells his wife:
'Something has just come up. I have a chance to go fishing
for a week. It's the opportunity of a lifetime and we leave right
away. So, honey, please pack my clothes, my fishing equipment
and especially my blue silk pyjamas. I'll be home in an hour to
pick them up.'

He goes home in a hurry and grabs everything and rushes off.
A week later he returns.

'Did you have a good trip, dear?' asks his wife.

'Oh yes it was great. But you forgot to pack my blue silk
pyjamas.'

'Oh no, I didn't. I put them in your tackle box.'

Q: What did the fish say when it hit a concrete wall?
A: Dam!

'I am never going to take my wife fishing with me, ever again!'
'That bad, huh?'

'She did everything wrong! She did every friggin' thing
wrong! She talked too much, made the boat rock constantly,
tried to stand up in the boat, baited the hook wrong, used the
wrong lures, and worst of all, she caught more fish than me!'

I think the only reason my husband likes to go fishing so much is that it's the only time he hears someone tell him, 'Wow, that's a big one!'

'What's the biggest fish you ever caught?'
'That would be the one that measured 35cm.'
'That's not so big!'
'Between the eyes.'

My wife gave me an ultimatum three weeks ago. She said, 'It's me or the fishing.' Gee I miss her.

Q: Why are fish so smart?
A: Because they swim in schools.

A fisherman came home one evening to find his eight-year-old son riding a new 10-speed bike.
'Boy', he yelled, 'where did you get the money for that bike? It must have cost $300!'
'Dad, I earned it hiking,' said his son. 'Every other night, while you've been fishing, Mr Green from the bait shop came to see Ma.
'He'd give me $20 and tell me to go take a hike.'

10 REASONS WHY YOU HAVE CHOSEN THE WRONG FISHING CHARTER SERVICE

1. The operator's got the engine manual sitting open on the console next to the controls.
2. He screams 'Yeehaa!' as he turns the boat away from the dock and pushes the throttle forward.
3. He thinks it's an asset that he can drive so fast that he gets the boat completely out of the water.

4. It takes him two hours and 25 minutes to reach your fishing destination on a five-hour charter.

5. He can't stop laughing when he realises that his brother the cop gave you a speeding ticket on your way to his boat, and says nothing about getting the ticket cancelled.

6. He casually tells you that on days he can't get a charter he's a delivery driver for Pizza Hut.

7. He goes on for hours about how boats are safer than cars, but only because there are fewer boats to hit. He runs aground three times during this oration.

8. He goes on for hours about his alien abduction experiences, with much detail given to the tests they supposedly performed on him.

9. The other fishing guides hold up protective religious icons as he passes by.

10. At the end of the day's fruitless fishing, he begs you to allow him to use your name as a reference.

'Do you really believe your husband when he tells you he goes fishing every weekend?' asked Jane's best friend.
'Why shouldn't I?' asked Jane.
'Well, maybe he is having an affair.'
'No way. He never returns with any fish.'

WHY BOATS ARE BETTER THAN WOMEN:

- Boats only need their fluids changed once a year.
- Boat's curves never sag.
- Boats last longer.
- Boats don't get pregnant.
- You can ride a boat any time of the month.
- Boats don't have parents.
- Boats don't whine unless something is really wrong.

- You can share your boat with your friends.
- If your boat makes too much noise, you can buy a muffler.
- You only need to get a new belt for your boat when the old one is really worn.
- If your boat smokes, you can do something about it.
- Boats don't care about how many other boats you have ridden.
- When riding, you and your boat both arrive at the same time.
- Boats don't care about how many other boats you have.
- Boats don't mind if you look at other boats, or if you buy boating magazines.
- If your boat is misaligned, you don't have to discuss politics to correct it.
- You can have a beer while riding your boat.
- You don't have to be jealous of the guy that works on your boat.
- You don't have to deal with priests or blood-tests to register your boat.
- You don't have to convince your boat that you're a boater and that you think that all boats are equals.
- If you say bad things to your boat, you don't have to apologise before you can ride it again.
- You can ride a boat as long as you want and it won't get sore.
- Your parents don't remain in touch with your old boat after you dump it.
- Boats always feel like going for a ride.
- Boats don't insult you if you are a bad boater.
- Boats don't care if you are late.
- You don't have to take a shower before riding your boat.
- It's always OK to use tie-downs on your boats.
- If your boat doesn't look good, you can paint it or get better parts.
- You can't get diseases from a boat you don't know very well.

Q: Where do fish keep their money?
A: In the river bank.

'I caught a 9kg salmon last week.'

'Were there any witnesses?'

'There sure were. If there hadn't been, it would have been 20kg.'

A priest was walking along the cliffs of Dover when he came upon two locals heaving another man up on the end of a rope.

'That's what I like to see,' said the priest, 'A man helping his fellow man.'

As he was walking away, one local remarked to the other, 'Well, he sure doesn't know the first thing about shark fishing.'

Three blondes are sitting by the side of a river holding fishing poles with the lines in the water. A game warden comes up behind them, taps them on the shoulder and says, 'Excuse me, ladies, I'd like to see your fishing licences.'

'We don't have any.' replies the first blonde.

'Well, if you're going to fish, you need fishing licences.'

'But officer, we aren't fishing. All we have are magnets at the end of our lines. We're collecting debris off the bottom of the river.'

The game warden lifts up all the lines and, sure enough, there are horseshoe magnets tied on the end of each line.

'Well, I know of no law against it,' he says. 'Take all the debris you want.'

And with that, the Game Warden leaves.

As soon as the Game Warden is out of sight, the three blondes start laughing hysterically.

'What a dumb fish cop,' the second blonde says to the other two, 'doesn't he know that there are steelhead in this river?'

Q: What is the difference between a fairy tale and a fish story?

A: A fairy tale begins with 'Once upon a time,' a fish story begins with 'This ain't no bullshit.'

One Saturday morning a man gets up early, dresses quietly, makes his lunch, puts on his long johns, grabs his dog and hooks up his boat to the truck.

When he pulls out of his garage the rain is pouring down, there's snow and sleet mixed in with the rain and the wind is blowing at over 30kph. He returns to the garage and goes back into the house. He turns the TV to the weather channel and he finds it is going to be very bad weather all day long, so he puts his boat back in the garage, quietly undresses and slips back into bed.

There he cuddles up to his wife's back, now with a different anticipation and whispers, 'The weather out there is terrible'.

'Yeah, can you believe my stupid husband is out fishing in it?' she says.

SURE WAYS TO GET A BITE ON A SLOW DAY

- Talk about changing spots
- Prepare another rod while one is out
- Lay your rod down unsecured
- Go for a sandwich
- Start to pull the boat anchor
- Use the worst fly you own
- Crack open your first beer
- Crack open your last beer
- Watch others fishing
- Start reeling in your lines at going home time
- Give your fishing rod to a female companion or child to hold
- Put your landing net out of reach
- Cast your line over an obstruction
- Let your line drift into impossible weeds
- Turn to look at the sunrise or sunset
- Decide that you need to take a leak

A fisherman's wife gave birth to twin boys. When the babies were side by side, they always looked in opposite directions, so they were named Forward and Away.

Years later the fisherman took his sons fishing, but they didn't return. Months passed, and the wife finally spotted her husband plodding sadly up the beach. He explained to her that during their trip, Forward had hooked an enormous fish. He had struggled for hours, when suddenly the fish pulled Forward into the water and they never saw him again.

'That's just terrible!' his wife cried.

'It was terrible all right. But you should have seen the one that got Away!'

'Do you think we'll catch any fish today?'
'Cod willing.'

There are two kinds of fishermen: those that fish for sport, and those that catch something.

'How was the fishing today Adrian?'
'Not very good, I only got fifty bites – one small fish and forty nine mosquitoes.'

Q: Why do they cut the heads off sardines?
A: So they don't bite each other in the can.

Wanted: Woman who can cook, clean, wash and make sweet love. Must have own boat. If interested, send a photo of the boat to . . .

'I'm going fishing' really means, 'I'm going to drink myself silly, get sunburnt and stand by a river with a stick in my hand, while the fish swim by in complete safety.'

A woman is in bed with her lover who also happens to be her husband's best friend. After they make love, the phone rings. Since it is the woman's house, she picks up the receiver. Her lover looks over at her and listens, only hearing her side of the conversation.

'Hello? Oh, hi. I'm so glad that you called,' she says speaking in a cheery voice.

'Really? That's wonderful. I am so happy for you, that sounds terrific.'

'Great!'

'Thanks.'

'OK.'

'Bye.'

She hangs up the telephone and her lover asks, 'Who was that?'

'That was my husband telling me all about the wonderful time he's having on his fishing trip with you.'

The Reverend Green encountered one of his parishioners returning from a day's fishing and engaged him in conversation.

'Ah, Lachlan,' he began in his best preaching tone 'You are a fine fisherman, but I am a fisher of men.'

Lachlan, determined to get home for his dinner, cut him short by replying, 'Aye, I was passing your church last Sunday and looked in the window, but you hadn't caught many.'

Mother's advice to daughter: Feed a man a fish and he'll eat for a day. But teach a man to fish and you get rid of him for the whole weekend.

Two men were walking down the street with two salmon each under their arms. Two Irishmen were walking in the opposite direction.

'How did you catch those?' asked the first Irishman.

'Well it's like this. Michael here holds my legs over the bridge, and I grab the salmon as they swim up the river. We got four salmon. A great day's fishing!'

So the fishless pair agreed to give it a try.

They got to the bridge and Sean called to his friend, 'Hold my legs now Paddy.'

After he had been hanging upside down for 30 minutes he cried, 'Pull me up! Pull me up!'

Paddy asked, 'Do you have a fish Sean?'

'No, there's a bloody train coming!'

FISHING IS BETTER THAN SEX BECAUSE:

- If you want to watch fishing on television, you don't have to subscribe to the Playboy channel.
- If your partner takes pictures or videotapes of you fishing, you don't have to worry about them showing up on the Internet if you become famous.
- If your regular fishing partner isn't available, s/he won't object if you fish with someone else.
- It is perfectly acceptable to pay a professional to fish with you once in a while.
- It's perfectly respectable to fish with a total stranger.
- Nobody expects you to fish with the same partner for the rest of your life.
- Nobody expects you to give up fishing if your partner loses interest in it.
- Nobody will ever tell you that you will go blind if you fish by yourself.
- The 10 commandments don't say anything about fishing.
- There are no fishing-transmitted diseases.
- When dealing with a fishing pro, you never have to wonder if they are really an undercover cop.

- When you see a really good fisherperson, you don't have to feel guilty about imagining the two of you fishing together.
- You can have a fishing calendar on your wall at the office, tell fishing jokes, and invite co-workers to fish with you without getting sued for harassment.
- You don't have to be a newlywed to plan a holiday primarily to enjoy your favourite activity.
- You don't have to go to a sleazy shop in a seedy neighbourhood to buy fishing stuff.
- You don't have to hide your fishing magazines.
- Your fishing partner doesn't get upset about people you fished with long ago.
- Your fishing partner will never say, 'Not again? We just fished last week! Is fishing all you ever think about?'

A country priest loves to fly fish. It's an obsession. So far this year the weather has been so bad that he hasn't had a chance to get his beloved wadders on and his favourite flies out of their box. Strangely though, every Sunday the weather has been good, but of course Sunday is the day he has to go to work.

The weather forecast for Sunday is good again so he calls a fellow priest, claiming to have lost his voice with the flu. He asks him to take over his sermon and on Sunday, the fly-fishing priest drives 100km to a river near the coast so that no one will recognise him.

An angel up in heaven is keeping watch and sees what the priest is doing. He tells God, who decides to do something about it.

With the first cast of the priest's line, a huge fish mouth gulps down the fly. For over an hour the priest runs up and down the river bank fighting the fish. At the end, when he finally lands the monster-sized fish, it turns out to be a world-record salmon.

Confused the angel asks God, 'Why did you let him catch that huge fish? I thought you were going to teach him a lesson.'

'I did. Who do you think he's going to tell?'

A woman goes into a shop to buy a rod and reel as a gift. She doesn't know which one to get so she just grabs one and goes over to the counter where there's a shop assistant wearing dark shades.

'Excuse me sir' she says, 'can you tell me anything about this rod and reel?'

The assistant replies, 'Ma'am I'm blind but if you drop it on the counter I can tell you everything you need to know about it from the sound it makes.'

She doesn't believe him, but drops it on the counter anyway.

He says, 'That's a six graphite rod with a Zebco 202 reel and 10lb test line. It's a good all around rod and reel and it's only $20.'

'It's amazing that you can tell all that just by the sound of it dropping on the counter. I think it's what I'm looking for so I'll take it.'

He walks behind the counter to the register, and in the meantime the woman breaks wind big-time. At first she is embarrassed but then realises that there is no way he could tell it was her as being blind he wouldn't know that she was the only person around.

The assistant rings up the sale and says, 'That will be $25.50.'

'But didn't you say it was $20?'

'Yes ma'am, the rod and reel is $20, but the duck call is $3, and the catfish stink bait is $2.50.'

A man, with two buckets of fish, was stopped by a game warden in a National Park, leaving a lake well known for its fishing. The warden asked the man, 'Do you have a licence to catch those fish?'

'No, sir. These are my pet fish.'

'Pet fish?'

'Yes, sir. Every night I take these fish down to the lake and let them swim around for a while. I whistle and they jump back into their buckets, and I then take 'em home.'

'That's a bunch of hooey! Fish can't do that.'

'Yes they can. Here, I'll show you. It really works.'

'OK I've got to see this.'

The man poured the fish into the river and stood and waited. After several minutes, the fishing inspector turned to the man and said, 'Well?'

'Well, what?' the man responded.

'When are you going to call them back?'

'Call who back?'

'The fish!'

'What fish?'

Joe and Bob are out fishing. A funeral service passes over the bridge they're fishing by, and Bob takes off his hat and puts it over his heart. He keeps it there until the funeral service has passed by.

'Gee Bob,' says Joe. 'I didn't know you had it in you.'

'It's the least I could do. After all I was married to her for 30 years.'

Steve was out on morning walk when he passed Ole's house and saw a sign that said 'Boat for Sale'. This confused Steve because he knew that Ole didn't own a boat, so he went in to ask Ole about it.

'Hey Ole,' said Steve, 'I noticed da sign in your yard dat says "Boat for Sale," but ya ain't ever been fishun and don't even have a boat. All ya have is your old John Deere tractor and combine harvester.'

'Yup, and they're boat for sale.'

Q: Where do you find most of the fish?

A Between the head and the tail.

Don't worry about eating fish from polluted waters. If you go fishing on a cold day, take the fish home and hang them by the head from a clothesline. The mercury will drop to the tail. Cut off the tail, and eat the rest of the fish. Easy as that!

Q: How can you tell when a fisherman is lying?

A: Watch his mouth real close – if it moves, he's lying.

Q: What do you say to a guy with his lure in the seaweed?

A: Your fly's down!

Q: Two fathers and two sons went fishing, how many people were there?

A: Three. They were all members of the same family – grandfather, father and son.

Q: Where do whales get weighed?

A: At a whaleweigh station.

Q: What kind of fish do you find in a bird cage?

A: A perch.

Q: What is the best way to communicate with a fish?

A: Drop it a line.

Q: What is the best way of stopping a fish from smelling?

A: Cut off its nose.

Q: What happened to the fishing boat that sank in piranha-infested waters?

A: It came back with a skeleton crew.

Q: What whizzes along a riverbed on three wheels?
A: A motor-pike with a side-carp.

Q: Where do fish wash?
A: In a river basin.

Q: What is the best fish on ice?
A: A skate.

Q: What swims in the sea, carries a machine gun, and makes you an offer you can't refuse?
A: The Codfather.

Q: What fish terrorises other fish?
A: Jack the Kipper.

Q: What do you give a seasick elephant?
A: Lots of room.

Mother: Have you given the goldfish fresh water today?
Son: No, they haven't finished the water I gave them yesterday.

Q: What swims and is highly dangerous?
A: A trout with a hand grenade.

Q: What did one sardine say to the other sardine when it saw a submarine?
A: There goes a can full of people.

Q: What do you call a neurotic octopus?
A: A crazy, mixed up squid.

Q: What do you call a baby whale that never stops crying?
A: A little blubber.

Q: What kind of sea creature eats its victims two by two?
A: Noah's shark.

Q: What side of a fish has the most scales?
A: The outside.

Q: How do you stick down an envelope under the water?
A: With a seal.

Q: What do sea monsters eat?
A: Fish and ships.

Q: What can fly under the water?
A: A bird in a submarine.

Q: What has antlers and sucks your blood?
A: A Moose-quito.

Q: What should you do if you find a shark in your bed?
A: Sleep somewhere else.

Q: What do you call a pike with a gun?
A: Sir.

First guy: You have no idea what I had to do to be able to come out fishing this weekend. I had to promise my wife that I will paint every room in the house next weekend.

Second guy: That's nothing, I had to promise my wife that I will build her a new deck for the pool.

Third guy: Man, you both have it easy! I had to promise my wife that I will remodel the kitchen for her.

Fourth guy: Why did you go to all that trouble? I just set my alarm for 5:30am and when it went off I gave my wife a nudge and said, 'Fishing or sex?' and she said, 'Don't forget your sweater.'

Q: Why did the lobster blush?
A: It saw the Queen Mary's bottom.

Q: Why did the fish blush?
A: Because it saw the seaweed.

Q: What lives under the sea and carries a lot of people?
A: An Octobus.

Q: Where do you find a crab with no legs?
A: Exactly where you left it.

YOU KNOW YOU ARE A FISHERMAN IF:

- You have a power worm dangling from your rear-view mirror because you think it makes a good air freshener.
- Your wedding party had to tie tin cans to the back of your bass boat.
- You call your boat 'sweetheart' and your wife 'skeeter'.
- Your local tackle shop has your credit card number on file.
- You keep a flipping stick by your favourite chair to change the TV channels with.
- You name your black lab 'Mercury' and your cat 'Evinrude'.
- Bass Pro Shop has a private line just for you.

- You have your name painted on a parking space at the launch ramp.
- You have a photo of your 5kg bass on your desk at work instead of your family.
- You consider cold sausages and crackers a complete meal.
- You think 'megabytes' means a great day fishing.
- You send your kid off to the first day of school with his shoes tied in a Palomar knot.
- You think there are four seasons – pre-spawn, spawn, post-spawn and hunting.
- Your $30,000 bass boat's trailer needs new tyres so you just 'borrow' the ones off your caravan.
- You trade your wife's van for a smaller vehicle so your boat will fit in the garage.
- Your kids know it's Saturday because the boat's gone.

Q: What did the boy octopus say to the girl octopus?
A: I want to hold your hand hand hand hand hand hand hand hand.

Q: What do you get if you cross a whale with a computer?
A: A four-tonne know it all.

Q: Why do they call him 'River'?
A: Because the biggest part of him is his mouth.

Q: Why do they call him 'Fish'?
A: Because he can't keep his mouth shut.

Q: What do you get is you cross a rose with a pike?
A: I don't know but I wouldn't put my nose too close to smell it.

Q: How do I avoid infection from biting insects?
A: That's easy – don't bite them.

Q: What sits at the bottom of the sea and shivers?
A: A nervous wreck.

Q: What has big sharp teeth, a tail, scales, and a trunk?
A: A pike going on holiday.

Q: What is the fastest fish in the sea?
A: Go-carp.

Q: If fish lived on land, which country would they live in?
A: Finland.

Q: What did one rock pool say to the other rock pool?
A: Show me your mussels.

Q: How do you kiss a pike?
A: Very carefully.

Three guys were fishing on a lake one day when Jesus walked across the water and joined them in the boat. When the three astonished men had settled down enough to speak, the first guy asked humbly, 'Jesus, I've suffered from back pain ever since I took shrapnel in the Vietnam War. Could you help me?'

'Of course, my son,' said Jesus.

He touched the man's back and he felt relief for the first time in years. The second guy, who wore very thick glasses and had a hard time reading and driving, asked if Jesus could do anything about his poor eyesight. Jesus smiled, removed the man's glasses and tossed them into the lake. When they hit the water, the man's eyes cleared and he could see everything distinctly. Jesus turned to the third guy, but he put his hands out defensively.

'Don't touch me!' he cried. 'I'm on a disability pension.'

THINGS NOT TO SAY IN A BAIT SHOP

- 'All right, who's going to be a sport and show me their favourite fishing hole?'
- 'Anyone know who owns the red pick-up out front that I just hit?'
- 'Look at all this antique tackle.'
- 'Let me tell you about a fish I once caught . . .'
- 'What! No high-tech lures? How can you people catch anything?'
- 'One of you has got to be named Bubba. Let me guess . . .'
- 'You do take travellers cheques, don't you?'
- 'Are those fish you caught or is that a family portrait?'
- 'I only use imported hooks.'
- 'I need a new rod. Do you have anything in blue to match my reel?'
- 'You call this live bait? Why, in New York we . . .'

A man went fishing one day. He looked over the side of his boat and saw a snake with a frog in its mouth. Feeling sorry for the frog, he reached down, gently took the frog from the snake, and set the frog free.

But then he felt sorry for the snake. He looked around the boat, but he had no food. All he had was a bottle of bourbon. So he opened the bottle and gave the snake a few shots.

The snake went off happy, the frog was happy, and the man was happy to have performed such good deeds. He thought everything was great until about 10 minutes passed and he heard something knock against the side of the boat. In stunned disbelief, the fisherman looked down and saw the snake was back with two other frogs!

GOLF

There was a young lady golfer named Duff,
With a lovely, luxuriant muff.
    In his haste to get in her,
    One eager beginner
Lost both of his balls in the rough.

Seamus O'Malley is playing golf when he takes a hard struck golf ball right in the crotch. Writhing in agony, he falls to the ground. As soon as he can manage, he takes himself to Doctor O'Connor.

'How bad is it doctor?' asks O'Malley, 'I'm going on my honeymoon next week and my girl-friend is a virgin in every way.'

'I'll have to put your penis in a splint, Seamus, to let it heal and keep it straight. Sure, it'll be fine by next week.'

The doctor takes four tongue compressors and forms a neat little four-sided bandage and wires it all together.

'An impressive work of art,' says the good doctor.

Seamus says nothing of this to his girlfriend. He marries her and goes off on his honeymoon. That night in the hotel room she rips off her blouse to revel a gorgeous set of breasts, a sight Seamus has not seen before.

'You're the first, Seamus,' she says. 'No one has ever touched these breasts.'

Seamus promptly drops his pants and replies, 'Here's something even fresher – it's still in the crate!'

One fine day in Ireland, a guy is out golfing and gets up to the 16th hole. He tees up and cranks one. Unfortunately, it goes into the woods on the side of the fairway. He goes looking for his ball and comes across a little guy with a huge bump on his head and the golf ball lying right beside him.

'Goodness,' says the golfer, and revives the poor little guy.

Upon awakening, the little guy says, 'Well, you caught me fair and square. I am a leprechaun. I will grant you three wishes.'

'I can't take anything from you, I'm just glad I didn't hurt you too badly,' says the guy, and walks away.

Watching the golfer depart, the leprechaun says, 'Well, he was a nice enough guy, and he did catch me, so I have to do something for him. I'll give him the three things that I would want. I'll give him unlimited money, a great golf game, and a great sex life.'

A year goes past and the same golfer is out golfing on the same course at the 16th hole. He gets up and hits one into the same woods and goes off looking for his ball. When he finds the ball he sees the same little guy and asks how he is doing.

The leprechaun says, 'I'm fine. And might I ask how your golf game is?'

'It's great! I hit under par every time.'

'I did that for you. And might I ask how your money is holding out?'

'That's the amazing thing, every time I put my hand in my pocket, I pull out a hundred dollar note.'

'I did that for you. And might I ask how your sex life is?'

Now the golfer looks at him a little shyly and says, 'Well, maybe once or twice a week.'

Floored the leprechaun stammers, 'Only once or twice a week?'

The golfer looks at him sheepishly and says, 'Well, that's not too bad for a Catholic priest in a small parish.'

ANAGRAMS

Nick Faldo	A fond lick
Tiger Woods	I'd worst ego

Gary Wolstenholme	Well, the moron's gay
Fred Couples	Rescued flop
Payne Stewart	Sweaty parent
Severiano Ballasteros	Resolves elaborate sin

There was a young golfer named Lear
Who went to jail for a year
For an act quite obscene,
On the very first green,
Under a sign saying, 'Enter course here.'

Texans are fabled for their grand style but when an oil tycoon appeared at a local British golf course, followed by a servant pulling a cushioned chaise lounge, his opponents thought that this was taking style too far.

'Are you going to make that poor caddy lug that couch all over the course after you?' he was asked.

'Caddy? Like hell,' drawled the Texan, 'That's my psychiatrist.'

'Caddy, why do you keep looking at your watch?'
'It's not a watch, sir. It's a compass.'

Two caddies were helping two aged Germans around their golf course. Failing yet again to get the ball in the air the worst golfer of the pair exclaimed, 'I suppose you have never seen any player worse than me?'

The caddy replied, 'There are plenty worse than you, sir, but they are no longer playing.'

A golfer named Sandy MacFarr
Went to bed with a Hollywood star
When he first saw her gash he
Cried, 'Quick, goot muh mashie!
Uh thunk uh c'n muk it in par.'

Caddying for the elderly beginner had required great patience. The old man was doddery but he was dogged and he had sworn to break 100 before the summer was out. In fact there was a bottle of whisky riding on it – his faithful caddy would receive it when the magic score had been broken.

Finally a day arrived when dogged persistence seemed about to pay off for both player and caddy. They were on the green at the 18th, and only 97 strokes had been accounted for. Player and caddy were excited and in the grip of such emotion it was small wonder that the player sent his first putt racing 3m past the hole.

In a flash the caddy had dropped the flagstick, picked up the ball and was crying excitedly. 'Well done, sir! You've done it. You've done it. Anyone would give you that.'

GOLF IS BETTER THAN SEX BECAUSE:

- If you damage a ball it is easy to replace it with a new one.
- The lay is always different.
- A hole in one is applauded.

'Well, caddy, How do you like my game?'
'Very good, sir. But personally I prefer golf'

Friendly golfer (to player searching for lost ball): What sort of a ball was it?
Caddy (butting in): A brand new one – never been properly hit yet.'

'Ah, easy! One long drive and a putt,' said the cocky golfer as he teed his ball and looked down the fairway to the green.

He swung mightily, and topped the ball, which dribbled forward and landed about a metre in front of him.

His caddy handed him a club and remarked, 'And now for one hell of a putt.'

A minister, a priest and a rabbi were golfing on the hottest day of the year. After 18 holes they were sweating and exhausted. They decided to take a dip in a pool and to hide their clothes in the bushes so that nobody would know they were there. They all stripped and jumped into the pond to cool down.

Feeling refreshed, they went to retrieve their clothes. As the three of them were crossing an open area in the nude, who should come along but the ladies auxiliary golf team. Caught unawares and unable to get to their clothes in time, the minister and the priest covered their privates. The rabbi covered his face.

After the ladies had left and they got their clothes back on, the minister and the priest asked the rabbi why he covered his face rather than his privates.

The rabbi replied, 'I don't know about you, but my congregation would recognise my face.'

O n the seventeenth hole, a very careful player was studying the green. First he got down on his hands and knees to check out the turf between his ball and the hole. Then he flicked several pieces of grass out of the way. Getting up, he held up a wet finger to try out the direction of the wind.

Then turning to his caddy he asked, 'Was the green mowed this morning?'

'Yes, sir.'

'Right to left or left to right?'

'Right to left, sir.'

The golfer putted, and missed the hole completely. He whirled on the caddy, 'What time?'

'T hat can't be my ball, caddy. It looks far too old,' said the player looking at a ball deep in the trees.

'It's a long time since we started, sir.'

Golfer: Well, I have never played this badly before!
Caddy: I didn't realise you had played before, sir.

A golfer and his caddy enjoyed a good argument, especially about what clubs to use. The caddy usually won, but this day, faced with a longish par three hole, the golfer decided that a 3-iron would be best.

'Take a 5-wood,' growled the caddy.

But the golfer stuck to his choice and the caddy watched gloomily as the ball sailed over the fairway, landed neatly on the green and rolled politely into the hole.

'You see,' grinned the triumphant golfer.

'You would have done better with your 5-wood.'

YOU KNOW YOUR BOSS IS A GOLFER IF:

- He has a golf ball on a string hanging from the rear vision mirror of his car.
- His daughter's wedding party was on the 19th hole of the golf course.
- He estimates a 'par' score for every task that he sets and awards 'eagles' or 'birdies' if you come in under budget.
- His pets are named 'Tiger' and 'JD'.
- He sets staggered drive off times for all of his staff.
- He insists that you sign off on your card at the end of each day.
- Sometimes he varies the workload by having you work with a different partner.
- When he asks, 'What's your handicap?' he is not talking about your limp.
- He buys a new car purely so that his clubs will fit easily in the boot.

Judge: Do you understand the nature of an oath?
Boy: Do I? I'm your caddy, remember!

After a series of disastrous holes, the amateur golfer, in an effort to smother his rage, laughed hollowly and said to his caddy, 'This golf is a funny game.'

'It's not supposed to be,' said the boy.

Golfer: Notice any improvement today, Jimmy?
Caddy: Yes, ma'am. You've had your hair done.

Golfer: Do you think my game is improving?
Caddy: Oh yes, sir! You miss the ball much closer than you used to.

One day, a Scotsman went golfing. After standing a while on the green he asked the boy standing beside him, 'Are you my caddy for today?'

'Yes,' answered the boy.

'Are you good at finding lost balls?'

'Oh yes, I find every lost ball.'

'OK, boy, then run and search for one, so we can start.'

Golfer: Caddy, do you think it is a sin to play golf on Sunday?
Caddy: The way you play, sir, it's a crime any day of the week!

Golfer: This is the worst golf course I've ever played on.
Caddy: This isn't the golf course, sir. We left that an hour ago.

A terrible golfer was playing a round of golf for which he had hired a caddy. The round proved to be somewhat tortuous for the caddy to watch and he was getting a bit exasperated by the poor play of his employer.

At one point the ball lay about 180m from the green and as

the golfer sized up his situation, he asked his caddy, 'Do you think I can get there with a 5-iron?'

'Eventually,' replied the caddy.

Golfer: I'd move heaven and earth to be able to break 100 on this course.

Caddy: Try heaven. You've already moved a fair amount of earth.

Bill was 26 over par by the eighth hole; he had landed a fleet of golf balls in the water hazard and dug himself into a trench fighting his way out of the rough. When his caddy coughed during a 12-inch putt, and the ball missed, he turned to him and exploded.

'You've got to be the worst caddy in the world!' he screamed.

'I doubt it,' replied the caddy. 'That would be too much of a coincidence.'

A hack golfer spends a day at a plush country club, playing golf and enjoying the luxury of a complimentary caddy. Being a shocking golfer, he plays poorly all day. Around about the 18th hole he spots a lake off to the left of the fairway.

He looks at the caddy and says, 'I've played so poorly all day; I think I'm going to go drown myself in that lake.'

'I don't think you could keep your head down that long,' says the caddy.

Man blames fate for other accidents that befall him, but takes full responsibility for a hole in one.

DICTIONARY OF GOLF

Ace: To complete a hole in a single stroke. The odds against this happening are about

50,000 to 1, so how you can claim you did it deliberately, especially as you had 11 at the previous hole, is beyond all good reason.

Addressing the ball:	Talking to the ball before it is hit, for example 'Please, please, pleeeeeese! Just go straight, you little bastard, just for once.'
Albatross:	A double eagle, or a score of three under par on a hole. Rarely employed as a tactic by the amateur golfer.
Approach-shot:	A shot which, if it had not gone into the water, would have swerved to the left and landed on the adjoining green, or involuntarily struck the club manager's Volvo in the car park.
Army:	Both the group of people that follow a particular golfer, as in Arnie's Army, or a phrase used to describe the inconsistent and erratic wayward shots of amateur golfers, as in 'left-right, left-right'.
Away:	The player whose ball lies farthest from the hole is 'away' and it is his turn to make the first putt. After his stroke is taken, if the ball still lies farthest from the hole, the player may kick the first bag and throw the first club.
Back nine:	The final 27 holes of an 18-hole golf course. Very character-building.
Backswing:	The part of the swing that takes place after the ball has been improperly addressed but before it has been sent to the wrong destination. Requires skill.
Bag rat:	Caddy – supposed to give you a club and advice, not lip.

Ball:	A dimpled, sphere with a weight of 40.5g and a diameter of 4.3cm that will enter a cup 10.9cm in diameter and 10.2cm deep after an average of 3.87 putts but, for most golfers, will not do what it is supposed to.
Banana ball:	A curvaceous slice, especially for those dogged with the birth defect of playing golf left-handed. For a right-hander, it is a ball that starts to the right and continues to curve right, until it nearly lands behind the golfer who hit it. For the leftie, the ball arcs beautifully left and usually lands 30m forward and 55m sideways. This shot is one reason why the word 'fore' is heard on the golf course, along with 'poop' and 'shit'.
Barky:	When one of your shots strikes a tree and you still make par for the hole, you have made a barky. Not recommended for that rare breed, the environmentalist golfer.
Beach:	The bunkers and other sand-covered areas at a golf course are known collectively as the beach, sometimes camel grass, and have brought many a good round to an early close, and many a potential career to an abrupt finish.
Birdie:	One under par, often called a Mulligan, the best of one or more practice swings, and a 6m 'gimme' putt.
Blow up:	To have your golf game come apart at the seams. Easily recognised: when your score is blowing up, so are you. Recognisable by behaviour including throwing clubs, cursing in several languages, going red in the face, and threatening to insert a 5-iron into the caddy.

Body language: Nervous leaning movements, particularly while putting, to 'persuade' the ball to go in a desired direction. If the ball fails to do so, these movements are often followed by a series of vulgar gestures and physical expressions, which re-appear later after nine beers at the nineteenth.

Bogey: The number of strokes needed to finish a hole by a golfer of average skill and above-average honesty. A contentious score, known to cause disputes and break friendships.

Boss of the moss: A golfer who is especially proficient on the green. Hacks need not apply.

Break: 1. The shifting or changing of the direction of a putt caused by the slope or slant of a green. 2. The splitting of the shaft of the putter caused by the rage or wrath of a player. 3. The shattering of the spirit of said player.

Bunker: A hazard consisting of an area of ground along a fairway or adjacent to a green from which a large amount of soil has been removed and replaced with a cavern made of sand designed to trap golfers. Archaeological digs have unearthed fragments of old balls, broken clubs and the remains of the occasional caddy.

Caddy: Individual who carries bags for golfers and assists them in the playing of the course. Ideally, a caddy should possess the eyes of a big-game hunter, the strength of a footballer, the patience of a diplomat and the memory of a Mafia witness. Many are just little smart-arses who can play a lot better than you.

Can:	The hole. The cup. The place to put your putts. See, over there! When you sink a putt, you canned it. Later, in the bar, when you have scored 127 for 18, your playing cops a canning from your mates, too.
Carpet:	The green. Soft, well-manicured fairways are also referred to as being 'like carpet.' Occasional resting place for the prone golfer when a late-breaking 60-footer rolls in the hole and the emotion of it all becomes too much.
Centre city:	A tee shot that lands directly in the centre of the fairway has gone to centre city. Most hackers visit the western suburbs.
Clubface:	The metal or wooden striking surface that is located on the front of a club head above the sole and between the toe and the heel. There is a specific point on every clubface called the 'sweet spot', which, when it connects with a ball, produces maximum accuracy and power as well as a solid, gratifying feeling of perfect contact. Most golfers have about the same success finding it as they do the G-spot. Hard to find, but on the rare occasion you do, it's like reaching Nirvana.
Clubhouse:	Place where the rules are prominently posted, and no-one reads them until there is a dispute.
Committee:	The duly authorised drafters of the rules. A group to be avoided at all costs.
Competition:	1. Form of play clearly established in the rules. 2. Death by a thousand cuts.
Course:	Area of play strictly regulated under the rules. Try and stay on it.

Courtesy:	1. Type of conduct specifically mandated by the rules. 2. If you must scratch your balls, don't use a jumbo tee.
Crap:	The said rules overseen by the said committee, who should be avoided at all costs.
Dawn patrol:	The golfers who are the first to play each day, so named because they start their march around the course at sunrise. Particularly skilled at playing the first two holes in the dark, they spend the rest of the day haranguing people about their exploits.
Delay:	Golfers are expected to play 'without undue delay'. The question of exactly what constitutes undue delay has been under intensive study for 30 years. Taking a leak in the bushes, sinking a beer, or reading *How I Play Golf* by Tiger Woods in between shots can all contribute to 'delay', but still may not be considered 'undue'.
Digger:	A golfer who takes a big divot with his iron shots. Sometimes the bloody sod goes further than the ball, provoking the cry from your playing partner, 'Play the divot!' Ignore him with dignity.
Divot:	Colourful Scottish word for the piece of turf scooped from the ground in front of the ball in the course of an iron shot. In Scotland, depending on its size, a divot is referred to as a 'wee tuftie', 'peg o' sward', 'snatch of haugh', 'fine tussock', 'glen' , 'firth', 'loch' and the biggest of them all, 'damned English divot' (anything larger than 3m). The professionals sweep the ball beautifully with a divot. Hackers dig for gold.

Dog track:	Derogatory term for a golf course that is not well maintained. You land the ball in every hole but the right one.
Double Bogey:	Two strokes over par. Positive types will describe a seven on a par-five as a combination birdie and eagle on the same hole.
Down and dirty:	Playing the ball 'as it lies'. No rolling the ball over or sitting it up. The way the game is meant to be played; your score is meaningless unless you play it down and dirty.
Dress:	Although clothes in a variety of styles are acceptable on a golf course, a few general pointers are worth keeping in mind when selecting an outfit. The combination of colours should be visible to an individual with normal eyesight looking out the window of a spacecraft in orbit. It should be made out of a fabric derived from a substance that was mined or refined rather than grown or raised. It should jam radar. It should be composed of no fewer than eight separate colours or shades and should bear a minimum of four distinct emblems, two of which are in foreign languages. When scuffed, the shoes should require repainting or re-stuccoing rather than shining. Any hat should be identifiable as such only by its position on the wearer's head.
Drive for show and putt for dough:	He who putts the best wins the most. The timeless golf cliché, shown every Sunday afternoon on network television.
Drive:	The initial shot on each hole, made with a special wood: the driver on par-four and

par-five holes, and with shorter woods or irons on par-three holes. Because the drive is so critical to the play of the hole, total concentration is essential, and thus, if the shot is spoiled because of some audible disturbance inadvertently caused by another player on the tee, such as a pair of shoelace tips clicking together or the wind whistling through an onlooker's eyelashes, it is customary to take the shot again. A very handy option for those who are dogged with the banana ball syndrome.

Dub: To miss-hit a shot badly, causing it to roll on the ground and come to a stop far short of its target. A dubber is the guy in the group ahead who takes 14 shots to reach the green and still insists he's having fun. Perhaps his marriage needs attending to.

Duffer: A golfer whose actual score on any given hole is ordinarily more than twice his or her reported score. Rarely gains membership at St Andrews.

Eagle: Unusually low score on a hole achieved by a golfer with an exceptionally good drive and one or two exceptionally good follow-up shots, or by a golfer with exceptionally good luck, or an exceptionally poor memory.

Elephant's ass: A poorly struck shot that is higher than it is long. Has been known to burn-up on re-entry.

Equipment: According to the rules of golf, equipment is 'anything that can be thrown, broken, kicked, twisted, torn, crushed, shredded or mangled; or propelled, driven or directed, either under its own power or by means of a transfer of momentum, into underbrush, trees or other overgrown terrain; or over the edge of a natural or artificially elevated area; or below the surface of any body of water, whether moving or impounded.' People keep buying it.

Etiquette: The rules of behaviour in golf. There isn't room here for a complete list, but a few of the more important ones are: Never put tees in your nose. Never sneeze into your glove. Never concede a chip shot. Never hold a ball for another player to hit. Never practice drives against a backboard. Never wear golf shoes to a dance.

Fade: 1. (Right-handed golfers) A shot that curves from left to right. 2. (Left-handed golfers) A shot that curves from right to left. Your chances of winning the E-grade monthly medal disappearing into the bushes.

Fan: To miss the ball completely. The air moves, but nothing else does. The silence after is deafening, followed by barley perceptible snickering. Has been known to lead to mental breakdown.

Fat, hit it: To hit the ground behind the ball first so that the shot has no spin and does not achieve the desired distance. Results often resemble an elephant's ass. A shot to be avoided.

Fight: To struggle with a particular golfing flaw. If all your poor shots are slices, you're said to be fighting a slice. If all your misses are hooks, you're said to be fighting a hook. If you miss all your short putts, you're said to be fighting a bad putter. If your rounds resemble boxing matches, take up crochet.

Flat bellies: The younger, thinner golfers on the PGA Tour. Coined by golfing legend Lee Trevino. On the other hand, the fat bellies are all playing the Masters circuit now and making more money in one tournament than they did in their entire career.

Flub: A shot that is too weak to register on conventional scorekeeping equipment. Eat more cereal at breakfast.

Fluff: A shot in which the club head strikes the ground behind the ball before hitting it, causing it to dribble forward one or two metres. Usually followed by shaking of the head, and muttering of dire threats.

Follow-through: The part of the swing that takes place after the ball has been hit but before the club has been thrown into the nearby water hazard. Can be spectacular and result in an appearance before the committee.

Fore: The first of several four-letter words exchanged between golfers as one group of players hits balls toward another in front of them on the course. Another f-word is often substituted.

Four-ball: A match in which two pairs of players each play their better ball against the other. Additional golf matches include: best-ball, in which one player plays against the better ball of two or the best ball of three players; three-ball, in which three players play against one another, each playing his or her own ball; and no-ball, in which two, three or four players, all of whom have lost all their balls, go to the clubhouse and play gin rummy.

Four-jack:	To take four putts on a hole. Makes perfect sense to a lot of people, but only tolerable for those who can drive the green on a par five.
Foursome:	Four golfers playing a round together. Three golfers are a threesome, and two form a twosome. Four ladies playing slowly are a 'gruesome'. Four men playing after a long lunch at the 19th hole are a 'fearsome'. A single attractive woman playing alone is a 'toothsome'. A husband and wife playing together are a 'quarrelsome'. A group of golfers who give advice while watching another group tee off is a 'meddlesome'. A single player with a large number of jokes is a 'tiresome'. And two younger men playing a fast, sub-par round are a 'loathsome'. And as for the old geezers in those frigging electric carts, why don't they give it away and play bowls?
Fried egg:	A ball buried in the sand, with a ring around it created on impact. Too many fried eggs will make you lose your appetite for the game.
Front nine:	The first half of an 18-hole golf course. A golfer who, by the end of the ninth hole, has shot within a few strokes of par for 18 is entitled to skip the second half of the course and head directly for the 19th hole and drink vast quantities of alcohol.
Frosty:	Nickname for the score of eight on a hole. Synonymous with 'snowman' because the figure eight resembles a snowman. A figure to be avoided.

Gaol: A place from which escape is nearly impossible. Particularly when you are still 320m from the green on a par four and have used up three shots.

Give: An agreement between two golfers with a shared fear of the short game to 'give' each other their next putt.

God squad: Name for the group of PGA Tour players who hold prayer meetings at professional golf tournaments and who thank God when they win as He always prefers born-again Christians to win tournaments.

Goer: A shot that goes much farther than normal for the club being used.

Golf bag: Portable container with compartments designed to hold clubs, balls and other golfing accessories including a flask for whisky.

Golf club: The basic golfing implement and a social organisation built around a golf course which has a distinct hierarchy that can be discovered by examining the car parking spaces and their labels. See committee and be warned.

Golf holiday: A chance for a group of blokes to go into the country for a few days without their spouses and children so that they can drink, gamble and play a bit of golf. Sometimes it can be combined with a conference so that the holiday becomes a tax deduction.

Golf lawyer: A player famous for knowing and constantly citing the rules. He will try to take advantage of your lack of knowledge to better his own score, so be careful.

Golf widow: Non-playing wife of an obsessive golfer.

Golf:	A pastime in which people get out of the house (office) to escape frustration and stress to play a game that causes frustration and stress.
Green:	A roughly circular area of smooth, lush grass where one 'putts for dough'.
Greens fees:	The charge for playing a round of golf. The more strokes one takes to play a hole the better value for money.
Grinder:	A player whose only mission is to achieve the best score possible. A hard worker. A serious player. To be avoided at all costs.
Grocery money:	Winnings from a golf bet that the winner pledges to spend on food and drink, or groceries, but which is usually spent at the 19th hole.
Grounder:	A golf shot that never leaves the ground.
Jelly legs:	A disability that afflicts nervous golfers. Especially debilitating when putting or surveying the end of night bar bill.
Jerk:	1. To pull a shot or putt left of the intended line. 2. A playing partner who pulls a shot or putt left of his intended line, but doesn't actually mean to.
Juicy:	A lie in the rough where the ball is sitting atop the grass, offering a clean approach. Can be so attractive that the player tends to pin the ears back and go for it, and the ball is last seen heading for the car park.
Keeping score:	Determines who wins the game after four or five hours of playing. Golf is the only game where the highest score loses, except maybe for the card game misere.

Kick: 1. The way the ball bounces, sometimes good and sometimes bad. 2. What a golfer does to his golf buggy when he is angry because he hit a bad shot.

Knee-knocker: An important putt to the outcome of the game, in the 1-1.5m range, that makes the putter nervous.

Knife: The toughest club to hit – a 1-iron. The old adage goes that if lightning starts looming in the distance, hold your 1-iron aloft, because not even God can hit a one iron.

Launched: Term for a drive that takes off like a jet plane and flies like a bird.

Leak oil: What a golfer does as his game begins to fall apart, a situation which can begin as early as the first tee.

Legs: 1. A ball is said to have legs if it continues to roll after landing. If it has too many legs it rolls past the hole and if it has not enough legs it does not make it to the hole. 2. The things that hang down from the daggy shorts of a weekend golfer.

Lie: 1. The place where the ball comes to rest after being hit by a golfer. 2. The number of strokes it took to get to the hole, as reported by that golfer.

Liz Taylor: A shot that's a little fat but not bad. Do not confuse with a Roseanne, which is very fat and not OK.

Local rules: A set of regulations that the committee makes up themselves for their own course so that the members minimise the faults in their own games.

Long and wrong: Description of a golfer who can hit the ball

	long distances but seldom in the right direction.
Looper:	Caddy.
Lost ball:	A missing ball. It is declared a lost ball if it can't be found after 10 seconds (opponent's ball) or 20 minutes (your own).
Meat and potatoes par four:	A long, straightforward par four that is uncomplicated and easy to play. If all things go right.
Military golf:	Having to march a long way, from side to side of the fairways, to retrieve balls hit in a game. Left, right. Left, right . . ..
Money player:	The golfer who makes the shots he needs to make under pressure and wins the bets. Only professionals and red-hot amateurs need apply.
Move:	The golf swing.
Muff:	To miss-hit a shot.
Needle:	Verbally teasing and taunting your opponents so that you put them off their game. Some go to water at the first hole.
Nineteenth Hole:	1. The only hole on which golfers do not complain about the number of shots they took. 2. A place where most golfers find their best lies.
Nuked:	When you hit a shot that achieves the absolute maximum distance for that club.
OB:	The abbreviation for the three saddest words in golf – out of bounds.
On fire:	You're on fire when everything you do works out just well. Then, having left the practice net, you stride to the first tee.
Oscar Brown:	Nickname used for out of bounds.
Overcook it:	To hit a shot too hard.

Par: The score that you should aim to end up
                  with at the end of the game. It almost never
                  happens.

Penalty: Strokes added to a golfer's score for play in
                  contravention of the rules. See committee.

Pencil hockey: When the scorekeeper fudges the score in
                  his own favour. Naughty, naughty, naughty.

Pin: The little sticky on the green thing that you
                  can just see from the tee and to where you
                  should be aiming your ball. It's amazing, in
                  the course of working your way up the
                  fairway, how often it goes out of your view.

Pipeline: The centre of the fairway, so named because
                  an irrigation pipe often runs down it. Not
                  usually a problem for most hacks.

Play it as it lies: One of the two fundamental dictates of
                  golf.

Playing through: This is what we invite the group behind us
                  to do so that they won't be waiting on the
                  tee for 40 minutes while we locate our balls.

Pond ball: An old, beat-up ball that won't be much of a
                  loss if it lands in the water. A seasoned
                  hacker has 31 in his bag.

Practice green: A place where a golfer goes to get an idea of
                  the lie and to make sure his balls go in the
                  hole. Usually leaves it all behind when he
                  hits the course.

Practice tee: The place where golfers go to work on their
                  faults and to try and convert a nasty hook
                  into a wicked slice. Takes time, but it works.

Pro shop: This is where the font of all knowledge, the
                  pro, hangs out. The temptations in this place
                  are: buy more lessons, buy more gear, buy
                  more equipment.

Pro:	A golf fanatic who is wise enough to stop neglecting his business by spending so much time on the course improving his game; and instead spends time getting paid for the privilege of improving his game by making it his business.
Pull:	To hit a shot straight but to the left of the intended target. It happens a lot.
Putt:	To hit a shot straight but to the left, the right, beyond, short of, over or around the intended target. A genuine putt actually goes in the hole.
Rainmaker:	A shot that is hit so high it travels close to the clouds.
Rake:	1. To pull the ball back into the hole casually with your putter after missing a putt. 2. The thing that lies in the bunker waiting for you to repair the damaged surface after you have taken many shots at escape. Step on it and it may well be the best pair of balls you will hit all day.
Reading the green:	Getting down on your haunches to look at the green and to pretend that you are able to predict where the ball will roll if you hit it at a certain speed. Best to just aim for the hole and hope. Besides, is holding your putter up, like the pros, really going to help?
Recovery shot:	A shot whose primary purpose is to get out of trouble – for the genuine hacker, usually every second shot.
Relaxation:	What you initially set out to do by taking up the game of golf but what you never get once you become a golfer.

Reload: 1. To tee up a second ball after a bad tee shot. 2. What you do when you are at the 19th and order another beer.

Robbed: 1. When a putt doesn't go as it should then the golfer says that he was robbed. 2. When you go back to the car and the stereo has been nicked while you were out on the course. At least you can't blame the caddy for that, because he has been right by your side snickering at you all day.

Roller coaster: Round of golf that has good and bad holes in it – like a roller coaster ride. Some have been known to hop off half way through.

Sand trap: A deep depression filled with sand which has the ability to induce deep depression.

Sandbagger: A golfer who falsely posts high scores in order to inflate his handicap, and then pounces at the next competition, to score maximum points, win the medal, and laugh all the way to the bar.

Scrambler: A golfer who plays somewhat erratically but manages to salvage good scores from inconsistent play.

Scratch: 1. A player who has a zero handicap. 2. A rat; louse; stinker. 3. What you do after you have spent the day retrieving balls from the scrub.

Scuff: A crappy shot that results from hitting the ground before hitting the ball.

Senior: An old bugger.

Set them up: 1. Improve your lie in the fairway. 2. What you ask the bartender to do with the beers.

Shag hags: 1. Container holding practice balls. 2. The groupies who hang around the clubrooms.

Shag:	1. To retrieve golf balls. 2. To go home and have sex with your partner after a good game.
Short hole:	Any par three.
Short stick:	1. The putter. 2. Your sitting member after a night in the clubrooms at the 19th hole.
Side:	Each nine holes—front and back.
Slam-dunk:	To putt or chip the ball into the hole with great force. Can be seen as a heroic charge at the ball, or the result of sheer desperation. The cup has been known to move as far as 5m back from one of these.
Slice:	A shot that curves to the right, and is the beginning of the 'left, right' military syndrome, which will dog you for the rest of the day.
Slick:	1. Term used to describe fast greens. 2. The most garish golf outfit of the day.
Spin:	1. One of a variety of spins applied to the ball to make it curve around obstacles, turn into the wind or stop dead where it lands. 2. The lies told in the club room after the game.
Spraying:	1. To be unpredictable in the manner and the direction you hit your balls. 2. To take a pee behind a tree.
Stance:	The proper positioning of the feet for a golf stroke. You must remember: Head down over the ball. Feet apart, not too much, not too little. Feet facing where you wish to hit the ball. Left arm straight. Right elbow bent. Hips loose. And more. Seemingly by the time you have the handle half way up your left nostril you're just about there.
Sticks:	1. Your clubs. 2. Things to throw at invading crows. 3. Things your clubs have been

reduced to you after a particularly serious tantrum on the 13th.

Stroke: 1. A forward movement of the club that is made with the intention of hitting and moving the ball. 2. A medical condition suffered by elderly golfers who should have stayed home in bed.

Texas wedge: Using a putter or another flat iron for a hefty punch shot out of the scrub. Great use for the 1-iron.

Top it: One of the worst things that can happen to the hack golfer, especially on the drive – the club skims across the top of the ball, just moving it forward a few metres. The wise caddy moves adroitly out of the way, in case he gets topped too.

Under the weather: That sickly feeling on an early Sunday morning, after a hefty night on the piss, when you look down to tee off at the first and see five balls in a pink haze. The worst-case scenario is a quiet chuck behind the bushes at the fifth. Never mind, a cold lunchtime ale will fix things up.

Undertaker: Many a funeral operator has been called to pick up the body of a dedicated golfer who has either had a stroke through the stress of it all, or collapsed with a smile on his face having scored that elusive albatross at the long par five.

Vardon, Harry: A really good golfer, like you will never be.

Venerable: The oldest member – recognised for his longevity, golfing prowess, gentlemanly manners and etiquette, his image only tarnished by the way he farts in his sleep when he is dozing in his favourite armchair in the member's lounge after one too many brandies.

Water hazard: A magnet for the hacker's ball. Lakes, rivers, creeks and dams are a nightmare for the nervous amateur. 'Don't hit in the water, don't hit in the water, don't hit in the water, don't hit in the water, don't hit in the water, don't hit in the water,' he repeats to himself over and over again. Splash.

Whack: The marvellous sound of the ball striking a nearby tree after a full-blooded drive, and which is last seen rocketing at head height into the next fairway.

Where the hell?: Agonised cry of the hacker when his tee-shot seems to disappear into thin air, witnessed by no-one as it left the launching pad. A search usually turns up absolutely nothing and another ball has to be found, or it is discovered 10m to the left, buried deep in a hedge, or more distressingly, still sitting on the tee.

X Factor: Some bastards just have it. That unerring ability to strike the ball beautiful, keep it in the middle of the fairway, and knock it in the hole with two, or sometimes one, caress of the putter. All smiles, they mark the card and move on. The rest of us have the Y Factor, as in, 'Why the hell did it go over there?'

X-ray vision: The great ability to find a seemingly lost ball in the rough. It's a sixth sense, and if you've got it, cultivate it. It can save you thousands.

Yachting: Almost as frustrating a game as golf.

Yahoo:	A wild thing on the golf course – loud clothes, loud style, loud mouth. Wants to bet you $20 on every hole. Trouble is, he often has the talent to back it up. Avoid him at all costs.
Yips:	A dreaded nervous condition, usually picked up by a pro or a serious amateur. When hovering over the putt, they get the shakes and can't control the stroke. The hacker usually gets the same feeling when reaching for the wallet to pay for his round of drinks at the 19th.
Zap:	When lightning strikes the bag and melts the clubs, leaving the golfer with a permanent ringing in the ears and a need to urinate whenever the microwave goes off. Let's hope it does not happen to you.
Zero:	The lowest number of Stableford points you can get – a very embarrassing moment, and an indication that you should give up the game and take up bowls.
Zoo:	The 19th about an hour before closing time.

KNOCK, KNOCK

Knock, knock.
Who's there?
Little old lady.
Little old lady who?
I didn't know you could yodel.

Knock, knock.
Who's there?
Aida.
Aida who?
Aida lot of sweets and now I've got tummy ache.

Knock, knock.
Who's there?
Ben.
Ben who?
Ben waiting, what took you so long?

Knock, knock.
Who's there?
Lettuce.
Lettuce, who?
Lettuce in, it's cold out here!

Knock, knock.
Who's there?
Acid.
Acid who?
Acid sit down and be quiet.

Knock, knock.
Who's there?
Dishes.
Dishes, who?
Dishes the stupidest knock-knock joke ever.

Knock, knock.
Who's there?
Doris.
Doris who?
Doris closed, that's why I'm knocking.

Knock, knock.
Who's there?
Ada.
Ada who?
Ada burger for lunch.

Knock, knock.
Who's there?
Adair.
Adair who?
Adair once but I'm bald now.

Knock, knock.
Who's there?
Adolf.
Adolf who?
Adolf ball hit me in the mouth.

Knock, knock.
Who's there?
Alaska.
Alaska who?
Alaska my friend the question then.

Knock, knock.
Who's there?
Aladdin.
Aladdin who?
Aladdin the street wants a word with you.

Knock, knock.
Who's there?
Alba.
Alba who?
Alba in the kitchen if you need me.

Knock, knock.
Who's there?
Alec.
Alec who?
Alec-tricity. Isn't that a shock.

Knock, knock.
Who's there?
Alexia.
Alexia who?
Alexia again to open this door.

Knock, knock.
Who's there?
Alfalfa.
Alfalfa who?
Alfalfa you, if you give me a kiss.

Knock, knock.
Who's there?
Alfie.
Alfie who?
Alfie terrible if you leave.

Knock, knock.
Who's there?
Alfred.
Alfred who?
Alfred the needle if you sew.

Knock, knock.
Who's there?
Allied.
Allied who?
Allied, so sue me.

Knock, knock.
Who's there?
Alma.
Alma who?
Alma-ny knock knock jokes can you take!

Knock, knock.
Who's there?
Amana.
Amana who?
Amana bad mood.

Knock, knock.
Who's there?
Ammonia.
Ammonia who?
Ammonia little kid.

Knock, knock.
Who's there?
Amory.
Amory who?
Amory Christmas and a happy new year.

Knock, knock.
Who's there?
Amy.
Amy who?
Amy fraid I've forgotten.

Knock, knock.
Who's there?
Annetta.
Annetta who?
Annetta wisecrack and you're out of here.

Knock, knock.
Who's there?
Augusta.
Augusta who?
Augusta go home now.

Knock, knock.
Who's there?
Boo!
Boo who?
Don't cry it's only a joke.

Knock, knock.
Who's there?
Button.
Button who?
Button in is not polite.

Knock, knock.
Who's there?
Carl.
Carl who?
Carl get you there quicker than walking.

Knock, knock.
Who's there?
Cash.
Cash who?
I knew you were nuts.

Knock, knock.
Who's there?
Cassie.
Cassie who?
Cassie the forest for the trees.

Knock, knock.
Who's there?
Celeste.
Celeste who?
Celeste time I'm going to tell you this.

Knock, knock.
Who's there?
Cereal.
Cereal who?
Cereal pleasure to meet you.

Knock, knock.
Who's there?
Colleen.
Colleen who?
Colleen up this mess.

Knock, knock.
Who's there?
Cologne.
Cologne who?
Cologne me names won't help.

Knock, knock.
Who's there?
Cosy.
Cosy who?
Cosy who's knocking.

Knock, knock.
Who's there?
Collier.
Collier who?
Collier big brother see if I care.

Knock, knock.
Who's there?
Lettuce.
Lettuce who?
Lettuce pray . . .

Knock, knock.
Who's there?
Hutch.
Hutch who?
Bless you.

LAWYERS

A solicitor from Dublin, while hunting in the west, brought down a fowl, which landed in a farmer's field. As the lawyer climbed over the wall to retrieve the bird, the elderly owner appeared, asking what he was doing.

The litigator replied, 'I shot that bird you see lying there, and now I'm about to pick it up.'

'This is my property you crossing into, and I'm telling you, yer not coming over,' said the old man.

'I'll have you know that I'm one of the best solicitors in all of Ireland, and if you don't let me retrieve my bird, I'll take ye to court for everything y'own!'

'Well now, being as how you're not from around here, you don't know how we settle things like this. You see now, here we use the three-kick method.'

'And what would that be?' asked the lawyer.

'First I kick you three times and then you do the same to me, and back and forth like that till one of us gives up.'

The attorney thought this over, and quickly decided he could easily take on the old codger, and agreed to the local custom. The old farmer walked slowly over to the lawyer. With his first kick he planted the toe of his heavy boot in the solicitor's groin dropping him to his knees. The second blow nearly wiped the lawyer's nose off his face. The attorney was flat on the ground when the farmer's third kick to the kidney almost finished him.

The lawyer dug deep for his every bit of will, dragged himself standing, and said, 'OK you old bugger, now it's my turn.

The old farmer just smiled and said, 'No, I believe I'll give up now. You can have the bird.'

A Sydney man was forced to take a day off from work to appear in court for a minor traffic summons. He grew increasingly restless as he waited hour after endless hour for his case to be heard. When his name was called late in the afternoon, he stood before the judge, only to hear that court would be adjourned for the rest of the afternoon and he would have to return the next day.

'What for?' he unwisely snapped at the magistrate.

His Honour, equally irked by a tedious day, roared, 'Twenty dollars for contempt of court. That's why!'

Then, noticing the man checking his wallet, the magistrate said, 'That's all right. You don't have to pay now.'

The young man replied, 'I'm just seeing if I have enough for two more words.'

Michael was in court for non-payment of maintenance to his ex-wife. The judge decided to increase his wife's allowance. So he told Michael, 'I have decided to increase this allowance and give your wife $50 per week.'

'Well,' Michael replied, 'you're a real gentleman sir. And I might even send her a few bob myself.'

'So let me get this straight,' the prosecutor says to the defendant, 'you came home from work early and found your wife in bed with a strange man.'

'That's correct,' says the defendant.

'You then take out a pistol and shoot your wife, killing her.'

'That's correct.'

'Then my question to you is, why did you shoot your wife and not her lover?' asked the prosecutor.

'It seemed easier, than shooting a different man every day.'

At a convention of biological scientists one researcher remarks to another, 'Did you know that in our lab we have switched from mice to lawyers for our experiments?' 'Really?' the other replied. 'Why did you switch?'

'Well, for three reasons. First we found that lawyers are far more plentiful. Second, the lab assistants don't get so attached to them. And thirdly, there are some things even a rat won't do. However, sometimes it is very hard to transfer our test results to human beings.'

A wedding occurred in a little village in Ireland. To keep tradition going, everyone got extremely drunk and the bride's and groom's families had a storming row and began wrecking the reception room, generally kicking the shit out of each other. The police were called in to break up the fight.

The following week, all members of both families appeared in court. The fight continued in the courtroom until the judge finally brought calm with the use of his gavel, shouting, 'Silence in the court!'

The courtroom went silent and Paddy, the best man, stood up and said, 'Judge, I was the best man at the wedding and I think I should explain what happened.'

The judge agreed and asked him to take the stand. Paddy began his explanation by informing the court that it is a traditional part of any wedding in this particular village that the best man got the first dance with bridge.

The judge says, 'OK.'

'Well,' said Paddy, 'after I'd finished the first dance, the music kept going so I continued dancing to the second song, and after that the music kept going and I was dancing to the third song when, all of a sudden, the groom leapt over the table, ran towards us and gave the bride an unmerciful kick right between her legs.'

Shocked, the judge instantly responded, 'God, that must have hurt!'

'Hurt?' Paddy replies. 'Shit, he broke three of my fingers!'

The pope and a lawyer find themselves together before the pearly gates. After a little polite small talk, St Peter shows up to usher them to their new heavenly station. After passing out wings, harps, halos and such, St Peter shows them to their new lodgings.

Peter brings them down on the front lawn of a huge palatial estate with all sorts of lavish trappings. This, Peter announces, is where the lawyer will be spending eternity.

'Holy Mary,' the pope thinks, 'If he's getting a place like this, I can hardly wait to see my heavenly reward!'

Peter leads the way but the landscape below begins to appear more and more mundane until they finally land on a street lined with dull brownstone houses. Pete indicates that the third stairs on the left will take the pope to his new domicile and turns to leave, wishing the pope the best.

The pope is quite taken aback and cries out, 'Hey Peter! What's the deal here? You put that lawyer in a beautiful estate home and I, spiritual leader of the whole world, end up in this dive?'

'Look here old fellow, this street is practically encrusted with spiritual leaders from many times and from many religions. We're putting you here with them so you can all get together and discuss dogma and philosophy. That other guy gets an elegant estate, because he's the first lawyer ever to make it up here.'

A very successful lawyer parked his brand-new BMW in front of his office, ready to show it off to his colleagues. As he got out, a truck passed too close and completely tore the door off of the driver's side. The counsellor immediately grabbed his mobile phone, dialled emergency, and within minutes a policeman pulled up. Before the officer had a chance to ask any questions, the lawyer started screaming hysterically. His BMW, which he had just picked up the day before, was now completely ruined and would never be the same, no matter what the panel-beater did to it.

When the lawyer finally wound down from his ranting and raving, the officer shook his head in disgust and disbelief. 'I can't believe how materialistic you lawyers are,' he said.

'You are so focused on your possessions that you don't notice anything else.'

'How can you say such a thing?' asked the lawyer.

'Don't you know that your left arm is missing from the elbow down? It must have been torn off when the truck hit you.'

'Ahhh!' screamed the lawyer. 'Where's my Rolex?'

O'Reilly, a dishonest lawyer, bribed a man on his client's jury to hold out for a charge of manslaughter, as opposed to the charge of murder which was brought by the state.

The jury was out for several days before they returned with the manslaughter verdict. When O'Reilly paid the corrupt juror, he asked him if he had a very difficult time convincing the other jurors to see things his way.

'I sure did,' the juror replied, 'the other eleven wanted to acquit.'

Q: What happens to a lawyer when he takes Viagra?
A: He gets taller.

LIGHT BULBS

How many sound men does it take to change a light bulb?
One, two; one, two; one, two . . .

How many sound men does it take to change a light bulb?
Hey man, I just do sound.

How many sound men does it take to change a light bulb?
One. Upon finding no replacement, he takes the original apart, repairs it with a chewing gum wrapper and gaffer tape, changes the screw mount to bayonet mount, finds an appropriate patch cable, and re-installs the bulb 20m from where it should have been, to the satisfaction of the rest of the band.

How many jazz musicians does it take to change a light bulb?
None. Jazz musicians can't afford light bulbs.

How many jazz musicians does it take to change a light bulb?
Don't worry about the changes. We'll fake it!

How many mathematical logicians does it take to replace a light bulb?
None. They can't do it, but they can prove that it can be done.

How many classical geometers does it take to replace a light bulb?
None. You can't do it with a straight edge and a compass.

How many constructivist mathematicians does it take to replace a light bulb?

None. They do not believe in infinitesimal rotations.

How many analysts does it take to change a light bulb?

Three. One to prove existence, one to prove uniqueness and one to derive a non-constructive algorithm to do it.

How many professors does it take to change a light bulb?

One. With eight research students, two programmers, three post-docs and a secretary to help him.

How many university lecturers does it take to change a light bulb?

Four. One to do it and three to co-author the paper.

How many graduate students does it take to change a light bulb?

Only one. But it takes nine years.

How many math department administrators does it take to change a light bulb?

None. What was wrong with the old one?

How many drummers does it take to change a light bulb?
None. They have a machine to do that.

How many altos does it take to change a light bulb?
None. They can't get that high.

How many bassists does it take to change a light bulb?
None. They're so macho they prefer to walk in the dark and bang their shins.

How many guitar players does it take to change a light bulb? Twelve. One to change the bulb and eleven to say they could do it better solo.

How many Grateful Dead fans does it take to change a light bulb?

12,001. One to change it, 2000 to record the event and take pictures of it, and 10,000 to follow it around until it burns out.

How many punk-rock musicians does it take to change a light bulb?

Two. One to screw in the bulb and the other to smash the old one on his forehead.

How many lead guitarists does it take to change a light bulb? None. They just steal somebody else's light.

How many bass players does it take to change a light bulb? None. They let the keyboard player do it with his left hand.

How many bass players does it take to change a light bulb? Don't bother. Just leave it out – no one will notice.

How many bass players does it take to change a light bulb? One, but the guitarist has to show him first.

How many bass players does it take to change a light bulb? Six. One to change it, and the other five to fight off the lead guitarists who are hogging the light.

How many strong men does it take to change a light bulb? 115. One to hold the bulb and 114 to rotate the house.

How many football players does it take to change a light bulb?
The entire team. A team is only as good as its weakest link.

How many generals does it take to change a light bulb?
One to change it and 1000 to rebuild it after it has been changed.

How many jugglers does it take to change a light bulb?
Only one, but you will need three light bulbs.

How many gods does it take to change a light bulb?
Two. One to hold the bulb and the other to rotate the planet.

How many cops does it take to change a light bulb?
None. It turned itself in.

How many physiotherapists does it take to change a light bulb?
   None. They just give the dead bulb some exercises to do and hope that it will be better in a week.

How many authors does it take to change a light bulb?
Two. One to screw it almost in and the other to give it a surprising twist at the end.

How many doctors does it take to change a light bulb?
None. They simply sign the death certificate and call the undertaker.

How many Irishmen does it take to change a light bulb?
Five. One to change the bulb and four to remark about how grand the old bulb was.

MILITARY

At the height of the Cold War, the Americans and Russians realised that if they continued in the usual manner they were going to blow up the whole world. They decided to settle the whole dispute with one dogfight. They'd have five years to breed the best fighting dog in the world and whichever side's dog won would be entitled to dominate the world. The losing side would have to lay down its arms.

The Russians found the biggest, meanest Doberman and the biggest, meanest Rottweiler in the entire world and bred them with the biggest, meanest Siberian wolves. They selected only the biggest and strongest puppy from each litter, killed his siblings, and gave him all the milk. They used steroids and trainers and after five years came up with the biggest, meanest dog the world had ever seen. Its cage needed steel bars that were 20cm thick and nobody could get near it.

When the day came for the fight, the Americans showed up with a strange animal. It was a 4m-long dachshund. Everyone felt sorry for the Americans because they knew there was no way that this dog could possibly last 10 seconds with the Russian dog.

When the cages were opened up, the dachshund came out and wrapped itself around the outside of the ring. It had the Russian dog almost completely surrounded. When the Russian dog leaned over to bite the dachshund's neck, the dachshund, in a snarling, vicious movement, reached out, opened up its enormous jaws, and consumed the Russian dog in one bite. There was nothing left of the Russian dog. The Russians shook their heads in disbelief.

'We don't understand how this could have happened. We had our best people working for five years with the meanest

Doberman and Rottweiler in the world and the biggest, meanest Siberian wolves,' they lamented.

'We looked at the problem from a different angle,' an American replied. 'We had our best plastic surgeons working for five years to make an alligator look like a Dachshund.'

A young officer was posted to a British army detachment in the desert. On his tour of the facility with the master sergeant, he noticed a group of camels.

'What are those for?' he asked.

'The men use them when they want to have sex.'

'Don't say another word, sergeant. That is the most disgusting thing I have ever heard. Get rid of those camels immediately!'

'Yes, sir.'

A few weeks went by and the young officer began to get rather horny. He called the sergeant over and asked, 'Where are the camels we used to have?'

The sergeant replied that he had sold them to a Bedouin that camped nearby.

'Take me to them, please.'

The officer and the sergeant went over to the Bedouin camp and found the camels. The officer told the sergeant to leave him alone with the camels, then picked out the most attractive one, and had sex with the camel.

On the way back to the camp, the officer asked, 'Sergeant, do the men actually enjoy sex with the camels?'

The sergeant looked at the officer in astonishment and exclaimed, 'Of course not! They use them to ride into town to where the girls are.'

A soldier serving overseas, far from home, was annoyed and upset when his girl wrote breaking off their engagement and asking for her photograph back. He went out and collected from his friends all the unwanted photographs of women that he could find. He bundled them all together and sent them to her with a note: 'Regret cannot remember which one is you. Please keep your photo and return the others.'

An army major visiting the sick soldiers in an army hospital approaches one of the patients and asks, 'What's your problem, soldier?'

'Chronic syphilis, sir!'

'What treatment are you getting?'

'Five minutes with the wire brush each day, sir!'

'What's your ambition?'

'To get back to the front lines, sir!'

'Good man!' says the major.

He goes to the next bed. 'What's your problem, soldier?'

'Chronic piles, sir!'

'What treatment are you getting?'

'Five minutes with the wire brush each day, sir!'

'What's your ambition?'

'To get back to the front lines, sir!'

'Good man!' says the major.

He goes to the next bed. 'What's your problem, soldier?'

'Chronic gum disease, sir!'

'What treatment are you getting?'

'Five minutes with the wire brush each day, sir!'

'What's your ambition?'

'To get to the front of the line and get the wire brush before the other two, sir!'

The captain called the sergeant in.

'Sarge, I just got a telegram that Private Jones' mother died yesterday. Better go tell him and send him in to see me.'

So the sergeant calls for his morning formation and lines up all the troops.

'Listen up, men,' says the sergeant. 'Johnson, step out and report to the mess hall for KP. Hoskins, step out and report for guard duty. Jones, step out and report to Personnel, your mother is dead. The rest of you are to report to the motor pool for maintenance.'

Later that day the captain called the sergeant into his office. 'Sergeant, that was a pretty cold way to inform Jones his mother died. Could you be a bit more tactful next time, please?'

'Yes, sir,' answered the sergeant.

A few months later, the captain called the sergeant in again. 'Sarge, I just got a telegram that Private McGrath's mother died. You'd better go tell him, and then send him in to see me. This time, please be more tactful.'

So the sergeant calls for his morning formation.

'OK, men, fall in and listen up. Everybody with a mother, take two steps forward. Not so fast, McGrath!'

MISCELLANEOUS

Two aerials meet on a roof – fall in love – get married. The ceremony was rubbish but the reception was brilliant.

I went to the butchers the other day and I bet him 50 bucks that he couldn't reach the meat off the top shelf. And he said, 'No, the steaks are too high.'

Two cows are standing next to each other in a field. Daisy says to Dolly, 'I was artificially inseminated this morning.'

'I don't believe you,' said Dolly.

'It's true, straight up, no bull!'

Q: How do you get four suits for a couple of dollars?
A: Buy a pack of cards.

Q: What did one elevator say to the other?
A: I think I'm coming down with something.

Q: What did one magnet say to the other magnet?
A: 'I find you very attractive.'

Sally: Why are you wearing garlic around your neck?
Jim: It keeps away vampires.
Sally: But there are no vampires.
Jim: See, it works.

A ghost walks into a bar.
'Sorry, we don't serve spirits here,' says the bartender.

Cannibal 1:   How do you make an explorer stew?
Cannibal 2:   Keep him waiting a few hours.

Once there was a boy named Odd. He was the butt of jokes his whole life, because of his name. Eventually he grew up to be a very successful fisherman and owner of three fish processing plants.

When Odd was about to die, he said, 'People have been teasing me my whole life and I don't want them doing that after I'm dead, so don't put my name on my gravestone.'

After Odd died, people saw his blank tombstone and said, 'That's odd.'

Two cows are in a field. One says to the other, 'So what do you think of mad cow disease?'

'What do I care? I'm a chicken.'

My friend drowned in a bowl of muesli. He was pulled in by a strong currant.

Last night I lay in my bed looking up at the stars in the sky and thinking to myself, 'Where the hell is the ceiling?'

The Seven Dwarfs go to the Vatican and are granted an audience with the pope.

'Dopey, my son,' says the pope. 'What can I do for you?'

Dopey asks, 'Excuse me, Your Excellency, but are there any dwarf nuns in Rome?'

The pope wrinkles his brow at this odd question, thinks for a minute and answers, 'No Dopey there are no dwarf nuns in Rome.'

In the background a few of the dwarfs start sniggering. Dopey turns around and gives them a glare, silencing them.

Dopey turns back, 'Your Worship, are there any dwarf nuns in all of Europe?'

The pope, puzzled now, again thinks for a moment and then answers, 'No Dopey, there are no dwarf nuns in Europe.'

The other dwarfs begin to giggle.

Dopey implores the pope, 'Mr Pope, are there any dwarf nuns anywhere in the world?'

'I'm sorry, my son, there are no dwarf nuns anywhere in the world.'

The other dwarfs collapse into a heap, rolling around in laughter. They're pounding the floor and tears are rolling down their cheeks as they begin chanting, 'Dopey screwed a penguin! Dopey screwed a penguin!'

An armless man walked into a bar that was empty except for the bartender. He ordered a drink and when he was served, he asked the bartender to get the money from his wallet in his pocket, since he had no arms. The bartender obliged.

He then asked if the bartender would tip the glass to his lips. The bartender did this until the man finished his drink. He then asked if the bartender would get a hanky from his pocket and wipe the foam from his lips. The bartender did this and commented that it must be very difficult not to have arms and have to ask someone to do nearly everything for him.

'Yes,' said the man. 'It is a bit embarrassing at times. By the way, where is your restroom?'

'The closest one is in the gas station three blocks down the street,' replied the barman quickly.

A beggar knocked on the door of a Toorak mansion. There was no immediate answer, so the bum kept knocking. For 15 minutes he kept this up. Finally, an angry millionaire opened the door.

The beggar asked, 'Can I have $2?'

'What the hell are you doing waking me up at 3am just for $2?' demanded the millionaire.

'Hey! I don't tell you how to run your business, so don't you dare tell me how to run mine!'

Porky was 18 years old, friendly, and eager to do things right. Unfortunately, he wasn't especially bright. He had just started his first job, as a delivery boy and general 'go-fer' at a furniture warehouse. His first task was to go out for coffee.

He walked into a nearby coffee shop carrying a large thermos. When the assistant finally noticed him, he held up the thermos.

'Is this big enough to hold six cups of coffee? he asked.

The assistant looked at the thermos, hesitated for a few seconds, then finally said, 'Yeah. It looks like about six cups to me.'

'Good,' Porky said. 'Give me two white, two black, and two decaf.'

Two hydrogen atoms walk into a bar.
'I think I've lost an electron,' says one.
'Are you sure?' asks the second.
'Yes, I'm positive.'

Two peanuts walk into a bar.
One was a-salted.

A jump-lead walks into a bar.
The barman says 'I'll serve you, but don't start anything.'

A sandwich walks into a bar.
The barman says 'Sorry we don't serve food in here.'

Aman walks into a bar with a roll of tarmac under his arm. He says 'Pint please, and one for the road.'

Radio Report of Duel between Alexander Shott and John Nott in June 1849:

Nott was shot and Shott was not. In this case, it is better to be Shott than Nott. Some said that Nott was not shot. But Shott says that he shot Nott. It may be that the shot Shott shot, shot Nott, or it may be possible that the shot Shott shot, shot Shott himself. We think, however, that the shot Shott shot, shot not Shott, but Nott.

Itold her, 'Your bank account's knotted,
You've spent so much more than allotted.'
    She said with a yawn,
    'I'm not overdrawn,
    It's just simply an under-deposit!'

Iwent to buy some camouflage trousers the other day but I couldn't find any.

Aguy goes to a girl's house for the first time, and she shows him into the living room. She excuses herself to go to the kitchen to make a drink, and as he's standing there alone, he notices a cute little vase on the mantel. He picks it up, and while he's looking at it, she walks back in.

'What's this?' he asks.

'Oh, my father's ashes are in there.'

Embarrassed he returns the vase to the mantle and apologises.

'Don't worry,' she says. 'The lazy bugger won't go to the kitchen to get an ashtray.'

Two guys are walking in the jungle. One is carrying a lamp post; the other one has a telephone booth.

'Why are you carrying a telephone booth?' the first asks the other.

'When the lions come, I put it down, get into it and I'll be safe,' he says. 'So, why are you carrying a lamp post?'

'When the lions come, I'll throw it away, so I can run faster.'

I went to a seafood disco last week, and pulled a mussel.

HOMER SIMPSON SINGS THE SOUND OF MUSIC

Dough, the stuff that buys me beer.
Ray, the guy that sells me beer.
Me, the guy who drinks the beer.
Far, the distance to my beer.
So, I think I'll have a beer.
La, la la la la la beer
Tea, No thanks, I'm drinking beer.
That will bring us back to (Looks into an empty glass)
D'oh!

An ice cream man was found lying on the floor of his van covered with hundreds and thousands. Police say that he topped himself.

Two elephants walk off a cliff. Boom, boom!

Apparently, one in five people in the world are Chinese. There are five people in my family, so one of them must be Chinese. It's either my mum or my dad. Or my older brother Colin. Or my younger brother Ho-Cha-Chu. But I think it is Colin.

Sal: Can you give me a lift?
Sam: Sure, you look great, the world's your oyster, go for it!

Two fat blokes in a pub, one says to the other, 'Your round.'
'So are you, you fat bastard!'

Two prostitutes standing on a street corner, one says to the other, 'Have you ever been picked up by the fuzz?'
'No, but I've often been swung around by the boobs.'

Ireland's worst air disaster occurred early this morning when a two-seater Cessna crashed into a cemetery. Irish search and rescue workers have recovered 1826 bodies so far and expect that number to climb as digging continues into the night.

I had a ploughman's lunch the other day. He wasn't very happy.

I was driving down the highway with my girl the other day when we both got a bit frisky. So we took the next exit, but it was a turn-off.

Mr and Mrs Potato had eyes for each other, and finally they got married and had a little sweet potato. They called her Yam. Of course, they wanted the best for Yam.

When it was time, they told her about the facts of life. They warned her about going out and getting half-baked, so she wouldn't get accidentally mashed, and get a bad name for herself like 'hot potato'.

Yam said 'Don't worry, no spud will get me into the sack and make a rotten potato out of me.'

But on the other hand she didn't want to stay home and become a couch potato either. And she wanted to get plenty of exercise to stay healthy, unlike her shoestring cousins.

When she went off to Europe, Mr and Mrs Potato told Yam to watch out for the hard boiled guys from Ireland. And the greasy guys from France called French fries. And in America, to watch out for the Indians so that she wouldn't get scalloped.

Yam said she would stay on the straight and narrow and wouldn't associate with those high class Sutton Supremes.

Mr and Mrs Potato sent Yam to Idaho PU (that's Potato University) so that when she graduated she'd really be in the chips. But in spite of all they did for her, one day Yam came home and announced she was going to marry Eddie McGuire.

Eddie McGuire! Mr and Mrs Potato were very upset. They told Yam she couldn't possibly marry Eddie McGuire, because he is just a common tater.

Two cannibals are eating a clown. One says to the other 'Does this taste funny to you?'

So I was in my car, and I was driving along, and my boss rang up, and he said, 'You've been promoted.'

And I swerved. And then he rang up a second time and said, 'You've been promoted again.'

And I swerved again. He rang up a third time and said, 'You're managing director.'

And I hit a tree and a policeman came up and said, 'What happened to you?'

And I said, 'I careered off the road.'

The phone was ringing. I picked it up, and said, 'Who's speaking please?'

'You are,' said a voice.

I rang up my local swimming pool. I said, 'Is that the local swimming pool?'

'It depends where you're calling from.'

I rang up a local building firm, I said, 'I want a skip outside my house.'

'I'm not stopping you.'

Q: What's brown and sounds like a bell?
A: Dung.

A very demanding customer was in a restaurant. First, he asked that the air-conditioning be turned up because he was too hot. Then he asked for it to be turned down because he was too cold. And so on for about half an hour.

Surprisingly, the waiter was very patient; he walked back and forth and never once got angry. Finally, a second customer asked him why he didn't throw the pest out.

'Oh it doesn't worry me,' said the waiter with a smile. 'We don't even have an air conditioner.'

Diner: Waiter, I can't eat this meal. Get me the manager.
Waiter: It's no use. He won't eat it either.

Diner: Waiter, there's a dead fly in my soup!
Waiter: Yes, sir, it's the hot water that kills them.

Diner: Waiter, I can't eat this.
Waiter: Why not sir?
Diner: You haven't given me a knife and fork.

Q: Why don't elephants pick their nose?
A: Because they don't know what to do with a 20kg boogie.

MORE BLONDE GAGS

A young blonde woman is distraught because she fears her husband is having an affair, so she goes to a gun shop and buys a handgun. The next day she comes home to find her husband in bed with a beautiful redhead.

She grabs the gun and holds it to her own head. The husband jumps out of bed, begging and pleading with her not to shoot herself.

Hysterically the blonde responds to the husband, 'Shut up. You're next!'

O n a plane bound for New York, the flight attendant approached a blonde sitting in the first-class section and requested that she move to economy since she did not have a first-class ticket.

The blonde replied, 'I'm blonde, I'm beautiful, I'm going to New York and I'm not moving.'

Not wanting to argue with a customer, the flight attendant asked the co-pilot to speak with her. He went to talk with the woman, asking her to please move out of the first-class section.

Again, the blonde replied, 'I'm blonde, I'm beautiful, I'm going to New York and I'm not moving.'

The co-pilot returned to the cockpit and asked the captain what to do. The captain said, 'I'm married to a blonde. I know how to handle this.'

He went to the first-class section and whispered in the blonde's ear. She immediately jumped up and ran to the economy section mumbling, 'Why didn't anyone just say so?'

Surprised, the flight attendant and the co-pilot asked what he said to her that finally convinced her to move from her seat.

He said, 'I told her the first-class section wasn't going to New York.'

A blonde walks into a hairdressing salon, wearing headphones. She says to the hairdresser, 'Please cut my hair, but, whatever you do, don't knock the headphones off!'

Alas, during the cutting, the hairdresser slips, and the headphones accidentally fall off. The blonde falls over dead. The shocked hairdresser picks up the headphones and listens.

The taped voice is saying, 'Breathe in, breathe out, breathe in, breathe out.'

A blonde decides to try horseback riding for the first time. She mounts the horse unassisted, and it springs into motion. It gallops along at a steady pace, but the blonde begins to slip from the saddle. In terror, she grabs for the horse's mane, but can't get a firm grip. She throws her arms around the horse's neck, but still slides down the side, while it gallops on.

The blonde tries to leap from the horse to safety. But her foot becomes entangled in the stirrup, and she is now in all sorts of trouble, with her head repeatedly banging against the ground as the horse continues its gallop. The blonde starts to lose consciousness.

Luckily, one of the checkout girls sees her predicament, rushes over, and unplugs the horse.

Then there was the blonde working at reception. A fellow worker came up and said, 'Would you like to buy a raffle ticket? Janice in production died suddenly last week. It's for her husband and four children.'

'No thanks,' said the blonde. 'I've already got a husband and two kids of my own.'

MUSIC

Once upon a time, there was a blind rabbit and blind snake, both living in the same neighbourhood. One beautiful day, the blind rabbit was hopping happily down the path toward his home, when he bumped into someone.

Apologizing profusely he explained, 'I am blind, and didn't see you there.'

'Perfectly all right,' said the snake, 'because I am blind, too, and did not see to step out of your way.'

A conversation followed, gradually becoming more intimate, and finally the snake said, 'This is the best conversation I have had with anyone for a long time. Would you mind if I felt you to see what you are like?'

'Why, no,' said the rabbit. 'Go right ahead.'

So the snake wrapped himself around the rabbit and shuffled and snuggled his coils, and said, 'You're soft and warm and fuzzy and cuddly. And those ears! You must be a rabbit.'

'Why, that's right!' said the rabbit. 'May I feel you?'

'Go right ahead.' said the snake, stretching himself out full length on the path.

The rabbit began to stroke the snake's body with his paws, then drew back in disgust.

'Yuck!' he said. 'You're cold and slimy. You must be a conductor!'

A maestro directing in Rome
Had a quaint way of driving it home.
Whoever he climbed
Had to keep her tail timed
To the beat of his old metronome.

Q: What's the difference between a soprano and the average boxer?
A: Stage makeup.

Q: What's the difference between a soprano and a Tenor?
A: About 10kg.

Q: What's the first thing a soprano does in the morning?
A: Puts on her clothes and goes home.

Q: What's the next thing a soprano does in the morning?
A: Looks for her instrument.

Q: What's the difference between a soprano and a Porsche?
A: Most musicians have never been in a Porsche.

Q: What's the definition of an alto?
A: A soprano who can sight read.

Q: What's the difference between an alto and a tenor?
A: Tenors don't have hair on their backs.

Q: What do you see if you look up a soprano's skirt?
A: A tenor.

Q: How do you tell if a tenor is dead?
A: The wine bottle is still full and the comics haven't been touched.

Q: Where is a tenor's resonance?
A: Where his brain should be.

Q: What's the definition of a male quartet?
A: Three men and a tenor.

Once a young tenor named Springer,
Got his testicles caught in a wringer.
  He hollered in pain
  As they rolled down the drain,
  'There goes my career as a singer!'

Q: What's the difference between a banjo and a chain saw?
A: The chain saw has greater dynamic range.

Q: What do you say to a banjo player in a three-piece suit?
A: 'Will the defendant please rise?'

Q: How do you get a guitar player to play softer?
A: Give him some sheet music.

Q: What do a vacuum cleaner and an electric guitar have in common?
A: Both suck when you plug them in.

Q: What's the best thing to play on a guitar?
A: Solitaire.

Did you hear about the electric bass player who was so bad that even the lead singer noticed?

Q: If you drop an accordion, a set of bagpipes and a viola off a 20-storey building, which one lands first?
A: Who cares?

Q: What's an accordion good for?
A: Learning how to fold a map.

Q: Why do bagpipe players walk while they play?
A: To get away from the noise.

Q: What's the difference between a puppy and a struggling singer-songwriter?

A: Eventually the puppy stops whining.

Q: What is the difference between a world war and a high school choir performance?

A: The performance causes more suffering.

Q: Why are conductor's hearts so coveted for transplants?

A: They've had so little use.

Did you hear about the planeload of conductors en route to the European Festival?

The good news: it crashed.

The bad news: there were three empty seats on board.

Q: Why is a conductor like a condom?

A: It's safer with one, but more fun without.

Q: What's the definition of an assistant conductor?

A: A mouse trying to become a rat.

Q: What's the difference between an opera conductor and a baby?

A: A baby sucks its fingers.

A girl went out on a date with a trumpet player, and when she came back her roommate asked, 'Well, how was it? Did his embouchure make him a great kisser?'

'No,' the first girl replied. 'That dry, tight, tiny little pucker; it was no fun at all.'

The next night she went out with a tuba player, and when she came back her roommate asked, 'Well, how was his kissing?'

'Ugh!' the first girl exclaimed. 'Those huge, rubbery, blubbery, slobbering slabs of meat; it was just gross!'

The next night she went out with a French horn player, and when she came back her roommate asked, 'Well, how was his kissing?'

'Well,' the first girl replied, 'his kissing was just so-so; but I loved the way he held me!'

Q: How do you tell the difference between a violinist and a dog?
A: The dog knows when to stop scratching.

Q: Why is a violinist like a SCUD missile?
A: Both are offensive and inaccurate.

Violinist: Oh, baby, I can play you just like my violin!
Violinist's wife: I'd rather have you play me like a harmonica.

Q: How do you make a cello sound beautiful?
A: Sell it and buy a violin.

Q: How do you make a double bass sound in tune?
A: Chop it up and make it into a xylophone.

Q: Why are harps like elderly parents?
A: Both are unforgiving and hard to get into and out of cars.

Q: How long does a harp stay in tune?
A: About 20 minutes, or until someone opens a door.

Q: Why is a concert grand better than a studio upright?
A: Because it makes a much bigger kabloom when dropped down a mine shaft.

Q: Why was the piano invented?
A: So the musician would have a place to put his beer.

The organ is the instrument of worship. In its sounding we sense the majesty of God, and in its ending we know the grace of God.

Q: How do you get two piccolos to play in unison?
A: Shoot one.

Q: What's the difference between a SCUD missile and a bad oboist?
A: A bad oboist can kill you.

Q: What's the difference between a saxophone and a lawn mower?
A: Lawn mowers sound better in small ensembles. Besides, the neighbours are upset if you borrow a lawnmower and don't return it.

Q: What's the difference between a baritone saxophone and a chain saw?
A: The exhaust.

The soprano, not being smart enough to use birth control, says to her saxophonist lover, 'Honey, I think you had better pull out now.'

He replies, 'Why? Am I sharp?'

Q: What's the range of a tuba?
A: Twenty metres if you've got a good arm!

Q: How do horn players traditionally greet each other?
A: 'Hi. I did that piece in junior high.'

Q: What do you get when you cross a French Horn player and a goalpost?
A: A goalpost that can't march.

Q: What is the difference between a French horn section and a '57 Chevy?
A: You can tune a '57 Chevy.

Q: How do you get your viola section to sound like the horn section?
A: Have them miss every other note.

It is difficult to trust a trombone player when his instrument changes shape as he plays it!

Q: How can you tell which kid on a playground is the child of a trombonist?
A: He doesn't know how to use the slide, and he can't swing.

Q: Why can't a gorilla play trumpet?
A: He's too sensitive.

Q: How do trumpet players traditionally greet each other?
A: 'Hi. I'm better than you.'

Q: How do you know when a trumpet player is at your door?
A: The doorbell shrieks!

Q: What's the difference between a soprano and a piranha?
A: The lipstick.

Q: What's the difference between a soprano and a terrorist?
A: You can negotiate with a terrorist.

Q: What do you call a groupie who hangs around and annoys musicians?
A: A bagpipe player.

In New York City, an out-of-work jazz drummer named Ed was thinking of throwing himself off a bridge. But then he ran into a former booking agent who told him about the fantastic opportunities for drummers in Iraq.

The agent said 'If you can find your way over there, just take my card and look up the bandleader named Faisal. He's the large guy with the beard wearing gold pyjamas and shoes that curl up at the toes.'

Ed borrowed enough money to get to Iraq. It took several days to arrange for passport, visas, transportation into Iraq and the shipping of his equipment, but he was finally on his way. He arrived in Baghdad and immediately started searching for Faisal. He found guys in pyjamas of every colour but gold.

Finally, in a small coffeehouse, he saw a huge man with a beard, wearing gold pyjamas and shoes that curled up at the toes! Ed approached him and asked if he was Faisal. He was. Ed gave him the agent's card and Faisal's face brightened into a huge smile.

'You're just in time. I need you for a gig tonight. Meet me at the market near the mosque at 7:30pm with your equipment.'

'But,' gasped Ed, 'what about a rehearsal?'

'No time. Don't worry.'

And with that, Faisal disappeared. Ed arrived in the market at 7pm to set up his gear. He introduced himself to the other musicians, who were all playing instruments he had never seen in his life. At 7:30pm sharp, Faisal appeared and hopped on the bandstand, his gold pyjamas glittering in the twilight. Without a word to the musicians, he lifted his arm for the downbeat.

'Wait.' shouted Ed. 'What are we playing?'

Faisal shot him a look of frustration and shouted back, 'Fake it! Just give me heavy after-beats on 7 and 13.'

Q: Why is it good that drummers have 50g more brains than horses?

A: So they don't disgrace themselves in parades.

Q: Did you hear about the time the bass player locked his keys
   in the car?
A: It took two hours to get the drummer out.

Q: What did the drummer get on his IQ test?
A: Drool.

OFFICE, BUSINESS & TECHNOLOGY

GUIDE TO REAL ESTATE SPEAK

Architect's delight:
Built to cut-down plans from a former chemical factory he had designed before the scheme fell through and he was deregistered.

Brilliant concept:
A two-story defoliating fir tree standing under a 10m all-glass dome, surrounded by a waterfall and a perfectly formed scale version of the sphinx.

Charming:
It's the size of a broom cupboard.

Quaint:
It's the size of a broom cupboard full of brooms.

Completely updated:
Stainless steel appliances, polished floorboards, paved court-yard, and not a smidgin of greenery in sight.

Contemporary:
Cheaply slapped together in a hurry to take advantage of the first home buyers grant.

Daring design:
Still a warehouse.

Garden outlook:
You get a good view of the neighbour's garden.

Much potential:
No one else has dared develop this, largely because the backyard sits on a disused mine shaft.

Must see to believe:	Unless you saw it, you'd never believe it.
One of a kind:	Ugly as sin. Nothing quite like it still standing.
Certified:	Actually, the architect has been certified.
National Trust–listed:	Look closer, and it actually reads 'National Truss–listed'. This was a former geriatric accommodation unit, and you can still smell the wee.
Renovator's delight:	A shit-heap.
Sea glimpses:	Take a chair into the bathroom, place it next to the toilet, get up on it, stand on your tippy-toes, crane your head to the left, and there – no, just there – is a flash of blue.
Sophisticated:	Black walls, flat roof, no windows. See Architect's delight.
On compact lot:	If you stretch your arms out, you will touch both fences at once.
Unique city home:	Was a former pasta-sauce factory; walls are concrete, roof is cold steel; smells of pepperoni.
Steeped in history:	There's mould on the walls.
You'll love it:	No, on second thoughts, you won't.

SIGNS YOUR CAT HAS LEARNED YOUR INTERNET PASSWORD

- You're getting email flames from some guy named Fluffy.
- There's kitty litter in your keyboard.
- You find you've been subscribed to strange newsgroups like alt.recreational.catnip.
- Your mouse has teeth marks in it, and a strange aroma of tuna.
- There are hate-mail messages to Apple Computers about their release of CyberDog in your sent messages.

- Your new ergonomic keyboard has a strange territorial scent to it.
- You keep finding new software around your house like CatinTax and WarCat II.
- On IRC you're known as the IronMouser.
- There are little carpal-tunnel braces near the scratching post.

COMPUTER DEFINITIONS

Bit:	A word used to describe the price of computers, as in 'our daughter's computer cost quite a bit.'
Boot:	What your friends give you because you spend too much time bragging about your computer skills.
Bug:	What your eyes do after you stare at the tiny green computer screen for more than 15 minutes.
Chips:	The fattening, non-nutritional food computer users eat to avoid having to leave their keyboards.
Cursor:	What you turn into when you can't get your computer to perform, as in 'you ~*%@& computer!'
Disk:	What goes out of your back after bending over a computer keyboard for seven hours at a time.
Dump:	The place all your former hobbies wind up soon after you install games on your computer.
Error:	What you made when you first walked into a computer showroom 'just to look.'
Expansion unit:	The new room you have to build on to your home to house your computer and all its peripherals.

File: What a secretary can now do to her nails 6 and a half hours a day, with a computer to do her day's work in 30 minutes.

Floppy: The condition of a constant computer user's stomach due to lack of exercise and a steady diet of junk food (see Chips).

Hardware: Tools, such as lawnmowers, rakes and other heavy equipment you haven't laid a finger on since getting your computer.

IBM: The kind of missile your family members and friends would like to drop on your computer so you'll pay attention to them again.

Menu: Something you'll never see again after buying a computer because you'll be too poor to eat in a restaurant.

Programs: Those things you used to look at on your television before you hooked your computer up.

Return: What lots of people do with their computers after they receive their first bill from their internet service provider.

Terminal: A place where you can find buses, trains and really good deals on hot computers.

Windows: What you heave the computer out of after you accidentally erase a program that took you three days to set up.

ANSWERING MACHINE MESSAGES

Twinkle, twinkle little star
How we wonder who you are.
Leave a message at the beep.
We'll call back before you sleep.

Twinkle, twinkle little star,
Betcha you're wondering where we are.

You're growing tired. Your eyelids are getting heavy. You feel very sleepy now. You are gradually losing your willpower and your ability to resist suggestions. When you hear the tone you will feel helplessly compelled to leave your name, number, and a message.

Now I lay me down to sleep;
Leave a message at the beep.
  If I should die before I wake,
  Remember to erase the tape.

This is you-know who. We are you-know-where. Leave your you-know-what you-know-when.

No, No! Not that! Anything but that! Not the beep! No! Please! Not the beep! Anything but the beep! AAAAIIIIEEEEEEEEEEEEE!

This is the Metropolitan Opera Amateur Audition Hotline. After the tone, sing Ave Maria.

Hello. I am David's answering machine. What are you?

Hi! John's answering machine is broken. This is his refrigerator. Please speak very slowly, and I'll stick your message to myself with one of these magnets.

Hello, this is Ron's toaster. Ron's new answering machine is in the shop for repairs, so please leave your message when the toast is done.

Hello, this is Sally's microwave. Her answering machine just eloped with her tape deck, so I'm stuck taking her calls. Say, if you want anything cooked while you leave your message, just hold it up to the phone.

Hi. Now you say something.

If you are a burglar, then we're probably at home cleaning our weapons right now and can't come to the phone. Otherwise, we aren't home, and it's safe to leave a message.

Please leave a message. However, you have the right to remain silent. Everything you say will be recorded and will be used by us.

We're not home, we're rarely home,
And when we're home, we're on the phone,
    So please leave a message at the tone!

Hi, I'm not home right now but my answering machine is, so talk to it instead.

Greetings, you have reached the Sixth Sense Detective Agency. We know who you are and what you want, so at the sound of the tone, just hang up.

Alpha Centauri Space Station. Commander Marlin can't come to the phone right now. He's either saving the universe from some dreaded, unnamed peril, or perhaps taking a nap. Leave your name and number after the beep and he will return your call.

(In a Darth Vader voice) Speak, worm!

A bubble in the space-time continuum has connected your line to a channeller in the 23rd century. Any message you leave will be broadcast into the future.

S teve has been captured by aliens in a flying saucer and can't come to the phone right now, but if you leave your name, phone number, and a message, I'll have him call you back as soon as he gets away. Read all about it in next week's tabloid.

OFFICE PRAYER

G rant me the serenity to accept the things I can't change, the courage to change the things I can't accept, and the wisdom to hide the bodies of those people I had to kill today because they pissed me off. Also, help me to be careful of the toes I step on today, as they may be connected to the ass I have to kiss tomorrow.

10 EXCUSES TO USE WHEN CAUGHT NAPPING AT YOUR DESK

1. . . . in the Lord Jesus' name, Amen.
2. They told me at the blood bank this might happen.
3. Damn! Why did you interrupt me? I had almost worked out a solution to our biggest problem.
4. I was doing Yoga exercises to relieve work-related stress.
5. Someone must've put decaf in the wrong pot.
6. I was testing my keyboard for drool resistance.
7. This is just a 15-minute powernap, as described in that time management course you sent me.
8. I wasn't sleeping! I was meditating on the mission statement and envisioning a new paradigm.
9. The coffee machine is broken.
10. Whew! Guess I left the top off the Liquid Paper! You got here just in time!

A site foreman had 10 very lazy men working for him, so one day he decided to trick them into doing some work for a change.

'I've got a really easy job today for the laziest one among you,' he announced. 'Will the laziest man please put his hand up?'

Nine hands went up.

'Why didn't you put your hand up?' he asked the 10th man.

'Too much trouble,' came the reply.

A shepherd was herding his flock in a remote pasture when suddenly a brand new Jeep Cherokee advanced out of a dust cloud towards him. The driver, a young man in a Hugo Boss suit, Gucci shoes, Ray Ban sunglasses and a YSL tie, leaned out of the window and said, 'If I can tell you exactly how many sheep you have in your flock, will you give me one?'

The shepherd looks at the yuppie, then at his peacefully grazing flock and calmly answers, 'Sure.'

The yuppie parks the car, whips out his laptop, connects it to a mobile phone, surfs to a NASA page on the internet where he calls up a GPS satellite navigation system, scans the area, opens up a database and some Excel spreadsheets with complex formulas.

Finally he prints out a 150 page report on his hi-tech miniaturised printer, turns to the shepherd and says, 'You have here exactly 1586 sheep.'

'This is correct, and as agreed you can take one of the sheep,' says the shepherd.

He watches the young man make a selection and bundle it in to his Cherokee.

Then he says: 'If I can tell you exactly what your business is, will you give me my property back?'

'OK, why not,' answers the young man.

'You are a consultant,' says the shepherd.

'This is correct,' says the yuppie, 'How did you guess that?

'Easy. You turn up here, although nobody invited you; you want to be paid for an answer to a question I never asked; and you gave me information I already knew.'

'Wow, pretty good.'

'Besides, you don't know Jack-shit about my business.'

'Hey, how do you come to that conclusion?'

'Because you took my dog.'

YOU WORK IN A GLOBAL CORPORATION IF:

- You sat at the same desk for four years and worked for three different companies.
- You worked for the same company for four years and sat at more than 10 different desks.
- You've been in the same job for four years and have had 10 different managers.
- You see a good-looking person and know it is a visitor.
- You order your business cards in 'half-orders' instead of whole boxes.
- When someone asks what you do for a living, you can't explain it in one sentence.
- You get really excited about a 2% pay raise.
- You use acronyms in your sentences.
- Art involves a white board.
- Your biggest loss from a system crash is that you lose your best jokes.
- You sit in a cubicle smaller than your bedroom closet.
- Weekends are those days your significant other makes you stay home.
- It's dark when you drive to and from work.
- Fun is when issues are assigned to someone else.
- The word 'opportunity' makes you shiver in fear.
- Free food leftover from meetings is your main staple.
- Being sick is defined as 'can't walk or admitted to hospital'.

- You're already late on the assignment you just got.
- Dilbert cartoons hang outside every cube and are read by your co-workers only.
- Your boss' favourite lines are 'when you get a few minutes' or 'when you're freed up'.
- You read this entire list and understood it all.

A man was eating in a restaurant and he dropped his spoon. The waiter was immediately at his table and took another spoon out of his pocket and gave it to the man. The man thanked him, and took a sip of his soup and then asked,

'Excuse me, but why do all the waiters have spoons in their pockets?'

The waiter said, 'Well sir, a time and motion survey in our restaurant showed that one in four customers drop their spoon just like you, so we always have a spare spoon on hand so we can give it to the customer so that he is not eating with the dirty one. It saves time as the waiter does not have to go back to the kitchen to retrieve a clean spoon. The management prides itself in the efficiency of the staff.'

Just as the waiter was about to walk back to the kitchen, the man noticed that there was a string hanging from his fly and the man said, 'Excuse me but why do you, and all the other waiters have a string hanging out of your flies?'

The waiter said, 'Well sir, a survey in our restaurant showed that the waiters can save time and serve more customers, if we do not wash our hands after using the toilet. So we use the string tied to our penises to pull it out of our trousers so we don't get our hands dirty.'

Then the man took another sip of his soup and replied, 'That's all very well, but how do you get it back in again?'

'Well I don't know about the others,' replied the waiter, 'But personally, I use the spoon.'

A man walks up to a woman in his office and tells her that her hair smells nice. The woman immediately goes into her supervisor's office and tells him that she wants to file a sexual harassment suit and explains why.

The supervisor is puzzled and says, 'What's wrong with your co-worker telling you that your hair smells nice.'

The woman replies, 'He's a midget.'

A blonde, a brunette, and a redhead all work at the same office for a female boss who always goes home early.

'Hey, girls,' says the brunette, 'let's go home early tomorrow. She'll never know.'

So the next day, they all leave right after the boss does. The brunette gets some extra gardening done, the redhead goes to a bar, and the blonde goes home to find her husband having sex with the female boss! She quietly sneaks out of the house and comes back at her normal time.

'That was fun,' says the brunette. 'We should do it again sometime.'

'No way,' says the blonde. 'I almost got caught.'

HOW TO ANNOY THE HELL OUT OF EVERYONE ELSE AT YOUR WORKPLACE

- Page yourself over the intercom. Don't disguise your voice.
- Find out where your boss shops and buy exactly the same outfits. Wear them one day after you boss does. This is especially effective if your boss is of a different gender than you.
- Make up nicknames for all your co-workers and refer to them only by these names, eg 'That's a good point, Sparky,' or 'No, I'm sorry, but I'm going to have to disagree with you there, Cha-Cha.'
- Highlight your shoes. Tell people you haven't lost them as much since you did this.

- Hang mosquito netting around your cubicle. When you emerge to get a coffee or a printout or whatever, slap yourself randomly the whole way.
- Put a chair facing a printer. Sit there all day and tell people you're waiting for your document.
- Every time someone asks you to do something, anything, ask them if they want fries with that.
- Encourage your colleagues to join you in a little synchronised chair-dancing.
- Feign an unnatural and hysterical fear of staplers.
- Send email messages saying there's free pizza or cake in the lunchroom. When people drift back to work complaining that they found none, lean back, pat your stomach and say, 'Oh you've got to be faster than that!'

YOU KNOW YOUR ACCOUNTANT IS A LITTLE CRAZY IF HE:

- Advises you to save postage by filing your taxes telepathically.
- Counts a family of possums living in your roof as dependents.
- Demands that you call him the 'Una-Countant'.
- Laughs at the demand for an audit.
- Has a GST form tattooed on his arm.
- Has written in several places on your tax forms, 'Give or take a million dollars'.
- Insists that there's no such number as four.
- Has on his wall, instead of a CPA licence, a framed photo of a shirtless Peter Costello.
- Tells you to put all your money into British cattle futures.
- Has on his desk, instead of a calculator, a broken VCR remote.

An engineer had an exceptional gift for fixing all things mechanical. After serving his company loyally for over 30 years, he happily retired. A few years later the company contacted him regarding an impossible problem they were having with one of their multi-million dollar machines. They had tried everything and everyone else to get the machine fixed, but to no avail.

In desperation, they called on the retired engineer who had solved so many of their problems in the past. The engineer reluctantly took the challenge. He spent a day studying the huge machine.

At the end of the day, he marked a small 'x' in chalk on a particular component of the machine and proudly stated, 'This is where your problem is'.

The part was replaced and the machine worked perfectly again. The company received a bill for $50,000 from the engineer for his service. They demanded an itemised accounting of his charges. The engineer responded briefly: One chalk mark: $1. Knowing where to put it: $49,999.

It was paid in full and the engineer retired again in peace.

YOU KNOW YOU'RE AN ENGINEER IF:

- At Christmas, it goes without saying that you will be the one to find the burnt-out bulb in the string of Christmas lights.
- For you, it becomes a moral dilemma to decide whether to buy flowers for your girlfriend or spend the money to upgrade the RAM on your computer.
- On an Alaskan Cruise, everyone else is on deck peering at the scenery, and you are still on a personal tour of the engine room.
- In college, you thought the summer break was metal fatigue failure.
- The only jokes you receive are through email.
- The salespeople at Computers 'R' Us can't answer any of your questions.
- You are always late to meetings.

- At an air show you know how fast the skydivers are falling.
- If you were in line on death row in a French prison and you found that the guillotine was not working properly, you would offer to fix it.
- You bought your wife a new CD-ROM for her birthday.
- You can quote scenes from any Monty Python movie.
- You can type 70 words per minute, but can't read your own handwriting.
- You can't write unless the paper has both horizontal and vertical lines.
- You comment to your wife that her straight hair is nice and parallel.
- You never have matching socks on.
- You save the power cord from a broken appliance.
- You have more friends on the Internet than in real life.
- You have never backed up your hard drive.
- You have never bought any new underwear or socks for yourself since you got married.
- You know what http stands for.
- You look forward to Christmas only to put together the kids' toys.
- You see a good design and still have to change it.
- You own a slide rule and you know how to use it.
- Your laptop computer cost more than your car.
- You think that when people around you yawn, it's because they didn't get enough sleep.

NEWTON'S LAW OF BALLS

Newton's Law of Balls: The Size of One's Balls is Inversely Related to the Size of One's Pay Packet. Thus:

1. The sport of choice for unemployed or incarcerated people is: basketball.

2. The sport of choice for maintenance level employees is: bowling.
3. The sport of choice for blue-collar workers is: football.
4. The sport of choice for supervisors is: cricket.
5. The sport of choice for middle management is: tennis.
6. The sport of choice for corporate officers is: golf.

Conclusion: The higher you rise in the corporate structure, the smaller your balls become.

BATHROOM POLICY – NOTICE TO EMPLOYEES

A bathroom trip policy will be established to provide a more consistent method of accounting for each employee's bathroom time and ensuring equal opportunity for all employees.

Under this policy a 'Bathroom Trip Bank' (BTB) will be established for each employee. On the first day of each month, employees will be given twenty (20) BTB credits. These credits may be accumulated indefinitely.

Within two weeks, the entrance doors to all restrooms will be equipped with personnel identification stations and computer-linked voice-print recognition devices. Each employee must provide two copies of voice-prints – one normal and one under stress.

Employees should acquaint themselves with the stations during the initial introduction period. If an employee's BTB balance reaches zero, the doors to the restroom will not unlock for that employee's voice until the first of the next month.

In addition, all restroom stalls are being equipped with timed paper roll retractors and pressure sensitive seats. If the stall is occupied for more than three minutes an alarm will sound. Thirty seconds after the alarm, the roll of paper will retract into the wall, the toilet will automatically flush, and the stall door will open. If the stall remains occupied, your picture will be taken.

The picture will then be posted on the bulletin board and the first of no more than two official warnings will be issued. If a person's picture appears for a third time, it will be grounds for immediate termination.

All supervisors have received advanced training on this policy. If you have any questions, please ask your supervisor.

OLD FOLKS

BEING OVER 60 HAS ITS ADVANTAGES

- No one expects you to run into a burning building.
- People call at 9pm and ask, 'Did I wake you?'
- People no longer view you as a hypochondriac.
- There's nothing left to learn the hard way.
- You can eat dinner at 4pm.
- You can live without sex, but not without glasses.
- You enjoy hearing about other people's operations.
- You get into a heated argument about pension plans.
- You have a party and the neighbours don't even realise it.
- You quit trying to hold your stomach in, no matter who walks into the room.
- You sing along with the elevator music.
- Your investment in health insurance is finally beginning to pay off.
- Your joints are more accurate weather gauges than the Bureau of Meteorology.
- Your secrets are safe with your friends because they can't remember them either.

Two old ladies were outside their nursing home having a smoke, when it started to rain. One of the ladies pulled out a condom, cut off the end, put it over her cigarette, and continued smoking.

'What's that?' asked the other lady.

'A condom.'

'Where'd you get it?'

'You can get them at any drugstore.'

The next day, the second lady hobbled into the local drugstore and announced to the pharmacist that she wanted to buy a package of condoms. The guy looked at her kind of strangely (she was, after all, in her 80s), but politely asked what brand she preferred.

'Doesn't matter,' she replied, 'as long as it fits a Camel.'

The drugs that we use when we're ailing
Go by different names for retailing
Tylenol's acetamenophen.
Advil's Ibuprofen.
And Viagra is Mycoxafailing . . .

Eighty-year-old Jessie bursts into the rec room of the men's retirement home. She holds her clenched fist in the air and announces, 'Anyone who can guess what's in my hand can have sex with me tonight!'

An elderly gentleman in the rear shouts out, 'An elephant?'

Jessie thinks a minute and says, 'Close enough.'

The wealthy old gentleman and his wife were celebrating their 35th wedding anniversary and their three grown sons joined them for dinner. The old man was rather irritated when he discovered none of the boys had bothered to bring a gift, and after the meal, he drew them aside.

'You're all grown men,' he said, 'and old enough to hear this. Your mother and I have never been legally married.'

'What?' gasped one of the sons, 'Do you mean to say we're all bastards?'

'Yes,' snapped the old man, 'and cheap ones, too!'

An old man who'd barely tried kissing
Soon discovered what he'd been missing.

When laid down on the sod,

He cried out, 'Oh, my God!

'All these years I just used it for pissing!'

THE MALE STAGES OF LIFE

Age	Drink
17	Beer
25	Vodka
35	Scotch
48	Double scotch
66	Milo

Age	Seduction Line
17	My parents are away for the weekend
25	My girlfriend is away for the weekend
35	My fiancée is away for the weekend
48	My wife is away for the weekend
66	My second wife is dead

Age	Favourite Sport
17	Sex
25	Sex
35	Sex
48	Sex
66	Napping

Age	Definition of a Successful Date
17	Tongue
25	Breakfast
35	She didn't set back my therapy
48	I didn't have to meet her kids
66	Got home alive

Age	Favourite Fantasy
17	Getting to third
25	Aeroplane sex
35	Ménage a trios
48	Taking the company public
66	Swiss maid/Nazi love slave

Age	House Pet
17	Roaches
25	Stoned college roommate
35	German shepherd
48	Children from first marriage
66	Barbie

Age	Ideal Age to Get Married
17	25
25	35
35	48
48	66
66	17

THE FEMALE STAGES OF LIFE

Age	Drink
17	Wine coolers
25	White wine
35	Red wine
48	Dom Perignon
66	Shot of Jack with an Ensure chaser

Age	Excuse for Refusing Dates
17	Need to wash my hair
25	Need to wash and condition my hair
35	Need to colour my hair

| 48 | Need to have François colour my hair |
| 66 | Need to have François colour my wig |

Age	**Favourite Sport**
17	Shopping
25	Shopping
35	Shopping
48	Shopping
66	Shopping

Age	**Definition of a Successful Date**
17	Burger King
25	Free meal
35	A diamond
48	A bigger diamond
66	Home Alone

Age	**Favourite Fantasy**
17	Tall, dark and handsome
25	Tall, dark and handsome with money
35	Tall, dark and handsome with money and a brain
48	A man with hair
66	A man

Age	**House Pet**
17	The cat
25	Unemployed boyfriend and the cat
35	German shepherd and the cat
48	Children from his first marriage and the cat
66	Retired husband who dabbles in taxidermy, stuffs the cat

Age	**Ideal Age to Get Married**
17	17
25	25

35   35
48   48
66   66

Age	Ideal Date
17	He offers to pay
25	He pays
35	He cooks breakfast the next morning
48	He cooks breakfast the next morning for the kids
66	He can chew breakfast

A woman saw a little wrinkled up man rocking in a chair on his porch.

'I couldn't help noticing how happy you look. What's your secret for a happy life?' she asked him.

'I smoke three packs of cigarettes a day. I also drink a case of whisky a week, eat lots of fatty foods, and never ever take any exercise.'

'That's amazing. Exactly how old are you?'

'Twenty-six.'

The most unfair thing about life is the way it ends. Life is tough. It takes a lot of your time. What do you get at the end of it? A death! What is that, a bonus?

The cycle is all backwards. You should die first. Get it out of the way. Then live in an old age home. You get kicked out when you're too young. You get a gold watch and you go to work.

You work forty years until you're young enough to enjoy your retirement. You do drugs and alcohol. You party. You get ready for High School. You go to primary school and become a kid. You play. You have no responsibilities.

You become a baby. You go into the womb. You spend your last nine months floating. You finish off as an orgasm.

A SAD TALE

My nookie days are over,
my pilot light is out.
What used to be my sex appeal,
is now my water spout.
Time was when, of its own accords,
from my trousers it would spring.
But now I have a full time job,
just to find the blasted thing.
It used to be embarrassing,
the way it would behave.
For every single morning,
it would stand and watch me shave.
But now as old age approaches,
it sure gives me the blues.
To see it hang its withered head,
and watch me tie my shoes.

THE BELL CURVE OF LIFE

At age 4	success is not peeing in your pants.
At age 10	success is making your own meals.
At age 12	success is having friends.
At age 18	success is having a driver's licence.
At age 20	success is having sex.
At age 35	success is having money.
At age 50	success is having money.
At age 60	success is having sex.
At age 70	success is having a driver's licence.
At age 75	success is having friends.
At age 80	success is making your own meals.
At age 85	success is not peeing in your pants.

PARTNERS & RELATIONSHIPS

If you love something, set it free. If it comes back, it was, and always will be yours. If it never returns, it was never yours to begin with.

If it just sits in your house, messes up your stuff, eats your food, uses your phone, takes your money, and never behaves as if you actually set it free in the first place, you either married it or gave birth to it.

WHY AREN'T YOU MARRIED?

- I was hoping to do something meaningful with my life.
- Because I just love hearing this question.
- Just lucky, I guess.
- It gives my mother something to live for.
- I'm waiting until I get to be your age.
- It didn't seem worth a blood test.
- I already have enough laundry to do, thank you.
- Because I think it would take all the spontaneity out of dating.
- They just opened a great singles bar on my block.
- I wouldn't want my parents to drop dead from sheer happiness.
- I don't want to have to support another person on my pay cheque.

PICK-UP LINES & THEIR COMEBACKS

Man: Haven't we met before?
MWoman: Perhaps. I'm the receptionist at the VD Clinic.

Man: Haven't I seen you someplace before?
MWoman: Yeah, that's why I don't go there anymore.

Man: Is that seat empty?
MWoman: Yes, and this one will be too if you sit down.

Man: Your place or mine?
MWoman: Both. You go to yours and I'll go to mine.

Man: So what do you do for a living?
MWoman: I'm a female impersonator.

Man: Hey, baby, what's your sign?
MWoman: Do not enter.

Man: How do you like your eggs in the morning?
MWoman: Unfertilised.

Man: Hey, come on, we're both here at this bar for the
             same reason.
    Woman: Yeah. Let's pick up some chicks.

Man: I know how to please a woman.
MWoman: Then please leave me alone.

Man: I want to give myself to you.
MWoman: Sorry, I don't accept cheap gifts.

Man: Your body is like a temple.
MWoman: Sorry, there are no services today.

Man: I'd go through anything for you.
MWoman: Good! Let's start with your bank account.

Man: I would go to the end of the world for you.
MWoman: Yes, but would you stay there?

A gay man decided he could no longer hide his sexuality from his parents. He went over to their house and found his mother in the kitchen cooking dinner. He sat down at the kitchen table, let out a big sigh, and said, 'Mum, I have something to tell you. I'm gay.'

His mother made no reply or gave any response, and the guy was about to repeat it to make sure she'd heard him, when she turned away from the pot she was stirring and said calmly, 'You're gay. Doesn't that mean you put other men's penises in your mouth?'

'Uh, yeah, mum, that's right.'

His mother went back to stirring the pot, then suddenly whirled around, whacked him over the head with her spoon and said, 'Well, then, don't you ever complain about my cooking again!'

Mrs Brown, who was a little on the chubby side, was at her weight-watchers meeting.

'My husband insists I come to these meetings because he would rather screw a woman with a trim figure,' she lamented to the woman next to her.

'Well,' the woman replied, 'what's wrong with that?'

'He likes to do it while I'm at these damn meetings.'

HE SAYS; SHE SAYS

He says: I don't know why you wear a bra; you've got nothing to put in it.

She says: You wear briefs, don't you?

He says: Do you love me just because my father left me a fortune?

She says: Not at all honey, I would love you no matter who left you the money.

He says: This coffee isn't fit for a pig!

She says: No problem, I'll get you some that is.

She says: What do you mean by coming home half drunk?

He says: It's not my fault. I ran out of money.

He says: Since I first laid eyes on you, I've wanted to make love to you in the worst way.

She says: Well, you succeeded.

He says: You have a flat chest and need to shave your legs, have you ever been mistaken for a man?

She says: No, have you?

He says: Why do you women always try to impress us with your looks, not with your brains?

She says: Because there is a bigger chance that a man is a moron than he is blind.

He says: What have you been doing with all the grocery money I gave you?

She says: Turn sideways and look in the mirror.

He says: Let's go out and have some fun tonight.
She says: OK, but if you get home before I do, leave the hall light on.

AROUND THE WORLD SEX LEGISLATION

- In Cali, Columbia, a woman may only have sex with her husband, and the first time this happens, her mother must be in the room to witness the act.
- The penalty for masturbation in Indonesia is decapitation.
- In Hong Kong, a betrayed wife is legally allowed to kill her adulterous husband, but may only do so with her bare hands. The husband's lover, on the other hand, may be killed in any manner desired.
- Most Middle Eastern countries recognise the following Islamic law:'After having sexual relations with a lamb, it is a mortal sin to eat its flesh.'
- In Lebanon, men are legally allowed to have sex with animals, but the animals must be female. Having sexual relations with a male animal is punishable by death.
- In Bahrain, a male doctor may legally examine a woman's genitals, but is forbidden from looking directly at them during the examination. He may only see their reflection in a mirror.
- Muslims are banned from looking at the genitals of a corpse. This also applies to undertakers. The sex organs of the deceased must be covered with a brick or piece of wood at all times.
- There are men in Guam whose full-time job is to travel the countryside and deflower young virgins, who pay them for the privilege. Reason: under Guam law, it is expressly forbidden for virgins to marry.
- Topless saleswomen are legal in Liverpool, England – but only in tropical fish stores.

- In Santa Cruz, Bolivia, it is illegal for a man to have sex with a woman and her daughter at the same time.
- In Maryland, USA, it is illegal to sell condoms from vending machines with one exception: prophylactics may be dispensed from a vending machine only 'in places where alcoholic beverages are sold for consumption on the premises.'

And God created Woman, and gave her three breasts. God spoke, saying to her, 'I have created thee as I see fit. Is there anything about thee that thou would prefer differently?'

And Woman spoke, saying, 'Lord, I am not made to birth whole litters. I need but two breasts.'

'Thou speakest wisely, as I have created thee with wisdom.'

There was a crack of lightning and a lingering odour of ozone, and it was done, and God stood holding the surplus breast in his hands.

'What are you going to do with that useless boob?' Woman asked.

And so it was, God created Man.

SEMINARS FOR WOMEN

- Gaining 2kg – is it the end of the world?
- Elementary map reading.
- How to programme your VCR.
- Football – not a game, a religion.
- PMS – it's your problem, not your man's.
- Your mate – selfish bastard, or victimised sensitive man?
- Makeup and driving – it's as simple as oil and water.
- Earning your own money.
- Lowering the toilet seat all by yourself.
- You, too, can fill up at a self-serve petrol station.

PICK-UP LINES NEVER TO REPEAT

- The word of the day is 'legs'. Let's go back to my place and spread the word.
- That outfit would look great in a crumpled heap on my bedroom floor tomorrow morning.
- I like every bone in your body, especially mine.
- How about you sit on my lap and we'll see what pops up?
- Baby I'm like milk, I'll do your body good.
- Is that a mirror in your pants, because I can see myself in them?
- Hey baby, let's play army. I'll lay down and you can blow me up.
- If I told you that you had a nice body, would you hold it against me?
- I want to kiss you passionately on the lips, and then move up to your belly-button.
- Is it hot in here, or is it just you?
- If you were a car door I would slam you all night long.
- How about you sit on my lap and we'll straighten things out.
- Baby, I'd run a mile for your vertical smile.
- If I could rearrange the alphabet I'd put U and I together.
- Can I have fries with that shake?
- I've got the F, the C and the K. All I need is U.
- You're so sweet you're giving me a toothache.
- Hey baby, can I tickle your belly-button from the inside?
- I'm new in town. Can I have directions to your house?
- Do you know CPR? Because you take my breath away.
- Do you know what would look good on you? Me.
- So do ya wanna see something really swell?
- I seem to have lost my number, can I have yours?
- I've got the hot dog and you've got the buns.
- Are we near the airport or is that just my heart taking off?
- I may not be Fred Flintstone, but I sure can make your bed rock.
- You have nice legs. What time do they open?

- Hey that dress looks nice. Can I talk you out of it?
- Is that a keg in your pants? Cause I'd just love to tap that ass.
- Are those pants from outer space? Cause that ass is out of this world.
- Are you a parking ticket, 'cause you have fine written all over you!

FALLING IN LOVE – BEFORE & AFTER

Before: Passion.
After: Ration.

Before: Don't stop!
After: Don't start.

Before: Turbocharged.
After: Jump-start.

Before: Twice a night.
After: Twice a month.

Before: Saturday Night Fever.
After: Monday Night Football.

Before: Idol.
After: Idle.

Before: Oysters.
After: Fishsticks.

Before: Is that all you're having?
After: Maybe you should just have a salad, honey.

Before: It's like I'm living in a dream.
BAfter: It's like he lives in a dorm.

Before: We agree on everything.
BAfter: Doesn't she have a mind of her own?

Before: Charming and Noble.
BAfter: Chernobyl.

Before: I love a woman with curves.
BAfter: I never said you were fat!

Before: He's completely lost without me.
BAfter: Why won't he ever ask for directions?

Before: You look so seductive in black.
BAfter: Your clothes are so depressing.

Before: She says she loves the way I take control of a
situation.
  After: She calls me a controlling, manipulative
egomaniacal prick.

Before: You take my breath away.
BAfter: I feel like I'm suffocating.

Before: I can hardly believe we found each other.
BAfter: I can't believe I ended up with someone like you.

Before: Time stood still.
BAfter: This relationship is going nowhere.

Before: Once upon a time.
BAfter: The end.

Q: How are husbands like lawn mowers?
A: They're hard to get started, they emit noxious odours, and half the time they don't work.

Q: How can you tell when a man is well hung?
A: When you can just barely slip your finger in between his neck and the noose.

Q: How do men define a 50-50 relationship?
A: We cook, they eat; we clean, they dirty; we iron, they wrinkle.

A nudist by the name of Rod Peet,
Loved to dance in the snow and the sleet,
But one chilly December
He froze every member,
And retired to a monkish retreat.

Q: How do men exercise on the beach?
A: By sucking in their stomachs every time they see a bikini.

Q: How do you get a man to stop biting his nails?
A: Make him wear shoes.

Q: How do you keep your husband from reading your email?
A: Rename the mail folder 'Instruction Manuals.'

Q: How does a man show he's planning for the future?
A: He buys two cases of beer instead of one.

Q: How is Colonel Sanders like the typical male?
A: He's only concerned with legs, breasts and thighs.

A young girl who was no good at tennis,
But at swimming was really a menace,
Took pains to explain,
'It depends how you train,
I was once a street-walker in Venice.'

Q: What do most men consider a gourmet restaurant?
A: Any place without a drive-thru window.

Q: What do you call the useless piece of skin on the end of a
    man's penis?
A: His body.

The spouse of a pretty young thing
Came home from the wars in the spring.
He was lame but he came
With his dame like a flame
A discharge is a wonderful thing.

'Have you ever met a man whose touch makes you tremble?'
'Yes.'
'Wow, who was he?'
'A dentist.'

Take anti-histamine tablets with your Viagra and achieve an
erection that's not to be sneezed at.

Q: What makes a man think about a candlelight dinner?
A: A power failure.

Q: What should you give a man who has everything?
A: A woman to show him how to work it.

My back aches, my pussy is sore;
I simply can't screw any more
  I'm covered with sweat
  And you haven't come yet
  And my God, it's a quarter to four!

Q: What do men and mascara have in common?
A: They both run at the first sign of emotion.

Q: What do men and pantyhose have in common?
A: They cling, run, or don't fit right in the crotch!

Q: What do you instantly know about a well-dressed man?
A: His wife is good at picking out clothes.

Q: What's a man's definition of a romantic evening?
A: Sex.

There was a young lady named Sue
Who preferred a stiff drink to a screw.
  But one leads to the other,
  And now she's a mother
  Let this be a lesson to you.

WHAT WOMEN REALLY MEAN IN PERSONAL ADVERTISEMENTS:

Affectionate:	Possessive.
Artist:	Unreliable.
Athletic:	Flat-chested.
Average looking:	Ugly.
Beautiful:	Pathological liar.
Commitment-minded:	Pick out curtains, now!

Communication important:	Just try to get a word in edgewise.
Contagious smile:	Bring your antibiotics.
Educated:	College dropout.
Emotionally secure:	Medicated.
Enjoys art and opera:	Snob.
Financially secure:	One pay cheque from the street.
Forty-ish:	48.
Free spirit:	Substance abuser.
Friendship first:	Trying to live down reputation as slut.
Gentle:	Comatose.
Good listener:	Borderline autistic.
Intuitive:	Your opinion doesn't count.
Light drinker:	Piss-pot.
Looks younger:	If viewed from far away in bad light.
Loves travel:	If you're paying.
New age:	All body hair, all the time.
Old-fashioned:	Lights out, missionary position only.
Open-minded:	Desperate.
Poet:	Depressive schizophrenic.
Reliable:	Frumpy.
Romantic:	Looks better by light of 40-watt globe.
Spiritual:	Involved with a cult.
Stable:	Boring.
Tall, thin:	Anorexic.
Tanned:	Wrinkled.
Writer:	Pompous.
Young at heart:	Toothless crone.

WHAT MEN REALLY MEAN IN PERSONAL ADVERTISEMENTS:

Artist:	Delicate ego, badly in need of massage.
Distinguished-looking:	Fat, grey and bald.
Educated:	Will always treat you like an idiot.
Forty-ish:	52 and looking for a 25-year-old.
Free Spirit:	Sleeps with your sister.
Good looking:	Arrogant bastard.
Huggable:	Overweight, more body hair than King Kong.
Open-minded:	Wants to sleep with your sister again.
Sensitive:	Needy.
Spiritual:	Once went to church with his grandmother.
Stable:	Occasional stalker, but never arrested.
Thoughtful:	Says please when demanding a beer.
Young at heart:	How young is your sister?

Q: What's a man's idea of honestly in a relationship?
A: Telling you his real name.

Q: What's the best way to force a man to do sit ups?
A: Put the remote control between his toes.

Q: What's the difference between Big Foot and intelligent man?
A: Big Foot's been spotted a several times.

Q: What's the smartest thing a man can say?
A: 'My wife says . . .'

Q: Why can't men get mad cow disease?
A: Because they're all pigs.

Q: Why do men like smart women?
A: Opposites attract.

Q: Why do men name their penises?
A: Because they don't like the idea of having a stranger make 90% of their decisions.

Most husbands can testify
To a wedding they can't deny.
'Cause they know where and when
They got married, but then,
What escapes them is exactly why.

Q: Why do men whistle when they're sitting on the toilet?
A: Because it helps them remember which end they need to wipe.

Q: Why do only 10% of men make it to heaven?
A: Because if they all went, it would be hell.

Q: What do you call a woman who knows where her husband is every night?
A: A widow.

Q: When do you care for a man's company?
A: When he owns it.

Q: What do men and sperm have in common?
A: They both have a one in a million chance of becoming a human being.

A couple is in bed sleeping when there's a rat-a-tat-tat on the door. The husband rolls over and looks at the clock, it's 3.30am.

'I'm not getting out of bed at this time,' he thinks, and rolls over.

There's a louder knock. So he drags himself out of bed, goes downstairs, opens the door, and a man is standing on the doorstep. It doesn't take the homeowner long to realise the man is drunk.

'Hi there,' slurs the stranger, 'Can you give me a push?'

'No, get lost. It's 3.30am and I was in bed.'

The man slams the door and goes back up to bed.

He tells his wife what happened and she says, 'That wasn't very nice of you. Remember that night we broke down in the pouring rain on the way to pick the kids up from the babysitter and you had to knock on that man's house to get us started again? What would have happened if he'd told us to get lost?'

'But the guy was drunk,' says the husband.

'It doesn't matter. He needs our help and it would be the Christian thing to help him.'

So the husband gets out of bed again, gets dressed, and goes downstairs. He opens the door, and not being able to see the stranger anywhere, he shouts, 'Hey, do you still want a push?'

And he hears a voice cry out, 'Yes please.'

'Where are you?'

'Over here, on the swing.'

I know of a fortunate Hindu
Who is sought in all towns that he's been to
By the ladies he knows,
Who are thrilled to the toes,
By the tricks he can make his foreskin do.

Winter is here with his grouch,
The time when you sneeze and you slouch.
You can't take your women
Canoein' or swimmin',
But a lot can be done on a couch.

Three women are having lunch, discussing their husbands.

'My husband is cheating on me, I just know it. I found a pair of stockings in his jacket pocket, and they weren't mine!' says the first woman.

'My husband is cheating on me, I just know it. I found a condom in his wallet, so I poked it full of holes with my sewing needle!' says the second woman.

The third woman fainted.

A girl on a southern plantation
Was the product of insemination.
So each Fathers' Day
She would send a bouquet
To a syringe in a faraway nation.

The nipples of Sarah Sarong,
When excited, were twelve inches long.
This embarrassed her lover
Who was pained to discover
She expected no less of his dong.

There was a young lady named Claire
Who possessed a magnificent pair
Or at least so I thought,
Till I saw one get caught
On a thorn, and begin losing air.

A cranky and pessimist Druid,
A defeatist, if only he knew it,
Said, 'The world's on the skids,
And I think having kids
Is a waste of good seminal fluid.'

A certain young man of St Paul
Consistently practiced withdrawal.
This quaint predilection
Created such friction,
He soon had no foreskin at all.

If men run the world, why can't they stop wearing neckties?
How intelligent is it to start the day by tying a noose around
your neck?

DEFINITIONS BY GENDER

Butt (but) n.
Female: The part of the body that every item of clothing
            manufactured makes look bigger.
Male: What you slap when someone's scored a goal. Also
            useful for mooning.

Commitment (ko-mit-ment) n.
Female: A desire to get married and raise a family.
Male: Not trying to pick up other women while out
            with one's girlfriend.

Communication (ko-myoo-ni-kay-shon) n.
Female: The open sharing of thoughts and feelings with
            one's partner.
Male: Scratching out a note before suddenly taking off
            for a weekend with the boys.

Entertainment (en-ter-tayn-ment) n.
Female: A good movie, concert, play or book.
Male: Anything that can be done while drinking.

Flatulence (flach-u-lens) n.
Female: An embarrassing by-product of digestion.
Male: An endless source of entertainment, self-
            expression and male bonding.

Making love (may-king luv) n.
Female: The greatest expression of intimacy a couple can
            achieve.
Male: Call it whatever you want just as long as we end
            up in bed.

Thingy (thing-ee) n.
Female: Any part under a car's hood.
Male: The strap fastener on a woman's bra.

Vulnerable (vul-ne-ra-bel) adj.
Female: Fully opening up emotionally to another.
Male: Riding a motorbike without a helmet.

There was a young girl named Sapphire
Who succumbed to her lover's desire
She says, 'It's a sin,
But now that it's in
Could you shove it a few inches higher?'

10 FACTS THAT EVERY MAN SHOULD KNOW ABOUT WOMEN

1. 'Oh, nothing,' has an entirely different meaning in woman-language than it does in man-language.
2. Only women understand the reason for 'guest towels' and the 'good china'.
3. Women do not want an honest answer to the question, 'How do I look?'

4. PMS really stands for: Permissible Man-Slaughter, Preposterous Mood Swings or Punish My Spouse.

5. Men can never catch women checking out other men; but women will always catch men checking out other women.

6. Women love to talk on the phone. A woman can visit her girlfriend for two weeks, and upon returning home, she will call the same friend and they will talk for three hours.

7. Women can't use a map without turning the map to correspond to the direction that they are heading.

8. All women seek equality with men until it comes to sharing the closet, taking out the rubbish, and picking up the cheque.

9. Women never check to see if the seat of the toilet is down. They seem to prefer taking a flying butt leap towards the bowl, and then becoming enraged because 'you left the seat up' instead of taking two seconds and lowering it themselves.

10. Women don't really care about a sense of humour in a guy, despite claims to the contrary. You don't see women trampling over Brad Pitt to get to Danny DeVito, do you?

Under the spreading chestnut tree
The village smithy sat,
   Amusing himself
   By abusing himself
And catching the load in his hat.

GREAT REASONS TO BE A GUY

- Your ass is never a factor in a job interview.
- Your orgasms are real. Always.
- Your last name stays put.
- Wedding plans take care of themselves.
- You don't have to curl up next to a hairy bottom every night.
- Chocolate is just another snack.
- Foreplay is optional.

- Car mechanics tell you the truth.
- You don't give a rat's ass if someone notices your new haircut.
- The world is your urinal.
- Hot wax never comes near your pubic area.
- Same work . . . more pay.
- Wrinkles add character.
- You don't have to leave the room to make emergency crotch adjustments.
- Wedding Dress $2000; Tux rental $100. Nuff said.
- People never glance at your chest when you're talking to them.
- Princess Di's death was just another obituary.
- New shoes don't cut, blister, or irreparably damage your feet.
- Porn movies are designed with you in mind.
- Your pals can be trusted never to trap you with, 'So, notice anything different?'

10 THINGS NOT TO SAY TO YOUR PREGNANT WIFE

1. 'Not to imply anything, but I don't think the kid weighs 10kg.'
2. 'Y'know, looking at her, you'd never guess that Elle McPherson has had a baby.'
3. 'Well, couldn't they induce labour? The 25th is the grand final.'
4. 'Fred at the office passed a stone the size of a pea. Boy, that's gotta hurt.'
5. 'I'm jealous. Why can't men experience the joy of childbirth?'
6. 'Are your ankles supposed to look like that?'
7. 'Get your own ice cream.'
8. 'Geez, you're looking awfully puffy today.'
9. 'Got milk?'
10. 'Man! That rose tattoo on your hip is the size of Madagascar!'

Withdrawal, according to Freud,
Is a very good thing to avoid.
  If practiced each day
  Your balls would decay
  To the size of a small adenoid.

Harold's wife bought a new line of expensive cosmetics
guaranteed to make her look years younger.

After applying her 'miracle' products, she asked, 'Darling, honestly, what age would you say I am?'

Looking over her carefully, Harold replied, 'Judging from your skin, 20; your hair, 18; and your figure, 25.'

'Oh, you flatter me!'

'Hey, wait a minute! I haven't added them up yet.'

HIS & HERS ROAD TRIP

Hers
1. Pulls off at wrong exit.
2. Opens window.
3. Asks directions from a knowledgeable police officer.
4. Arrives at destination presently.

His
1. Pulls off at wrong exit, absolutely positive it's the correct one.
2. Drives 5km into wilderness, still thinks he's right.
3. Drives an extra 5km just in case.
4. Finally rolls down window just to get fresh air.
5. Pulls up at a service station.
6. Gets three hot-dogs, a soft-drink and a packet of chips.
7. Asks person behind counter how to get back onto the highway.
8. Nods knowledgeably without really listening.
9. Gets back into car.

10. Laughs at the idea of looking at a map.
11. Drives down a dirt road with no streetlights insisting this is the way back because the guy from the service station says it was.
12. Almost hits a dog.
13. Curses the night.
14. Curses you.
15. Curses the third hot dog.
16. Yells at you for suggesting the map again.
17. Admits he didn't want to go to Christmas at your sister's anyway.
18. He hates your sister.
19. Ever since she called him a pernicious weasel last Christmas.
20. He had to look up pernicious when he got home.
21. Couldn't find a dictionary.
22. Finally found a dictionary.
23. Couldn't spell pernicious.
24. Seethes at the memory of it all.

Women will never be equal to men until they can walk down the street bald and still think they are beautiful.

Q: How many men does it take to open a beer?
A: None. It should be opened by the time she brings it to the couch.

A proper young man named Mal Grissing
Announced he had given up kissing.
'I strike out at once
For something that counts,
And besides my girl's front teeth are missing.'

RELATIONSHIP DICTIONARY

Attraction: Associating horniness with a particular person.

Birth control: Avoiding pregnancy through such tactics as swallowing special pills, inserting a diaphragm, using a condom, and dating repulsive men.

Dating: The process of spending enormous amounts of money, time and energy to get better acquainted with a person whom you don't especially like in the present and will learn to like a lot less in the future.

Easy: A term used to describe a woman who has the sexual morals of a man.

Eye contact: A method used by one person to indicate that they are interested in another. Despite being advised to do so, many men have difficulty looking a woman directly in the eyes, not necessarily due to shyness, but usually due to the fact that a woman's eyes are not located on her breasts.

Friend: A person in your acquaintance who has some flaw which makes sleeping with him/her totally unappealing.

Indifference: A woman's feeling towards a man, which is interpreted by the man to be playing hard to get.

Interesting: A word a man uses to describe a woman who lets him do all the talking.

Irritating habit: What the endearing little qualities that initially attract two people to each other turn into after a few months together.

Love at first sight: What occurs when two extremely horny, but not entirely choosy, people meet.

Kathleen came home from a women's liberation meeting, and told her husband Mike that the meeting had been about free love.

'Surely you don't believe in free love?' said Mike.

'Have I ever sent you a bill?'

A couple was told to individually write a sentence using the words 'sex' and 'love'.

The woman wrote, 'When two people love each other very much, like Bob and I do, it is morally acceptable for them to engage in sex.'

Bob wrote, 'I love sex.'

FIVE QUOTES FOR MARRIED MEN

1. I married Miss Right. I just didn't know her first name was Always.
2. It's not true that married men live longer than single men. It only seems longer.
3. Losing a wife can be hard. In my case, it was almost impossible.
4. A man is incomplete until he is married. After that, he is finished.
5. I haven't spoken to my wife for 18 months – I don't like to interrupt her.

Q: What do you do if a bird shits on your car?
A: You never take her out again.

A man is dating three women and wants to decide which to marry. He decides to give them a test. He gives each woman a present of $5000 and watches to see what they do with the money.

The first does a total make over. She goes to a fancy beauty salon, gets her hair done, gets new make up, and buys several new outfits to dress up very nicely for the man. She tells him that she has done this to be more attractive for him because she loves him. The man is impressed.

The second goes shopping to buy the man gifts. She gets him a new set of golf clubs, some new gizmos for his computer, and some expensive clothes. As she presents these gifts, she tells him that she has spent all the money on him because she loves him so much. Again, the man is impressed.

The third invests the money in the stock market. She earns several times the 5,000. She gives him back his $5000 and reinvests the remainder in a joint account. She tells him that she wants to save for their future because she loves him. Obviously, the man is impressed.

He thinks for a long time about what each woman has done with the money he's given her. Then, he marries the one with the biggest boobs.

Peter wakes up at home with a huge hangover. He forces himself to open his eyes and the first thing he sees is a couple of Panadol and a glass of water on the side table. He sits down and sees his clothing in front of him, all clean and pressed. Peter looks around the room and sees that it is in perfect order, spotlessly clean. So is the rest of the house.

He takes the Panadol and notices a note on the table 'Honey, breakfast is on the stove, I left early to go shopping. Love you.'

So he goes to the kitchen and sure enough there is a hot breakfast and the morning newspaper. His daughter is also at the table, eating.

Peter asks, 'Victoria, what happened last night?'

'Well, you came home after 3am, drunk and delirious. Broke some furniture, puked in the hallway, and gave yourself a black eye when you stumbled into the door.'

'So, why is everything so clean, and why is breakfast on the table waiting for me?'

'Oh that! Well, Mum dragged you to the bedroom, and when she tried to take your pants off, you said, "Lady, leave me alone, I'm married."'

CONDOMS

Coca Cola condoms:	The real thing.
Energizer:	It keeps going and going and going.
KFC condoms:	Finger-licking good.
M&M condom:	It melts in your mouth, not in your hands.
Maxwell House:	Good to the last drop.
Microsoft:	Where do you want to go today?
Nike condoms:	Just do it.
Pringles condoms:	Once you pop, you can't stop.
Star Trek condoms:	Boldly go where no man has gone before.
Toyota condoms:	Oh what a feeling.

Three gay men died, and were going to be cremated. Their lovers happened to be at the funeral home at the same time, and were discussing what they planned to do with the ashes.

'My Ryan loved to fly,' said the first man, 'so I'm going up in a plane to scatter his ashes in the sky.'

'My Ross was a good fisherman,' said the second, 'so I'm going to scatter his ashes in our favourite lake.'

'My Jack was such a good lover,' said the third, 'I think I'm going to dump his ashes in a pot of chilli, so he can tear my ass up just one more time.'

THINGS MEN SHOULD KNOW ABOUT WOMEN

- The female always makes the rules.
- The rules are subject to change at any time without prior notification.

- No male can possibly know all the rules.
- The female is never wrong.
- If the female is wrong, it is because of a flagrant misunderstanding which was a direct result of something the male did or said wrong.
- The female can change her mind at any time.
- The male must never change his mind without express written consent from the female.
- The female has every right to be angry or upset at any time.
- The male must remain calm at all times, unless the female wants him to be angry or upset.
- The female must not, under any circumstances, let the male know whether or not she wants him to be angry or upset.
- The male is expected to mind read at all times.
- The male who doesn't abide by the rules, can't take the heat, lacks a backbone, and is a wimp.
- Any attempt to document the rules could result in bodily harm.
- At no time can the male make such comments as 'insignificant' and 'is that all?' when the female is complaining.
- If the female has PMS, all the rules are null and void.

There was a young maid from Madras
Who had a magnificent ass;
Not rounded and pink,
As you probably think
It was grey, had long ears, and ate grass.

10 THINGS THAT ONLY WOMEN UNDERSTAND

1. Cats' facial expressions.
2. The need for the same style of shoes in different colours.
3. Why bean sprouts aren't just weeds.
4. Fat clothes.

5. Taking a car trip without trying to beat your best time.
6. The difference between beige, off-white, and eggshell.
7. Cutting your hair to make it grow faster.
8. Eyelash curlers.
9. The inaccuracy of every bathroom scale ever made.
10. That a cuddle does not necessarily need to turn into full-blown sex.

Husband and wife are getting all snugly in bed. Just as things are starting to heat up the wife stops and says, 'I don't feel like it tonight. I just want you to hold me.'

'What?' says the husband.

The wife explains that he must not be in tune with her emotional needs as a woman. Realising that nothing is going to happen tonight he rolls over and goes to sleep. The next day the husband takes her shopping at a big department store. He walks through the entire store loading his wife up with goodies. Her arms are full of expensive clothes, jewellery, shoes and make-up. The wife is so excited; she can barely walk to the cash register as she is carrying so many things.

But her husband stops her. 'No, no, no, honey we're not going to buy all this stuff!'

The wife looks confused.

'No honey – I just want you to hold this stuff for a while.'

The wife's face starts to turn red as her husband says 'You must not be in tune with my financial needs as a man!'

Three married couples, aged 20, 30 and 40 years old, wish to join the Orthodox Church of Sexual Repression. Near the end of the interview, the priest informs them that before they can be accepted they will have to pass one small test. They will have to abstain from all sex for a month. They agree to try.

A month later, they are having their final interview with the cleric. He asks the 40-year-old couple how they went.

'Well, it wasn't too hard. I spent a lot of time in the workshop and my partner has a garden, so we had plenty of other things to do. We did OK,' the husband says.

'Very good, my children,' says the priest. 'You are welcome in the Church.'

'And how well did you manage?' he asks the 30-year-old couple.

'It was pretty difficult,' the husband answers. 'We thought about it all the time. We had to sleep in different beds and we prayed a lot. But we were celibate for the entire month.'

'Very good, my children, you also are welcome in the Church.'

'And how about you?' he asks the 20-year-old couple.

'Not too good, I'm afraid, Father. We did OK for the first week,' the man says sheepishly. 'By the second week we were going crazy with lust. Then one day during the third week my wife dropped a head of lettuce, and when she bent over to pick it up, I weakened and took her right there.'

'I'm sorry my son, you are not welcome in the Church'

'Yeah, and we're not too welcome in the Safeway supermarket anymore, either.'

For sale by owner: Complete set of Encyclopaedia Britannica, 45 volumes. Excellent condition. $1000 or best offer. No longer needed. Got married last weekend. Wife knows f#*#ing everything.

A new study has just been released mapping women's thoughts on marriage. The results were somewhat surprising:

85% of women think their ass has grown too big since getting married.

10% of women think their ass is just as big as it was when they got married.

The other 5% say that they don't care, they love him and would have married him anyway.

My wife suggested a book for me to read to enhance our relationship. It's called Women are from Venus, Men are Wrong.

After a day at the office a man gets home from work. When he comes through the door his wife greets him and says, 'Hi, Honey. Notice anything different about me?'

'Oh, I don't know. You got your hair done.'

'Nope, try again.'

'Oh, you bought a new dress.'

'Nope, keep trying.'

'You got your nails done.'

'No, try again.'

'I give up. I'm too tired to play twenty questions.'

'I'm wearing a gas mask.'

A boy and his date were parked on a back road some distance from town, doing what boys and girls do on back roads some distance from town. The girl stopped the boy.

'I really should have mentioned this earlier, but I'm actually a hooker and I charge $20 for sex,' she said.

The boy reluctantly paid her, and they did their thing.

After a cigarette, the boy just sat in the driver's seat looking out the window.

'Why aren't we going anywhere?' asked the girl.

'Well, I should have mentioned this before, but I'm actually a taxi driver, and the fare back to town is $25.'

Women want a relationship without the complication of unnecessary sex. Men want sex without the complication of an unnecessary relationship.

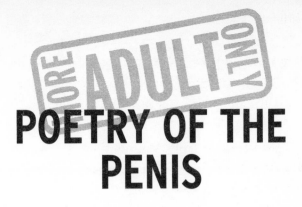

POETRY OF THE PENIS

There once was a man named MacBride
Who fell in a privy and died.
He had a young brother,
Who fell in another,
And now they're in turd side by side.

There was a young student from Boston
Who drove around in an Austin.
There was room for his ass
And a gallon of gas.
But his balls hung out and he lost 'em.

There was a young fellow named Paul
Who confessed, 'I have only one ball
But the size of my prick
Is God's dirtiest trick
For my girls always ask, 'Is that all?'

There was a young man of Devizes
Whose balls were of differing sizes.
One was so small
It was nothing at all
The other took numerous prizes.

A fussy young fellow named Lear
Used to wash off his bollocks with beer.

Said he, 'By the gods,
This is good for the cods
Look, they are always so full of good cheer.'

There once was a man from Madras
Whose balls were constructed of brass
When jangled together
They played Stormy Weather
And lightning shot out of his ass!

Floating idly by through the air
A circus performer named Blair
Tied a sizeable rock
To the end of his cock
And shattered a balcony chair.

There was a young man whose dong
Was prodigiously, massively long
Down the sides of his whang,
Two testes did hang
Which attracted a curious throng.

There was a young man of Malacca
Who always slept on his left knacker.
One Saturday night
He slept on his right,
And his knacker went off like a cracker.

There was a young fellow of Harrow
Whose john was the size of a marrow.
He said to his tart,
'How's this for a start?
My balls are outside in a barrow.'

Did you hear about young Henry Lockett?
He was blown down the street by a rocket.
The force of the blast
Blew his balls up his arse,
And his pecker was found in his pocket.

There was an old man of Tagore
Whose tool was a yard long or more,
So he wore the damn thing
In a surgical sling
To keep it from wiping the floor.

A man with a fever so dire,
Had testes which burned like a pyre.
He was heard to exclaim,
As they put out the flame,
'Goodness gracious, great balls of fire.'

A young man maintained that his trigger
Was so big, there weren't any bigger.
But this long and thick pud
Was so heavy it could
Scarcely lift up its head. It lacked vigour.

There once was a man named Mort
Whose dick was incredibly short
He climbed into bed
And his lady friend said,
'That's not a dick, it's a wart.'

The favourite pastime of grandfather
Was tickling his balls with a feather.
But the thing he liked best
Of all of the rest,
Was knocking them gently together.

I lost my arm in the army,
I lost my leg in the navy,
I lost my balls
At Niagara Falls,
And I lost my cock in a lady.

Ivan Stravinsky Skavar
Had the world's biggest cock, by far
Such was its strain
When he went by train
That it travelled in its own separate car.

There once was a man named Crockett
Who stuck his cock in a socket.
Some son-of-a-bitch
Turned on the switch
And Crockett went up like a rocket.

LET ME TELL YOU ABOUT MY DICK

- My dick is so big, it graduated a year ahead of me in high school.
- My dick is so big, it has a roadie.
- My dick is so big, I have to call it Mr Dick in front of company.
- My dick is so big, it won't return Spielberg's calls.
- My dick is so big, it was overthrown in a coup. It's now known as the People's Democratic Republic of My Dick.
- My dick is so big, it has casters.
- My dick is so big, it lives next door.
- My dick is so big, it votes.
- No matter where I go, my dick always gets there first.
- My dick takes longer lunches than I do.
- My dick is so big, it has feet.
- My dick is so big, it has investors and a CEO.
- My dick is so big, we use it at parties as a limbo pole.
- My dick is so big, it has an opening act.

- My dick is so big, every time I get hard-on I cause a solar eclipse.
- My dick is so big, Trump owns it.
- My dick is so big, I can never sit in the front row.
- My dick is so big, it has its own dick.
- My dick is so big, it only does one show a night.
- My dick is so big, you can ski down it.
- My dick is so big, it has elbows.
- My dick is so big, I have to check it as luggage when I fly.
- My dick is so big, it has a personal trainer.
- If you cut my dick in two, you can count the rings and tell how old I am.
- I sat in the front row at the theatre once, and conducted the orchestra through the entire score of Cats.
- My dick is so big, it has a retractable dome.
- My dick is so big, it has its own gravity.
- My dick is so big, it has a basement.
- My dick is so big, it has cable.
- My dick is so big, it violates 17 zoning laws.
- My dick is so big, I can braid it.
- My dick is so big, it passes through 11 time zones.
- My dick is so big, I can sit on it.
- My dick is so big, it can chew gum.
- My dick is so big, it only tips with hundreds.
- My dick is so big, investors want to build an amusement park on it.
- My dick is so big, you're standing on it.
- My dick is so big, it only comes into work when it feels like it.
- My dick is so big, it plays golf with the prime minister.
- My dick is so big, it charges money for its autograph.
- My dick is so big, the tip of it celebrated the arrival of the new millennium 40 minutes before my balls did.
- My dick is so big, it has an agent.
- So, let's have lunch with my dick. My dick's people will call your dick's people . . .

POLITICS

A secretary for a foreign embassy was entertaining a wealthy ambassador during lunch at a very expensive restaurant in uptown New York. The ambassador was so enthralled by the beauty and presence of this secretary that he asked her to marry him.

The secretary was startled, but remembered that her boss told her never to insult foreign dignitaries, so she decided to let him down easy.

'I'll only marry you under three conditions,' she said.

'Anything, anything,' said the ambassador.

'First, you must buy me a 14-carat gold wedding band with a 72-carat diamond, along with a 70cm studded matching necklace for our engagement.'

Without hesitation, the ambassador picked up his cellular phone, called his personal accountant, told him the instructions, and said, 'Yes, yes, I buy, I buy!'

The secretary thought that her first request was too easy, so she thought of a more difficult situation.

'Second, I want you to build me a 58-acre mansion in the richest part of the Poconos along with a 40-acre summer home in the sweetest vineyards of France.'

The ambassador picked up his phone, called his personal broker in New York, then called another broker in France, and after a quick conversation, he said, 'Yes, yes, I build, I build!'

The secretary was very startled, and knew she must think of a final request that would be impossible to live up to.

'Finally,' she said. 'I'll only marry you if you have a 25cm penis.'

A sad face befell the ambassador, and he cupped his face in his hands. After weeping in his native language for a few minutes, the ambassador slowly lifted his head and said, 'Ok, ok, I cut, I cut!'

A young man joined the army and signed up with the paratroopers. He went though the standard training, completed the practice jumps from higher and higher structures, and finally went to take his first jump from an aeroplane. The next day, he phoned his father to tell him the news.

'So, did you jump?' his father asked.

'Well, let me tell you what happened. We got up in the plane, and the sergeant opened up the door and asked for volunteers. About a dozen men got up and just walked out of the plane!'

'Is that when you jumped?'

'Um, not yet. Then the sergeant started to grab the other men one at a time and throw them out the door.'

'Did you jump then?' asked his father.

'I'm getting to that. Everyone else had jumped, and I was the last man left on the plane. I told the Sergeant that I was too scared to jump. He told me to get off the plane or he'd kick my arse.'

'So, did you jump?'

'Not then. He tried to push me out of the plane, but I grabbed onto the door and refused to go. Finally he called over the jumpmaster. The jumpmaster is this great big guy, about six-foot five, and 17 stone.

He said to me, "Boy, are you going to jump or not?"

I said, "No, sir. I'm too scared."

So the jumpmaster pulled down his zip and exposed himself.

He said, "Boy, either you jump out of that door, or you and I are going to have some wild time."'

'So, did you jump?' asked the father.

'Well, a little, at first.'

The CIA were conducting a job interview for only highly qualified people. After all the background checks, interviews and testing were done, there were three finalists: two men and a woman.

For the final test, the CIA agents took one of the men to a large metal door and handed him a gun.

'We must know that you will follow your instructions, no matter what the circumstances,' said the agent.

'Inside this room, you will find your wife sitting in a chair. Kill her!'

The man said, 'You can't be serious. I could never shoot my wife.'

'Then you're not the right man for this job. Take your wife and go home.'

The second man was given the same instructions. He took the gun and went into the room. All was quiet for about five minutes.

Then the man came out with tears in his eyes. 'I tried, but I can't kill my wife.'

'You don't have what it takes. Take your wife and go home.'

Finally, it was the woman's turn. She was given the same instructions to kill her husband. She took the gun and went into the room. Shots were heard, one shot after another. They heard screaming, crashing, banging on the walls.

After a few minutes, all was quiet. The door opened slowly and there stood the woman. She wiped the sweat from her brow.

'This gun is loaded with blanks,' she said. 'I had to beat him to death with the chair.'

President George W Bush was visiting an elementary school. After the typical civics presentation, he announced, 'All right, boys and girls, you can ask me questions now.'

A little boy named Bobby raised his hand and said, 'Mr President, I have three questions. First, how did you win the election with fewer votes than Gore? Second, why are you using the US Patriot Act to limit Americans' civil liberties? And third, why hasn't the US caught Osama Bin Laden yet?'

The president said, 'Well, Bobby –'

But suddenly, the bell sounded, everything came to a halt, and all the kids ran out to the playground. After lunch the kids were back in class and the president said, 'I'm sorry we were interrupted by the bell. Now, where were we. Oh, yes, you can ask me questions.'

A little girl raised her hand and said, 'Mr President, I have five questions. First, how did you win the election with fewer votes than Gore? Second, why are you using the US Patriot Act to limit Americans' civil liberties? Third, why hasn't the US caught Osama Bin Laden yet? Fourth, why did the bell go off 20 minutes early? And fifth, where's Bobby?'

A colonel on his way home from work at the pentagon came to a dead halt in traffic and thought to himself, 'Wow, this traffic seems worse than usual. Nothing's even moving.'

He noticed a police officer walking back and forth between the lines of cars so he rolled down his window and asked, 'Excuse me, officer, what's the hold up?'

The officer replies, 'President Bush is just so depressed about being behind in the polls that he stopped his motorcade in the middle of the highway. He says he can't find donators to give him money for his campaign and he's threatening to douse himself in gasoline and set himself on fire. I'm walking around taking up a collection for him.'

'Oh really? How much have you collected so far?'

'So far only about three hundred gallons, but I've got a lot of folks still siphoning!'

Defence Secretary Donald Rumsfeld still believes we will find weapons of mass destruction in Iraq – and Santa at the North Pole.

A large group of Taliban soldiers are moving down a road when they hear a voice call from behind a sand dune.

'One US soldier is better than 10 Taliban.'

The Taliban commander quickly sends 10 of his best soldiers over the dune, whereupon a gun-battle breaks out and continues for a few minutes. Then there's silence.

The same voice calls out, 'One US soldier is better than one hundred Taliban.'

Furious, the Taliban commander sends his next best 100 troops over the dune, and instantly a huge gunfight commences. After 10 minutes of battle, again there's silence.

The voice calls out, 'One US soldier is better than one thousand Taliban.'

The enraged Taliban commander musters one thousand fighters and sends them across the dune. Cannons, rockets and machine gun fire ring out as a huge battle is fought. Then silence.

Eventually one wounded Taliban fighter crawls back over the dune and with his dying words he tells his commander, 'Don't send any more men. It's a trap. There's two of them.'

Seamus O'Brien had been hailed the most intelligent Irishman for three years running. He had topped all the Irish quiz shows and it was suggested by the Irish Mensa board that he should go over to England and enter Mastermind. He did, and won a place on the show.

On they evening of the competition, Seamus climbed on stage from the studio audience and placed himself on the famous leather chair, and made himself comfortable. The lights dimmed and a spotlight picked out his face.

The host, Magnus said, 'Seamus, What subject are you studying?'

Seamus responded, 'Irish History'.

'Very well,' said Magnus. 'Your first question is, in what year did the Easter Uprising take place?'

Seamus responded, 'Pass.'

The host looked a little shocked at this, but continued, 'Who was the leader of the Easter Uprising?'

Seamus responded, 'Pass.'

'How long did the Easter Uprising last?'

'Pass.'

Instantly, a voice shouted from the crowd, 'Good Man Seamus. Tell the English bastards nothing.'

John Kerry said that America needs to be able to trust their president. Hillary Clinton said, 'Tell me about it.'

Many years after Bill Clinton had been president of the United States a famous biographer was interviewing him.

'Bill, what were your best and worst decisions during the presidency?' he asked.

Bill thought deeply and then said, 'Monica Lewinsky! I'd have to say Monica was my best, as well as my worst, decision.'

'How could that be?' asked the surprised biographer.

Bill smiled and shook his head, 'I'd have to say she was both my best and my worst decision for the same reason.'

'And what was that reason?'

Bill squirmed in his chair and answered, 'Monica had a big mouth.'

The president's loud protestation
On his fall to the intern's temptation
'This affair is still moral
As long as it's oral
Straight screwing I save for the nation.'

Said Bill Clinton to young Ms Lewinsky
We don't want to leave clues like Kaczynski,

Since you look such a mess,
Use the hem of your dress
And wipe that stuff off of your chinsky.

Send the missiles!' Bill cried, 'On the double
Reduce those Afghanis to rubble.'
It made sense, he decided
As his missile unguided
Was the thing that got him into trouble.

Miss Jones,' Clinton said with affection,
Be so kind as to check my erection.'
But Paula, so silly
Misunderstood Billy,
And thought he said, 'Wreck my election.'

The Cork-born Father O'Connor's reputation for castigating
the British from the pulpit was legendary. However, the
congregation in his new parish of Boston, Massachusetts, tired of
him lambasting the Brits for the horrors they inflicted upon the
Irish for generations. Ultimately, the Archbishop opted to send
the good father to a small hamlet in the far reaches of Tennessee
where, His Grace said, 'The folks know nothing of England and
couldn't care less. So knock off the Brit-bashing and you'll better
serve the holy mother church.'

Several weeks later, when Father O'Connor stood in the
pulpit to deliver his first sermon to his new congregation, the
local bishop, who knew of O'Connor's reputation, was in
attendance to check up on him.

'My dear brethren,' Father O'Connor began, 'this morning I'd
like to talk about the last supper.'

'Not bad,' thought the bishop, 'Safe enough ground.'

'Now, the lesson to be learned from the last supper, where
Christ knew He'd been betrayed, is that the sin of betrayal is the

worst sin of all. It's a sin never forgiven by God or man,' thundered Father O'Connor.

'Fair enough,' thought the bishop.

'Christ looked around at His apostles.

"Was it you Peter, who betrayed me?" He asked.

"Not I my Lord," answered Peter.

"Was it you John?"

"Not I my Lord."

'Christ asked each of them in turn and finally came to Judas, who was sitting at the end of the table, his head bowed. Was it you, Judas, who betrayed me? asked Christ, and Judas responded, "Wot? Me? Cor, not on yer bloody life, Mi'lud."'

A sergeant and a private were patrolling the streets in Baghdad. There was a 9pm curfew in place. Suddenly private Slattery shot a man walking down a lane.

The sergeant screamed, 'Slattery its only 8.45, why did you shoot him?'

Slattery replied, 'Well I know where he lives and he would never have made it by 9.00.'

They called off the investigation of President Clinton due to a lack of evidence.

It turns out he didn't tell her to lie, he told her to kneel.

Only Clinton can take our mind off a sex scandal with another sex scandal.

Tony and Cherie Blair are on a trip back to their old home town. They're almost out of fuel, so Tony pulls into a service station on the outskirts of town. The attendant runs out of the station to serve them when Cherie realises it's an old boyfriend from school. She and the attendant chat as he puts petrol in their car and cleans the windows. Then they all say good-bye.

As Tony pulls the car onto the road, he turns to Cherie and says, 'Now aren't you glad you married me and not him? You could've been the wife of a grease monkey!'

To which Cherie replies, 'No, Tony. If I had married him, you'd be pumping gas and he would be prime minister.'

When the Clintons were in the white house, officials estimated that during the three weeks from early December through to Christmas, the president and first lady shook hands with 100,000 white house visitors. Hillary thought it was just her civic responsibility as first lady. Bill thought it was a great way to meet new chicks.

A new American ambassador was being entertained by an African diplomat. They'd spent the day discussing what the country had received from the Russians before the new government kicked them out.

'The Russians built us a power plant, a highway, and an airport. Plus, we learned to drink vodka and play Russian roulette.'

The American frowned. 'Russian roulette's not a very nice game.'

The diplomat smiled. 'That's why we developed African roulette. If you want to have good relations with our country, you'll have to play. I'll show you how.'

He pushed a buzzer, and a moment later, six magnificently built, nude women were ushered in.

'You can choose any one of these women to give you oral sex,' he told the American.

'That's great,' the ambassador said, 'but it doesn't seem much like Russian roulette.'

'Oh, yes it is. One of them is a cannibal.'

A suicide bomber shows up at the pearly gates and St Peter comes out to greet him. St Peter takes one look and says 'I don't think you can get in here.'

'Who wants in? You've got 20 minutes to get the hell out!'

Saddam Hussein and George W Bush meet up in Baghdad for a round of talks in a new peace process. When George sits down, he notices three buttons on the side of Saddam's chair.

They begin talking and after about five minutes Saddam presses the first button. A boxing glove springs out of a box on the desk and punches Bush on the face. Confused, Bush carries on talking, as Saddam falls about laughing. A few minutes later he presses the second button, and this time a big boot comes out and kicks Bush in the shin. Again, Saddam laughs, and again Bush carries on talking, not wanting to be put off the bigger issue.

But when Saddam presses the third button and another boot comes out and kicks Bush in the privates, he's finally had enough.

'I'm going back home!' he tells the Iraqi. 'We'll finish these talks in two weeks – on my territory!'

A fortnight passes and Saddam flies to the States for talks. As the two men sit down, Hussein notices three buttons on Bush's chair and prepares himself for the Yank's revenge.

They begin talking and Bush presses the first button. Saddam ducks, but nothing happens. Bush snickers. A few seconds later, he presses the second button. Saddam jumps up, but again nothing happens. Bush roars with laughter. When he presses the third button, Saddam jumps up again, and again nothing happens. Bush falls on the floor in a fit of hysterics.

'Sod this,' says Saddam. 'I'm going back to Baghdad.'

Bush says through tears of laughter, 'What Baghdad?'

Saddam Hussein is sitting at home when the phone rings. He picks it up and says 'Hello'.

The voice at the end of the phone says 'Hello Mr Hussein, it's Paddy here. I'm just ringing to let you know that we've declared war on your country.'

Saddam smiles to himself, 'Come on Paddy', he says, 'there's no point you declaring war on us, you wouldn't stand a chance.'

Paddy replies, 'No, no, we've had ourselves a meeting, and we've decided to declare war on you.'

So Saddam says, 'OK Paddy, now listen, I've got an air force of over a thousand planes, what kind of air force have you got to match that? It'd be over in no time.'

'Well my lad's got himself a hot-air balloon, and my brother used to work at an airport.'

Hussein laughs, 'Oh come on, and you've not got a hope'.

'Hold on a sec, Mr Hussein, we'll just have a quick meeting.' So off he goes and has a quick meeting and returns to the phone. 'Are you still there Mr Hussein? Yes, well we've had our meeting, and we've decided that we're still going to declare war.'

'Right then Paddy, well you know, as well as the air force, we've also got about a thousand tanks. How are you going to match that?'

'Well, I've got an old Austin, and my cousin down the road has got a tractor.'

'Get real, that's no match at all.'

'Hold on, I'll just go and have another meeting.' Paddy leaves the phone for a few minutes and returns.

'Are you still there Mr Hussein? Yes, well we've had our meeting, and we've decided that we're still going to declare war.'

Saddam thinks this is just amazing, 'Well how many soldiers have you got Paddy?'

'Well, there's me, my kid, me four cousins, and they all have sons, and there's Michael down the road. I reckon I could get together about 30.'

Laughing openly now Saddam replies, 'Come on Paddy, I've got 10,000 highly trained fighting men at my disposal. I think you'd better go and have another meeting.'

'I will', says Paddy, 'I will.'

He goes away and comes back. 'Are you still there Mr Hussein? Yes, well we've had our meeting, and we've decided that we're not going to declare war on you after all.'

'At last,' replies Saddam, 'What made you change your mind?'

'Well, it's those 10,000 soldiers you see. We can't declare war on you because we've not got the facilities to keep all those prisoners!'

During a recent publicity outing, Cherie Blair sneaked off to visit a fortune teller of some local repute. In a dark and hazy room, peering into a crystal ball, the mystic delivered grave news.

'There's no easy way to say this, so I'll just be blunt: Prepare yourself to be a widow. Your husband will die a violent and horrible death this year.'

Visibly shaken, Cherie stared at the woman's lined face, then at the single flickering candle, then down at her hands. She took a few deep breaths to compose herself. But she drew herself up to ask the important question. She simply had to know. She met the fortune teller's gaze, steadied her voice, and asked, 'Will I be acquitted?'

A salesman was travelling between towns in America when he got a flat tyre in the middle of nowhere. Checking the spare, he found it was also flat. His only option was to flag down a passing motorist and get a ride to the nearest town.

The first vehicle to stop was an old man in a truck. He yelled out the window to the salesman, 'Need a lift?'

'Yes, I do,' replied the salesman.

'Are you a Democrat or Republican?'

'A Republican.'

'Get screwed!' yelled the old man as he sped off.

The next person to stop rolled down the window and asked the same question, to which the salesman gave the same answer, 'Republican.'

The driver gave him the finger and drove off. The salesman thought it over, and decided maybe he should change his approach, since there appeared to be few Republicans in this area.

The next car to stop was a red convertible driven by a beautiful blonde. She smiled seductively and asked him if he were a Democrat or Republican.

'Democrat!' shouted the salesman.

'Hop in!' replied the blonde.

Driving down the road, he can't help but stare at the gorgeous woman in the seat next to him. She looked lovely. The wind was blowing through her hair, she had perfect breasts and a short skirt that continued to ride higher and higher up her thighs. He began to lust over her.

Finally, he yelled 'Stop the car!'

She slammed on the brakes, and, as soon as the car stopped he jumped out.

'What's the matter?' she asked.

'I can't take it!' he replied. 'I've only been a Democrat for five minutes and already I want to sleep with a woman I've only just met!'

Murphy sat in a Belfast confessional. 'Bless me, Father, for I have sinned,' he said. 'I've blown up three hundred miles of English railroad!'

'All right, my son,' admonished the priest. 'For penance, do the stations!'

An English MP was addressing a crowd in Belfast. He stated to the masses 'I was born an Englishman, I've lived an Englishman, and by God I shall die an Englishman!'

From the back of the crowd, a voice yelled, 'Shite, man have ye no bloody ambition?'

The mistress of a big English house called her Irish maid and pointed out the dust still on top of the piano.

'Mary,' she said, 'I could write my name in this dust.'

'Isn't education a grand thing, ma'am?' said Mary.

The Supreme Court has ruled that there can't be a Nativity Scene in Washington DC this Christmas season. This isn't for any religious reason, they simply have not been able to find three wise men and a virgin in the nation's capitol.

There was no problem, however, finding enough asses to fill the stable.

A busload of politicians was driving down a country road when suddenly the bus ran off the road and crashed into a tree in an old farmer's field. The old farmer went over to investigate. He then dug a hole to bury the politicians.

A few days later the local sheriff came out, saw the crashed bus, and asked the old farmer where all the politicians had gone. The old farmer said he had buried them.

The sheriff asked the old farmer, 'Were they all dead?'

'Well, some of them said they weren't, but you know how them politicians lie.'

'**T**hings are more like they are now than they have ever been.' – President Gerald Ford

'**C**apital punishment is our society's recognition of the sanctity of human life.'

- Orrin Hatch, Senator from Utah, explaining his support of the death penalty.

'**C**hina is a big country, inhabited by many Chinese.'
- Charles de Gaulle, ex-French president

'**I** stand by all the mis-statements.'
- Dan Quayle, defending himself against criticism for making verbal gaffes.

'**G**erald Ford was a Communist'
- Ronald Reagan in a speech. He later indicated he meant to say 'Congressman'.

'**O**utside of the killings, Washington DC has one of the lowest crime rates in the country.'
- Mayor Marion Barry, Washington DC

'**T**his is a great day for France!'
- President Richard Nixon while attending Charles De Gaulle's funeral.

'**T**his is the worst disaster in California since I was elected.'
- California Governor Pat Brown, discussing a local flood.

'**F**acts are stupid things.'
- Ronald Reagan

A reporter heard George W Bush and one of his underlings talking in the hallway.
'Mr President, how do we know for sure Iraq has weapons of mass destruction?' asked the underling.
'You think we're stupid boy? We made copies of all the receipts.'

A Canadian, Osama bin Laden and George W Bush are out walking together one day. They come across a lantern. A genie pops out of it, granting each man one wish.

The Canadian says, 'I'm a farmer, my dad was a farmer, and my son will also farm. I want the land to be forever fertile in Canada.'

With a blink of the genie's eye, poof! the land in Canada is made forever fertile for farming.

Bin Laden is amazed, so he says, 'I want a wall around Afghanistan, so that no infidels, Jews or Americans can come into our precious state.'

Again, with a blink of the genie's eye, poof! there is a huge wall around Afghanistan.

George W Bush, says, 'I'm very curious, please tell me more about this wall.'

The Genie explains, 'Well, it's about 15,000 feet high, 500 feet thick and completely surrounds the country; nothing can get in or out - it's virtually impenetrable.'

George W Bush says, 'Fill it with water.'

B ill and Hillary are at the first baseball game of the year. The crowd is roaring as one of Clinton's advisers whispers something into his ear. Bill immediately stands up and throws Hillary out onto the field. The crowd goes deathly silent and the advisor says, 'No, sir, what I said was, they want you to throw out the first pitch.'

Q: How do you stop a Taliban tank?
A: Shoot the guy pushing it.

N elson Mandela, Bill Gates, and David Suzuki were all killed in a horrific aeroplane crash. They arrived at the gates of heaven and were greeted by God sitting on a great golden throne.

God addressed David Suzuki first. 'David, what do you believe in?'

Suzuki replied, 'I believe that man has destroyed the earth with his rampant greed and lust for industrialisation. If we are to continue to survive we must begin to respect the environment and learn to live in harmony with our surroundings.'

God was impressed and asked Suzuki to sit on his left. He then turned to Nelson Mandela and asked what he believes in.

Mandela replied, 'I believe in the equality of all men and women – be they black or white. I believe in fighting vehemently for your ideals, no matter what the personal sacrifice is.'

God was equally impressed and invited Mandela to sit on his right side.

God then addressed Bill Gates.

'Bill, what do you believe in?'

Bill Gates said, 'I believe you're in my chair.'

The president was out walking on a beautiful snowy day, when he saw that somebody had urinated on the white house lawn. In large loopy letters it spelt out 'the president sucks.'

Infuriated, he called on the secret service to work out who had done it. In a few hours, they came to him and told him that there was some bad news and some worse news.

'Give me the bad news first,' said the president.

'The bad news is that the urine is the vice president's.'

'How could he do this to me? What could be worse than that?'

'The handwriting is the first lady's.'

On one of his first nights in the white house George Dubya is woken by the ghost of George Washington. Bush is frightened, but asks, 'George, what is the best thing I could do to help the country?'

Washington advises him, 'Be honest above all else and set an honourable example, just as I did.'

This makes Bush somewhat uncomfortable but he manages to get back to sleep. The next night, the ghost of Thomas Jefferson moves through the dark bedroom.

'Tom,' Dubya asks, 'what is the best thing I could do to help the country?'

Jefferson replies, 'Throw away your prepared remarks and speak eloquently and extemporaneously from your heart.'

Bush isn't sleeping well at all the next night, and sees another figure moving in the shadows. It's Abraham Lincoln's ghost.

'A right winger, finally!' Dubya thinks, 'At last I'll get some advice that I can use.'

So he asks the ghost, 'Abe, what is the best thing I could do to help the country?'

Abe answers, 'Go see a play.'

THE DIFFERENCE BETWEEN LEFT-WING AND RIGHT-WING VIEWS

- Right-wing boys always expect to grow up and marry right-wing girls to please their parents. But they always date left-wing girls because they think they're entitled to a little fun first.
- Left-wingers step on bugs. Right-wingers call an exterminator.
- Left-wingers eat the big fish they catch. Right-wingers have them mounted.
- Left-wingers sit on the dock and fish. Right-wingers expect to have someone else drive the boat.
- Left-wingers make a lot of plans, but don't do much with them. Right-wingers are still following the plans their grandfathers made.

A party of Democrats was climbing in the Alps, when they realised that they were hopelessly lost. One of them got out the map, and studied it for some time. He turned it this way and that. He looked at the direction of the sun, consulted his compass and sighted familiar landmarks.

Finally he turned to the group and said, 'OK see that big mountain over there?'

'Yes,' answered the others eagerly.

'Well, according to the map, we're standing on top of it.'

One day God was hanging out at the pearly gates with St Paul. 'I need to find someone to run for president,' he said after a while.

Attentive to his boss' needs, St Paul started naming a few qualified candidates.

'Nah, I want that guy,' God said, pointing to a drunken Texas governor pissing off a balcony.

'You've got to be kidding,' said St Paul, 'Not only is he dumber than a box of rocks, he's got drinking and drug problems.'

'I don't care,' said God, 'This is the guy.'

Perplexed, St Paul asked: 'What's the problem, Lord? Art thou angry with the Americans?'

'No,' said God, 'I made a bet with the devil that I could get a village idiot to run for president.'

'But won't that work in the devil's favour, oh Lord?'

'That's all right. He'll never get Florida.'

Three surgeons were at the pub arguing over who was the best surgeon.

'One day,' the first one says, 'this guy came in with all his fingers in a bag of frozen peas. I sewed them back onto his hands, and he's now playing piano for the queen of England!'

'Oh, that's nothing,' retorts the second one. 'One day this guy came in with his arms and legs cut off. I sewed them back onto his body and now he's on the Olympic track and swimming teams!'

'Pff!' snorts the third one. 'One day a guy high on cocaine was riding his horse when he was hit by a freight train. Unfortunately the bloke was decapitated and all that remained of the horse was it's ass, so I sewed the horse's ass to the body and now he is the prime minister of Britain!'

It was the first day of school and the teacher decided she would like to review her students' knowledge of American history.

She asked, 'Who said "Give me liberty, or give me Death"?'

She saw a sea of blank faces, except for the new boy Martinez who had just immigrated from Mexico. He replied, 'Patrick Henry 1775.'

'Very good'! she exclaimed. 'Now, who can tell me who said "Government of the people, by the people, for the people, shall not perish from the earth"?'

Again, no response except for Martinez, 'Abraham Lincoln, 1863.'

The teacher snapped at the class, 'Class, you should be ashamed. Martinez, who is new to our country, knows more about its history than you do.'

She heard a loud whisper. 'Screw the Mexicans.'

'Who said that?' she demanded.

Martinez put his hand up, 'Jim Bowie. 1836.'

At that point, a student in the back said, 'I'm gonna puke.'

The teacher glares, and asks 'All right! Now, who said that?'

Again, Martinez says 'George Bush Senior to the Japanese prime minister. 1991.'

Now furious, another student yells, 'Oh yeah? Suck this!'

Martinez jumps out of his chair waving his hand and shouts to the teacher, 'Bill Clinton, to Monica Lewinsky. 1997!'

Now with almost a mob hysteria someone said, 'You little shit. If you say anything I'll kill you.'

Martinez frantically yells at the top of his voice, 'Gary Condit to Chandra Levy, 2001.'

The teacher fainted. As the class gathered around her on the floor, someone said, 'Oh shit, now we're in big trouble!'

Martinez said, 'Saddam Hussein, 2003.'

A little old lady calls 911. When the operator answers she yells, 'Help, send the police to my house right away! There's a damn Democrat on my front porch and he's playing with himself.'

'What?' the operator exclaims.

'I said there is a damn Democrat on my front porch playing with himself and he's weird; I don't know him and I'm afraid! Please send the police!' the little old lady says.

'Well, now, how do you know he's a Democrat?'

'Because, you damn fool, if he was a Republican, he'd be screwing somebody!'

C helsea Clinton burst into the room shouting, 'Dad! Mom! I have some great news! Nick asked me to marry him. We are getting married next month.'

Bill takes Chelsea in the back and says, 'As you might have heard, I have been known to fool around with other women on occasions. Your boyfriend Nick happens to be the product of one of my liaisons. He is my son and is your half-brother.'

Chelsea runs out of the office screaming, 'Not another brother!'

She rushes to her mother's side, telling her all about dad's shameful behaviour and how every man she dates turns out to be one of her father's illegitimate sons.

Hillary begins to laugh and says, 'Don't pay any attention to him. He isn't really your father anyway.'

T wo terrorists are chatting. One of them opens his wallet and flips through pictures.

'You see, this is my oldest. He's a martyr. Here's my second son. He's a martyr, too.'

The second terrorist says, gently, 'Ah, they blow up so fast, don't they?'

A son asked his father, 'What can you tell me about politics? I have to learn about it for school tomorrow.'

The father thought a little and said, 'OK, son, the best way I can describe politics is to use an analogy. Let's say that I'm a capitalist because I'm the breadwinner. Your mother will be the government because she controls everything. Our maid will be the working class because she works for us. You will be the people because you answer to us. And your baby brother will be the future. Does that help any?'

The little boy said, 'Well, dad, I don't know, but I'll think about what you said.'

Later that night, after everyone had gone to bed, the little boy was awoken by his baby brother's crying. He went to his brother and realised that he had a dirty nappy. So he went down the hall to his parent's bedroom to tell his parents.

His father's side of the bed was empty, and try as he could his mother wouldn't wake up. He then saw a light on in the guest room down the hall, and through the crack in the door he saw that his father was in bed with the maid.

The son then turned and went back to bed. The next morning, he said to his father at the breakfast table, 'Dad, I think I understand politics much better now.'

'Excellent, my boy,' he answered, 'What have you learned?'

The little boy thought for a minute and said, 'I learned that capitalism is screwing the working class, government is sound asleep ignoring the people, and the future's full of crap.'

While visiting England, George Bush is invited to tea with the Queen. He asks her what her leadership philosophy is. She says that it is to surround herself with intelligent people. Bush asks how she knows if they're intelligent.

'I know by asking them the right questions,' says the Queen. 'Allow me to demonstrate.'

Bush watches as the Queen phones Tony Blair and says, 'Mr Prime Minister, please answer this question: your mother has a child, and your father has a child, and this child is not your brother or sister. Who is it?'

Tony Blair responds, 'It's me, ma'am.'

'Correct. Thank you and good-bye, sir,' says the Queen. She hangs up and says, 'Did you get that, Mr Bush?'

Bush nods: 'Yes ma'am. Thanks a lot. I'll definitely be using that!'

Bush, upon returning to Washington, decides he'd better put the chairman of the senate foreign relations committee to the test. Bush summons Jesse Helms to the white house and says, 'Senator Helms, I wonder if you can answer a question for me.'

'Why, of course, sir. What's on your mind?'

Bush poses the question: 'Uhh, your mother has a child, and your father has a child, and this child is not your brother or your sister. Who is it?'

Helms ponders this and finally asks, 'Can I think about it and get back to you?'

Bush agrees, and Helms leaves. He immediately calls a meeting of other senior right wing senators, and they puzzle over the question for several hours, but nobody can come up with an answer. Finally, in desperation, Helms calls Colin Powell at the state department and explains his problem.

'Now lookee here, son, your mother has a child, and your father has a child, and this child is not your brother or your sister. Who is it?'

Powell answers immediately, 'It's me, of course.'

Much relieved, Helms rushes back to the white house, finds George Bush, and exclaims, 'I know the answer, sir! I know who it is! It's Colin Powell!'

And Bush replies in disgust, 'Wrong, you dumb shit, it's Tony Blair!'

The president was woken one night by an urgent call from the pentagon.

'Mr President,' said the four-star general, barely able to contain himself, 'There's good news and bad news.'

'Oh, no,' muttered the president, 'Well, let me have the bad news first.'

'The bad news, sir, is that we've been invaded by creatures from another planet.'

'Gosh, and the good news?'

'The good news, sir, is that they eat reporters and piss oil.'

A reporter cornered George W Bush at a press conference and said, 'Many say the only reason you were elected president is due to the enormous power and influence of your father.'

'That notion is ridiculous!' retorted George Junior, 'It doesn't matter how powerful the man is. He is only allowed to vote once!'

Five surgeons are discussing who makes the best patients on the operating table.

The first surgeon says, 'I like to see accountants on my operating table, because when you open them up, everything inside is numbered.'

The second responds, 'Yeah, but you should try electricians! Everything inside them is colour-coded.'

The third surgeon says, 'No, I really think librarians are the best, everything inside them is in alphabetical order.'

The fourth surgeon chimes in, 'You know, I like construction workers. Those guys always understand when the job takes longer than you said it would and are not worried if you have a few parts left over at the end.'

But the fifth surgeon shuts them all up when he observes, 'You're all wrong. Politicians are the easiest to operate on. They have no guts, no heart, and no spine. And the head and arse are interchangeable.'

Einstein dies and goes to heaven. At the pearly gates, St Peter tells him, 'You look like Einstein, but you have no idea the lengths that some people will go to in order to sneak into heaven. Can you prove who you really are?'

Einstein ponders for a few seconds and asks, 'Could I have a blackboard and some chalk?'

St Peter snaps his fingers and a blackboard and chalk instantly appear. Einstein describes with arcane mathematics and symbols his theory of relativity. St Peter is suitably impressed.

'You really are Einstein!' he says. 'Welcome to heaven!'

The next to arrive is Picasso. Once again, St Peter asks for credentials.

Picasso asks, 'Mind if I use that blackboard and chalk?'

St Peter says, 'Go ahead.'

Picasso erases Einstein's equations and sketches a truly stunning mural with just a few strokes of chalk. St Peter claps.

'Surely you are the great artist you claim to be!' he says. 'Come on in!'

Then St Peter looks up and sees George W Bush.

St Peter scratches his head and says, 'Einstein and Picasso both managed to prove their identity. How can you prove yours?'

George W looks bewildered and says, 'Who are Einstein and Picasso?'

St Peter sighs and says, 'Come on in, George.'

15 BIZARRE, BUT TRUE, LAWS . . .

1. It is illegal in Newcastle, Wyoming to have sex in a butcher shop's meat freezer.
2. In Atlanta, Georgia, it is illegal to tie a giraffe to a telephone pole or street lamp.
3. Duelling is legal in Paraguay as long as both parties are registered blood donors.

4. Federal law forbids recycling used eyeglasses in the United States.
5. Dancing cheek to cheek is prohibited in California.
6. It is illegal in Texas to take more than three sips of beer at a time while standing.
7. In Alabama it is illegal for a driver to be blindfolded while operating a vehicle.
8. Clergyman shall not tell a funny story from the pulpit in West Virginia.
9. In Arkansas, law states that the name must be pronounced 'Arkansaw'.
10. In North Carolina it is illegal for elephants to be used to plough cotton fields.
11. After 14 January in Maine you will be fined for having your Christmas decorations still up.
12. It is illegal to have sex on a parked motorcycle in London.
13. Dog-catchers are required to be psychoanalysed by a psychiatrist to determine if they are qualified to chase stray mutts in Texas.
14. In Virginia it is against the law to advertise on tombstones.
15. In Tennessee it is illegal to lasso a fish.

Monica Lewinsky was taking some of her clothes to the dry-cleaners. The man behind the counter was hard of hearing. She was holding a dress up and pointing at stains on the front of it, when she realised that the man was looking confused.

The old man put a hand up to his ear, and said, 'Come again?'

'No,' said Monica, 'It's red wine this time!'

Cherie Blair dies and goes to heaven. She is standing outside the pearly gates when she notices a wall of clocks behind St Peter. Curious she asks him why he has so many

'Ah,' he says, 'They are truth clocks. Every person has their own clock, and whenever they tell a lie the hands on their clock moves forward one minute.'

Cherie looks up and sees Pope John Paul II's clock. The time on his clock shows one minute past twelve, meaning that he has only told one lie in his entire life.

She then sees Mother Teresa's clock. Amazingly the hands on her clock are unmoved. She has never told a lie, or even a fib!

Cherie then starts to wonder where her husband's clock is. She asks St Peter to point it out to her. St Peter looks a little uncomfortable as he says, 'It's hanging in Jesus' office. He's using it as a ceiling fan.'

While on a state visit to England, George Bush met the queen.

He said to her, 'Your Majesty, I think you are onto something here. As I'm the president, I'm thinking of changing how my great country is referred to, and I'm thinking that it should become a kingdom.'

The queen replied, 'I'm sorry Mr Bush, but to be a kingdom, you have to have a king in charge - and you're not a king.'

George Bush thought about this for a while and then said, 'How about a principality then?'

The queen replied, 'Again, to be a principality your head of state must be a prince - and you're not a prince, Mr Bush.'

Bush thought long and hard and came up with, 'How about an empire then?'

The queen, getting a little annoyed by now, replied, 'Sorry again, Mr Bush, but to be an empire you must have an emperor in charge - and you are not an emperor.'

Before George Bush could utter another word, the queen said: 'I think you're doing quite nicely as a country.'

PRESIDENT GEORGE W BUSH

There was one kind of embarrassing moment when President Bush was asked if he ever went AWOL and he said, 'No, we have EarthLink.'

Bush made the declaration, 'I'm a war president.' It's a pity that he didn't tell the American public that back in 2000 before they voted him in.

President Bush wants to lead the world to more peace. More peace – can we take any more of this peace? It has worked so well in the Middle East, let's spread the peace around a little bit more (not).

Former president Bill Clinton won a Grammy in the spoken word category. Who would have thought that Bill Clinton would be a Grammy winner and that Janet Jackson would be the subject of a government sex investigation!

Remember the good old days when the only thing the president was trying to cover up was a stain?

President Bush was asked if his commission investigating Iraq was bipartisan. He replied, 'A person's sexuality should play no role in this.'

The white house is enraged by the suggestion that President Bush was AWOL during Vietnam. However, under an obscure perversion of the Patriot Act, actual Vietnam combat veterans will be reclassified as show-offs.

Bush the younger has two things going for him that his father never had. One – an easy charm with regular people; and two – the power to make them disappear without a trial.

For some reason, the two words this president just can't seem to say are 'sorry' and 'nuclear'.

George Bush sent his warmest regards to ex-president, Ronald Reagan, on his 93rd birthday and asked if he wanted to be on his committee looking in on intelligence failures. Oh, and Reagan has Alzheimer's.

The Bush administration started broadcasting an Arabic language satellite TV channel in the Middle East. Launching it, President Bush said the channel will tell people the truth about what the United States is doing in the Middle East, which is pretty good considering that he doesn't really know what is going on.

They say Bush's popularity is falling so fast, his new secret service codename is 'Howard Dean'.

President Bush is now launching an investigation into pre-war intelligence over weapons of mass destruction. If we find out that we were wrong, do we have to put Saddam Hussein back in the hole?

President Bush's approval rating is now down under 50 percent. So now what he's going to have to do is let Saddam go so we can capture him again.

President Bush has appointed a commission to answer one big question about pre-war Iraq: how did American oil get under their sand?

This Iraqi intelligence scandal is growing. Americans are asking, 'What did President Bush not know?' and 'When did he mispronounce it?'

Critics are now saying that his dad got him out of going to Vietnam. However, his dad did get him to go to Iraq.

Boeing is working on an invisible fighter jet so nobody can see who's flying it. Didn't George Bush fly this in the National Guard?

The white house released President Bush's military records from the National Guard, which include a rare photo of Bush in an F-102 flown by his chauffeur.

A reporter asked George W Bush if he was a deserter. Bush answered, 'No, I skip the pie and the ice cream. I'm not a big deserter.'

Who cares if Bush didn't do his job in the National Guard 30 years ago? Personally, I'm more afraid of the job he's doing now.

In the same week an issue of Time magazine asked if President Bush has a credibility problem and the cover of the Newsweek magazine asked who really killed Jesus. And in both cases, it proved the same thing – it's hard to get good intelligence in the Middle East.

New questions are emerging about President Bush's service in the National Guard, like where he was for six months in 1972?, and why did he refuse to take a routine physical? President Bush has vowed to get to the bottom of this right after election day.

The white house chief of staff asked President Clinton, 'What should we do about the Abortion Bill, Mr President?' Clinton replied 'Just pay it.'

One day Bill Clinton and Al Gore are pissing in the same bathroom. Bill notices that Al has a huge dick.

'Shit', he says; 'how did you ever make your dick that big?'

'Well', Al tells him, 'Every night before I go to bed, I beat it on the bedpost 50 times. This also works wonders before sex.'

So, that night, Clinton sneaks in late, and starts beating the bedpost with his dick.

Hillary rolls over and says, 'Is that you, Al?'

Clinton, Dole and Perot are on a long flight in Air Force One. Perot pulls out a $100 bill and says 'I'm going to throw this $100 bill out and make someone down below happy.'

Dole, not wanting to be outdone, says, 'If that was my $100 bill, I would split it into two $50 bills and make two people down below happy.'

Of course Clinton doesn't want these two candidates to outdo him, so he pipes in, 'I would instead take 100 $1 bills and throw them out to make 100 people just a little happier.'

At this point the pilot, who has overheard all this bragging and can't stand it anymore, comes out and says, 'I think I'll throw all three of you out of this plane and make 250 million people happy.'

George W Bush and his driver were heading for Air Force One and were passing a farm. A pig jumped out in the road suddenly. The driver tried to get out of the way, but he hit him.

He went in the farm to explain what had happened. He came out with a beer, a cigar, and tons of money.

Bush saw this and said, 'My God, what did you tell them?'

The driver replied, 'I told them that I'm George W Bush's driver and I just killed the pig.'

JANET JACKSON'S BREAST

The congressional hearings began into the Janet Jackson half-time Super Bowl scandal. It's interesting that they won't look into Iraq, and they are not looking into Enron. But Janet Jackson's bra, they're looking into that.

As a result of Janet Jackson's performance at the Super Bowl, the Grammys were on a five-minute delay so they can take out any mistakes. Dick Cheney wants to use this technology on Bush's speeches.

Bin Laden's been forced into hiding, Saddam Hussein is being interrogated, Janet Jackson is under investigation. 'We'll get to the bottom of this!'

After the game, President Bush phones the winning team, the Patriots, and former president Clinton called Janet Jackson.

GAY MARRIAGES

The Massachusetts court decision to allow gay marriages this week may prove to be a divisive issue in the upcoming presidential election. President Bush is likely torn because he has to protect what he sees as a sacred institution and yet he knows gay marriage would boost the economy because you know those gay guys would go all out. A vote to allow gay marriage is a vote for a fabulous economy.

GEORGE W BUSH & THE NATIONAL GUARD

The Ninja were Japanese warriors who could make themselves invisible whenever there was a war. Kind of like George W Bush.

The white house has now released military documents that 'prove' George Bush met his requirements for the National Guard. Big deal, there's documents that prove Al Gore won the election.

Embarrassing moment in the white house: They were looking around while searching for George Bush's military records and found some old Al Gore ballots.

President Bush says that he can't find any of his National Guard records from the 70s. Oh sure, but he's got no problem finding photos of John Kerry with Jane Fonda from the 70s.

There's this huge controversy over the fact that President Bush apparently received credit for National Guard service in Alabama in '72 and '73 even though his commanding officers are saying he never reported. What's even more disturbing is that he received enough credits to graduate from Yale.

The white house announced today that during the Vietnam War, President Bush was listed as MIA — Missing in Alabama.

Bush did have an explanation - he said he did go to Alabama but when he didn't find any weapons of mass destruction, he went back to Texas.

President Bush stopped off at a bass pro fishing store to pick up a fishing reel, some line and some rubber worms. He's going to disappear and go fishing. So he must think he's back in the National Guard.

QUOTES

'They are taking these holes by the neck and squeezing the birdies out of them.'
- Australian Women's Golf Open commentator.

'Here we are in the Holy Land of Israel – a Mecca for tourists.'
- BBC

'In a sense it's a one-man shown, except there are two men involved – Hartson and Berkovic, and a third man, the goalkeeper.'
- BBC 1

'I'd be surprised if all 22 players are on the field at the end of the game – one's already been sent off.'
- Sky Sports

'They've really got the bit between their legs now.'
- Pulse Sport

'Liz Taylor is recovering in hospital after having had a benign tuna removed from just behind her right ear.'
- Capital Radio

Peter Snow: In a sense, Deng Xiaoping's death was inevitable, wasn't it?

Expert: Yes.
- Channel 4 News

'**R**obert Lee was able to do some running on his groin for the first time.'
- The Observer

'**A**s Phil de Glanville said, each game is unique, and this one is no different to any other.'
- BBC1

'**I**t's like learning to play golf. Just when you think you've cracked it, they move the goalposts.'
- Southern Counties Radio

'**I** . . . that particular honeymoon has completely burst.'
- BBC1

'**I** . . .an idea someone picks up and runs with, only to find they've painted themselves into a corner.'
- BBC1

'**C**ystitis is a living death, it really is. Nobody ever talks about it, but if I was faced with a choice between having my arms removed and getting cystitis, I'd wave goodbye to my arms quite happily.'
- Q Magazine

'**S**ex is an anticlimax after that!'
- Grand National-winning jockey Mick Fitzgerald

'**W**ell, you gave the horse a wonderful ride, everyone saw that.'
- BBC

'**J**ulian Dicks is everywhere. It's like they've got eleven Dicks on the field.'
- Metro Radio

'**M**orcelli has the four fastest 1500m times ever. And all those times are at 1500m.'
– BBC1

Listener: My most embarrassing moment was when my artificial leg fell off at the altar on my wedding day.

Simon Fanshawe: How awful! Do you still have an artificial leg?

– Talk radio

'**T**he part that says 'pump on', that probably means to switch the pump on.'
– BBC

Interviewer: So did you see which train crashed into which train first?

15-year-old: No, they both ran into each other at the same time.

– Radio 4

'**T**he lack of money is evident but you've got 12,000 volunteers who'll break their back to make sure it's a success.'
– Today Program (on the Paralympics)

'**Y**ou weigh up the pros and cons and try to put them in chronological order.'
– Radio 5 Live

REDNECK GAGS

A Jewish family invited their uneducated neighbours over for a holiday dinner. The first course was set in front of them and their hostess announced, 'This is soup made with matzo balls.'

Seeing two large matzo balls in the soup, the redneck man was very hesitant to taste this strange looking brew. The Jewish couple gently urged him to try it.

'Just give it a taste. If you don't like it, you don't have to finish it,' they said reassuringly.

Finally, he agreed to give it a try. He dug his spoon in, picked up a small piece of matzo ball with some soup in the spoon and gingerly tasted it. He was surprised to realise how good it was, and he quickly finished the soup.

'I must say, that was quite delicious,' he said, 'but I was wondering – are there other parts of the matzo you can eat?'

HILLBILLY STATE RESIDENCY APPLICATION

Name (tick appropriate box):

☐ Billy-Bob   ☐ Billy-Mae
☐ Billy-Joe   ☐ Billy-Jack
☐ Billy-Ray   ☐ Billy-Cart
☐ Billy-Sue

Age: _____

Sex: ☐ M ☐ F ☐ N/A

Shoe Size:

Left _____

Right _____

Occupation:

☐ Farmer   ☐ Hairdresser

☐ Mechanic   ☐ Unemployed

Spouse's Name: _____

Relationship with spouse:

☐ Sister   ☐ Mother

☐ Brother   ☐ Father

☐ Aunt   ☐ Son

☐ Uncle   ☐ Daughter

☐ Cousin   ☐ Pet

Number of children living in household: _____

Number that are yours: _____

Mother's Name: _____

Father's Name: _____

(If not sure, leave blank)

Education: 1 2 3 4 (Circle highest grade completed)

Do you ☐ own or ☐ rent your mobile home? (Check appropriate box)

Total number of vehicles you own _____

Number of vehicles that still crank _____

Number of vehicles in front yard _____

Number of vehicles in back yard _____

Number of vehicles on cement blocks _____

Total number of firearms you own _____
Number of firearms in truck _____
Number of firearms in bedroom _____
Number of firearms in bathroom _____
Number of firearms in kitchen _____
Number of firearms in shed _____

Model and year of your pickup: _____194__

Number of times you've seen a UFO _____
Number of times you've seen Elvis _____
Number of times you've seen Elvis in a UFO _____

How often do you bathe?
☐ Weekly   ☐ Monthly   ☐ Not Applicable

Colour of teeth:
☐Yellow   ☐Black
☐Brownish-Yellow   ☐N/A
☐Brown

Brand of chewing tobacco you prefer: _____

How far is your home from a paved road? _____
Have you ever seen a paved road? _____

RELIGIOUS JOKES

Forrest Gump dies and goes to heaven. The gates are closed, however, and Forrest approaches the gatekeeper. It is St Peter himself.

'Well, Forrest, it's certainly good to see you. We have heard a lot about you. It's now our policy to administer an entrance examination which you must pass before you can get into heaven,' says St Pete.

'Nobody ever told me about any entrance exams,' says Forrest. 'Sure hope the test ain't too hard; life was a big enough test as it was. But I guess, like Mama always used to say, the test will be like a box of chocolates – you never know what you've got until you take a bite. So dish her up to me now. I'm a-ready, St Pete.'

'The test I have for you is only three questions. The first one is, 'What days of the week begin with the letter 'T'? Second, how many seconds are there in a year?, and third, what is God's first name? Take your time, think about it and come back to me when you reckon that you have the answers.'

Forrest goes away to think the questions over. He returns the next day.

St Peter waves him up and asks, 'Now that you have had a chance to think the questions over, tell me your answers.'

Forrest says, 'Well, the first one, how many days of the week begin with the letter 'T'? Shucks, that one's easy. That'd be today and tomorrow!'

The saint's eyes open wide and he exclaims, 'Forrest! That's not what I was thinking, but, you do have a point, and I guess I didn't specify, so I give you credit for that answer. How about the next one. How many seconds in a year?'

'Now that one's harder,' says Forest. 'But, I thunk and thunk about that, and I guess the only answer can be twelve.'

Astounded, St Peter says, 'Twelve! Twelve! Forrest, how in heaven's name could you come up with twelve seconds in a year?'

Forrest says, 'Shucks, there gotta be twelve: January second, February second, March second –'

'Hold it,' interrupts St Peter. 'I see where you're going with it. And I guess I see your point, though that wasn't quite what I had in mind. But I'll give you credit for that one too. Let's go on with the next and final question. Can you tell me God's first name?'

Forrest says, 'Well sure, I know God's first name. Everybody probably knows it. It's Howard.'

'Howard?' asks St Peter. 'What makes you think it's Howard?'

Forrest answers, 'It's in the prayer.'

'The prayer?' asks St Peter. 'Which prayer?'

'The Lord's Prayer,' responds Forest: 'Our Father, who art in heaven, Howard be thy name . . .'

Four priests board a train for a long journey to a church council conference. Shortly into the trip, one priest says 'Well, we've all worked together for many years, but don't really know one another. I suggest we tell each other one of our sins to get better acquainted.'

They look nervously at each other but nod OK.

The first priest says, 'Since I suggested it, I'll go first. With me it's the drink. Once a year I take off my collar and go out of town to a pub and drink myself blind for a few days. Get it out of my system.'

They all look at each other again nervously, but the next priest slowly starts, 'Well, with me, it's the gambling. Periodically, I nick the money out of the poor box and go to the races. Spend it all! But I get it out of my system.'

The third, who is really nervous now reluctantly says, 'This is very difficult. My sin is worse. I take off my collar and go into the red light district, pick out a lass, and spend a week in the saddle. But I really get it out of my system.'

They all look at the fourth priest, waiting, but he doesn't say anything.

One of the others speaks up, 'Come now, we've all told our innermost faults. It's your turn.'

He looks at the others and starts hesitantly 'Well, I'm an inveterate gossip, and I can't wait to get off this train!'

There was a young Rabbi from Peru
Who was vainly attempting to screw
His wife said 'Oi vey'
If you keep up this way
The Messiah will come before you.'

Once upon a time in the kingdom of heaven, God went missing for seven days. Eventually, Michael the Archangel found him.

He inquired of God, 'Where have you been?'

God sighed a deep sigh of satisfaction and proudly pointed downwards through the clouds; 'Look son, look what I have made.'

Archangel Michael looked puzzled and said, 'What is it?'

God replied, 'It's another planet but I'm after putting life on it. I've named it Earth and there's going to be a balance between everything on it. For example, there's North America and South America. North America is going to be rich and South America is going to be poor, and the narrow bit joining them – that's going to be a hot spot. Now look over here. I've put a continent of whites in the north and another one of blacks in the south.'

And then the archangel said, 'And what's that green dot there?'

And God said 'Ahhh that's the Emerald Isle – that's a very special place. That's going to be the most glorious spot on earth;

beautiful mountains, lakes, rivers, streams, and an exquisite coastline. These people here are going to be great characters, and they're going to be found travelling the world. They'll be playwrights and poets and singers and songwriters. And I'm going to give them this black liquid which they're going to go mad on, and for which people will come from the far corners of the earth to imbibe. Michael the Archangel gasped in wonder and admiration. But then, seemingly startled, he proclaimed: 'Hold on a second, what about the balance? You said there was going to be a balance.'

God replied wisely. 'Wait until you see the neighbours I'm going to give them.'

And God populated the earth with green and yellow vegetables of all kinds, so Man and Woman would live long and healthy lives.

And Satan created McDonald's, with its double-cheeseburgers and super-sized fries. And Man gained kilos.

And God created the healthy yoghurt, that Woman might keep her figure that Man found so fair.

And Satan froze the yoghurt, and brought forth chocolate, nuts and brightly coloured sprinkles to put on the yoghurt. And Woman gained kilos.

And God said, 'Try my crispy fresh salad'.

And Satan brought forth creamy dressings, bacon bits, and shredded cheese. And Man gained kilos.

And God brought forth running shoes, and Man resolved to lose those extra kilos.

And Satan brought forth cable TV with remote control so Man would not have to work to change channels. And Man gained kilos.

And God said, 'You're running up the score, Devil'. And God bought forth the potato, a vegetable naturally low in fat and brimming with nutrition.

And Satan peeled off the healthful skin and sliced the starchy centre into chips and deep-fried them. He created sour cream dip also, and Man clutched his remote control, and ate the potato chips swaddled in cholesterol.

And Satan saw that and said, 'It is good'. And Man went into cardiac arrest.

And God sighed and created quadruple bypass surgery. And Satan created private health insurance.

There was a young lady from Kew
Who said, as the curate withdrew,
   'I prefer the dear vicar;
   He's longer and thicker.
   Besides, he comes quicker than you.'

Q: What do you get when you cross a Jehovah's Witness and a skinhead?
A: Someone who comes knocking on your door at 8am on a Sunday and tells you to piss off.

On a flight from Shannon to New York, Father Maguire finds himself seated next to a rabbi who introduces himself as Rabbi Klein. He is returning home to New York after a lovely holiday in Ireland.

Shortly after Father Maguire asks, 'Rabbi. Is it true that you people never eat pork?'

'Never,' replies the rabbi.

'Surely, at some time in your life you must have tasted pork. Come on, now, huh?'

'Well, Father, I guess since we're both in the same racket I can tell you. Yes, I did stray once and eat pork.'

'Ah, I thought so,' says Father Maguire, a broad smile of satisfaction on his rotund face.

'Now, Father,' said the rabbi, 'it's my turn. You guys are supposed to be celibate, right?'

'Oh, dear God, yes. Absolutely!'

'Ah, come on, man. I levelled with you. Was there ever a time you strayed?'

Sheepishly, Father Maguire says, 'Well, truth to tell, there was a time, yes. Once, a long time ago.'

'I see,' says the rabbi. 'Beats the hell out of pork, don't you think?'

Three men die in a car accident on Christmas Eve. They all find themselves at the pearly gates waiting to enter heaven. Here St Peter greets them and tells them that if they wish to enter into heaven they must present something 'Christmassy'.

The first man searches his pockets, and finds some pine needles from the family's Christmas tree. He is let in.

The second man presents a bow and some ribbon, from presents that were opened earlier in that night. So he is also allowed in.

The third man pulls out a pair of black lace panties.

Confused at this last offering, St Peter says in a booming voice, 'I fail to see the relevance. How do these represent Christmas?'

To which the third man sheepishly replies, 'Oh, they're Carol's.'

In the Garden of Eden sat Adam
Massaging the bust of his madam
He chuckled with mirth,
For he knew that on Earth
There were only two boobs, and he had 'em.

A man wonders if having sex on the Sabbath is a sin because he is not sure if sex is work or play. He asks a priest for his opinion on this question.

The priest says, after consulting the Bible, 'My son, after an exhaustive search I am positive sex is work and is not permitted on Sundays.'

The man thinks, 'What does a priest know of sex?'

He goes to a minister, an experienced married man, for the answer. He queries the minister and receives the same reply, 'Sex is work and not for the Sabbath!'

Not pleased with the reply, he seeks out the ultimate authority, a man of thousands of years of tradition and knowledge – a Rabbi.

The Rabbi ponders the question and states, 'My son, sex is definitely play.'

'Rabbi, how can you be so sure when so many others tell me sex is work?' asks the man.

The Rabbi answers softly, 'If sex were work, my wife would have the maid do it!'

Father O'Malley, the new priest, is nervous about hearing confessions, so he asks the older priest to sit in on his sessions. The new priest hears a couple of confessions, and then the old priest asks him to step out of the confessional for a few suggestions.

The old priest suggests, 'Cross you arms over your chest, and rub your chin with one hand.'

The new priest tries this and achieves a concerned, thoughtful look.

The old priest says, 'Good. Now try saying things like, "I see, yes, go on, I understand" and "how did you feel about that?"'

The new priest tries saying those things and sounds caring and compassionate.

The old priest says, 'Wonderful! Now, don't you think that's a little better than slapping your knee and saying "No shit? What happened next?"'

From the depths of the crypt at St Giles
Came a scream that was hear round for miles.
Said the vicar, 'Goodness Gracious,
It's Father Ignatius,
He's forgotten the Bishop has piles.'

An Irish priest and a Rabbi get into a car accident. They both get out of their cars and stumble over to the side of the road.

The Rabbi says, 'Oi vey! What a wreck!'

The priest asks him, 'Are you all right, Rabbi?'

The Rabbi responds, 'Just a little shaken.'

The priest pulls a flask of whisky from his coat and says, 'Here, drink some of this it will calm your nerves.'

The Rabbi takes the flask and drinks it down and says, 'Well, what are we going to tell the police?'

'Well,' the priest says, 'I don't know what you will be telling them. But I'll be telling them I wasn't the one drinking.'

A man sick of the outside world decided to join a monastery in Tibet. One of the stipulations for acceptance into this most holy order was that he was only permitted to say two words every five years.

For the first five years he eats rice, sleeps on a wooden bed, and has only one blanket with holes in it. He tends to the fields and looks after livestock everyday.

After five years the head monk comes to him and says he can use his two words to which he replies, 'More blankets.'

Now the man is warm at night on his wooden bed with all his blankets but still he only eats rice and tends to the fields and livestock everyday.

Another five years pass and the head monk comes to him again and says that he can use two more words.

He replies, 'More food.'

He now sleeps on his wooden bed with all his blankets and

eats gourmet food every day but he still has to tend to the fields and livestock.

Another five years passes and the head monk comes again to him and says, 'You may use two words now.'

The man replies, 'I'm leaving.'

'Good,' said the head monk, 'all you've done is bloody complain since you got here.'

Easter Sunday a young boy, Stan Snead,
Popped a stiff one as long as a reed.
And did he turn beet red,
When Pastor Fred loudly said,
'He is risen. He is risen indeed!'

Pat was found dead in his back yard, and as the weather was a bit on the warm side, the wake was limited to only two days, so his mortal remains wouldn't take a bad turn. At the appointed time, his friends laid him in the box, nailed it shut and started down the hill into the churchyard.

As it was a long, sloping path and the mourners were appropriately tipsy, one fellow lurched into the gatepost as they entered the graveyard. Suddenly a loud knocking came from in the box. Paddy was alive!

They opened the box up and he sat up, wide eyed, and they all said, 'Sure, it's a miracle of God!'

All rejoiced and they went back and had a few more drinks but later that day, the poor lad died. Really died. Stone cold dead.

They bundled him back into his box, and as they huffed and puffed down the hill the next morning, the priest said, 'Careful now, boys; mind ye don't bump the gatepost again'

Father Ryan is seated next to a rabbi on a flight from Shannon to NYC.

The flight attendant asks the good father, 'Cocktail, sir?'

Infuriated, the good father responds, 'I'd sooner commit adultery.'

She asks the rabbi, 'How about you, sir?'

The rabbi responds, 'I'll have what he's having.'

The bishop of Winchester Junction
Found his phallus would no longer function.
So in black crepe he wound it,
Tied a lily around it,
And solemnly gave it last unction.

A newly arrived novitiate, Sister Bridget, young, fresh and eager to please, was summoned by her Mother Superior to assist the aging Sister Maureen on her daily round of errands in the local village.

So off they went, with young Sister Bridget studiously taking note of each and every road and stop they made as they pedalled their way about, on the convent's two ancient bicycles.

After a while they finished their tasks and stopped for a break and a cup of tea. Then they started back to the convent. Sister Bridget took the lead, only to find that a road they had taken was now impassable due to heavy repairs going on.

Sister Maureen told her not to worry, she knew another way, so off they went again, wobbling and jostling down tiny lanes paved with cobblestones in a manner that gave young Sister Bridget cause for concern.

Somewhat breathlessly she called out to Sister Maureen and said 'I've never come this way before'.

'Don't you be alarmed now,' said Sister Maureen, 'it's just those lovely cobblestones.'

Jeff and Mike are killed in an accident and as Jeff arrives at the pearly gates, he is met by St Peter.

'Where's my friend Mike?' Jeff asks the old Saint.

St Peter replies, 'Mike wasn't as fortunate as you, instead of heaven, he went in the other direction.'

Jeff is deeply concerned by this and asks, 'Well, could I see Mike just one more time?'

St Peter agrees to this, so they walk over to the edge of heaven and look down. Jeff sees Mike down in hell with a sexy blonde on one side of him and a keg of beer on the other.

'I really don't mean to complain,' Jeff says, 'but Mike seems to be having a pretty nice time down in hell.'

'Look a little closer,' says St Peter. 'The keg has a hole in it, and the blonde doesn't.'

Adam was walking around the Garden of Eden hanging his head and aimlessly kicking rocks, so God asked him, 'What is wrong with you?'

'Oh I don't know God. I'm feeling kind of down. I don't have anyone to talk to,' said Adam.

'Don't worry,' said God 'I'm going to make you a companion, and it will be a woman. She will gather food for you, cook for you and, when you discover clothing, she'll wash it for you. She will always agree with every decision you make. She will bear your children and never ask you to get up in the middle of the night to take care of them. She will not nag you, and will always be the first to admit she was wrong when you've had a disagreement. She will never have a headache, and will freely give you love and passion whenever you need it.'

'What will a woman like this cost?' asked Adam.

God replied, 'An arm and a leg.'

'Oh dear, said Adam. 'I'm quite attached to my arm and my leg. What can I get for a rib?'

Young O'Donnell rushed into a church, placed his rifle under a pew and entered the confessional.

'Father,' he said, trying to catch his breath, 'I've just shot down two British lieutenants!' There was no response, so he went on. 'I also knocked off a British captain!'

When there was still no response from the priest, O'Donnell said, 'Father, have ye fainted?'

'Of course I haven't fainted,' replied the confessor. 'I'm waiting for you to stop talking politics and commence confessing your sins!'

A new priest at his first mass was so nervous he could hardly speak. After mass he asked the monsignor how he had done.

The monsignor replied, 'When I am worried about getting nervous on the pulpit, I put a glass of vodka next to the water glass. If I start to get nervous, I take a sip.'

So the next Sunday he took the monsignor's advice. At the beginning of the sermon, he got nervous and took a drink. He talked up a storm. Upon his return to his office after mass, he found the following note on the door:

Father, that was an exemplary sermon, and I can see the vodka is helping. But just one or two points you might want to consider next time:

1. Sip the vodka, don't gulp. And just have the one, not the entire bottle.
2. There are 10 commandments, not 12.
3. There are 12 disciples, not 10.
4. Jesus was consecrated, not constipated.
5. Jacob wagered his donkey, he did not bet his ass.
6. We do not refer to Jesus Christ as 'the late JC'.
7. The Father, Son, and Holy Ghost are not referred to as 'Daddy, Junior and the Spook.'
8. David slew Goliath, he did not kick the crap out of him.
9. When David was hit by a rock and knocked off his donkey, don't say he was stoned off his ass.
10. We do not refer to the cross as the 'Big T.'

11. When Jesus broke the bread at the Last Supper he said, 'Take this and eat it for it is my body'. He did not say 'Eat me'.
12. The recommended grace before a meal is not 'Rub-A-Dub-Dub, thanks for the grub, yeah God'.
13. Next Sunday there will be a taffy pulling contest at St Peter's, not a peter pulling contest at St Taffy's.

Apart from that, you were great.

A musician arrived at the pearly gates.

'What did you do when you were alive?' asked St Peter.

'I was the principal trombone player of the London Symphony Orchestra,' replied the musician.

'Excellent! We have a vacancy in our celestial symphony orchestra for a trombonist. Why don't you turn up for the next rehearsal.'

When the time for the next rehearsal arrived our friend turned up with his heavenly trombone. As he took his seat, God moved, in a mysterious way, to the podium and tapped his baton to bring the players to attention.

Our friend turned to the angelic second trombonist and whispered, 'So, what's God like as a conductor?'

'Oh, he's OK most of the time, but occasionally he thinks he's von Karajan.'

There was a straight parson named Stings
Who talked about God and such things.
But his secret desire
Was to join a mixed choir
With nice ladies with whom he'd have flings.

One day Mrs Jones went to have a talk with the minister at the local church.

'Reverend,' she said, 'I have a problem, my husband keeps

falling asleep during your sermons. It's very embarrassing. What should I do?'

'I have an idea,' said the minister. 'Take this hat-pin with you. I will be able to tell when Mr Jones is sleeping, and I will motion to you at specific times. When I motion, you give him a good poke in the leg.'

In church the following Sunday, Mr Jones dozed off. Noticing this, the preacher put his plan to work.

'And who made the ultimate sacrifice for you?' he said, nodding to Mrs Jones.

'Jesus!' Jones cried, as his wife jabbed him the leg with the hat-pin.

'Yes, you are right, Mr Jones,' said the minister.

Soon, Mr Jones nodded off again. Again, the minister noticed.

'Who is your redeemer?' he asked the congregation, motioning towards Mrs Jones.

'Oh God!' Mr Jones cried out, as he was stuck again with the hat-pin.

'Right again,' said the minister, smiling.

Before long, Mr Jones again winked off. However, this time the minister did not notice. As he picked up the tempo of his sermon, he made a motion that Mrs Jones mistook as the signal to bayonet her husband with the hat-pin again .

The minister asked, 'And what did Eve say to Adam after she bore him his 99th son?'

Mrs Jones poked her husband, who yelled, 'You stick that goddamned thing in me one more time and I'll break it in half and shove it up your arse!'

Quinn stumbled out of a saloon right into the arms of Father O'Flaherty.

'Inebriated again!' declared the priest. 'Shame on you! When are you going to straighten out your life?'

'Father,' asked Quinn, 'What causes arthritis?'

'I'll tell you what causes it! Drinking cheap whisky, gambling and carousing around with loose women. How long have you had arthritis?'

'I don't,' slurred Quinn. 'The Bishop has it!'

Three pastors and their wives were car-pooling their way back from a revival meeting when their van slid off the side of a cliff and sadly, they were all killed. They arrived at the pearly gates together. Peter called the first couple forward and began to examine the journal in which their life story was written. He looked up at the first preacher and spoke sharply.

'You hypocrite!' he boomed, 'All you ever cared about in your life was money! You've hoarded money all your life! You were the wealthiest person in your whole community. In fact, so smitten with money were you that you even went out and married a woman named Penny. Money is evil and will never buy you happiness!'

The preacher and his wife were obviously shaken and meekly cast their eyes down and were chastened.

But St Peter softened and said, 'Well, you did preach the gospel, so I won't send you off to hell but you can't come in the front gate. You must walk all the way around heaven and enter by the back door. Off you go!'

So the couple went shamefully on their way. St Peter then turned to the next pastor and his wife.

'All you ever talked and cared about was alcohol and where you would get your next drink! In fact, you have been drunk nearly every time you preached. You were so consumed with alcohol and drinking that you married a woman named Brandy!'

The pastor hung his head and nodded in shame.

'However, you too preached a powerful sermon, despite

being drunk, so you have also been spared the everlasting flames of hell. Nevertheless, you have to walk all the way around heaven and enter in the back way. Off with you!'

The couple slowly shuffled off. He then turned his attention to the third and final couple, pointing an accusing finger at them. But, before he could begin to speak the pastor held up his hand in order to silence St Pete.

He turned to his wife and said, 'We'd better start walking, Fanny.'

There was a young lady of Tottenham
Whose manners – well, she had forgotten 'em
While at tea at the vicar's
She took off her knickers
Explaining she felt much too hot in 'em.

Devil: Why so miserable?
Larry: What do you think? I'm in hell.
Devil: Hell's not so bad. We actually have a lot of fun down here. You like a drink, Larry?
Larry: Sure, I like a drink.
Devil: Well you're going to love Mondays then. On Mondays that's all we do – drink. Beer, whisky, tequila, Guinness, wine coolers, diet drinks. We drink till we throw up and then we drink some more!
Larry: Gee that sounds great.
Devil: You a smoker?
Larry: You better believe it! I love smoking.
Devil: OK! You're going to love Tuesdays. On Tuesdays we get the finest Cuban cigars, and smoke our lungs out. If you get cancer – no problem – you're already dead, remember?
Larry: Wow. That's awesome!
Devil: I bet you like to gamble.

Larry:	Why, yes, as a matter of fact, I do. Love the gambling.
Devil:	Cause Wednesday you can gamble all you want. Blackjack, Roulette, Poker, Slots, Craps, whatever. If you go bankrupt – who cares, you're dead anyhow.
Devil:	You into drugs?
Larry:	Are you kidding? I love drugs! You don't mean . . .
Devil:	I do! Thursday is drug day. Help yourself to a great big bowl of crack. Or smack. Smoke a bong the size of a submarine. You can do all the drugs you want and if you overdose, that's OK – you're dead – so, who cares! OD as much as you like!
Larry:	Gee whiz, I never realised that hell was such a great place!!
Devil:	See, now you're getting the hang of it! Now Larry, tell me, are you gay?
Larry:	Ah, no.
Devil:	Ooooh. Well Larry, I'm afraid you're really gonna hate Fridays.

A young Irish girl goes into her priest on Saturday morning for confession.

'Father, forgive me for I have thinned.'

'You've thinned?'

'Yes, I went out with me boyfriend Friday night. He held me hand twice, kissed me three times, and made love to me two times.'

'Daughter! I want you to go straight home, squeeze seven lemons into a glass, and drink it straight down.'

'Will that wash away me thin?'

'No, but it will get that silly smile off your face.'

St Peter was manning the gates of heaven when some English soccer supporters walked up.

St Peter went to God and said 'God there are English soccer

supporters here. You know what those lager louts are like. What do I do?'

'Peter,' said God, 'this is heaven, the place where we treat everyone with respect, and in turn, you are treated the same. Just carry on as normal and treat them how you usually do,' said God.

St Peter went back to his post.

All of a sudden St Peter runs back towards God, shouting, 'They're gone! They're gone!'

'What, the soccer supporters?' quizzed God.

'No Lord,' said St Peter, 'the pearly gates!'

A wealthy farmer went to church one Sunday. After the service he said to the priest, 'Father, that was a damned good sermon you gave, damned good!'

'I'm happy you liked it,' said the priest. 'But I wish you wouldn't use those terms in expressing yourself.'

'I can't help it,' said the rich farmer. 'I still think it was a damned good sermon. In fact, I liked it so much I put $100 in the collection basket.'

'Holy shit, did you?' replied the priest.

The church service was under way and the collection plate was being passed around.

When the preacher saw a $100 bill in the plate, he was so surprised that he stopped the service and asked, 'Will whoever put the $100 bill in the plate, please stand up?'

A young, gay man in the congregation stood up.

The preacher told him, 'I am so impressed that you would donate such a large sum. Since you put that money in the plate I think that it is only fair that you should choose three hymns.'

Excitedly, the gay guy looked around, and said, 'Well, I'll take him and him and him.'

There once was a boring young Reverend
Who preached till it seemed he would never end.
His hearers, en masse,
Got a pain in the ass,
And prayed for relief of their nether end.

The good Lord decided to make a companion for Adam. He summoned St Peter to his side.

'My dear Peter,' he said. I have a little job for you. I want you to make a being who is similar to man, yet different, and one who can offer man comfort, companionship and pleasure. I will call this being 'woman'.'

So St Peter set about creating a being who was similar to man, yet was different in ways that would be appealing, and that could provide physical pleasure to man. When St Peter had finished creating this woman, he summoned the Lord to look at his work.

'Ah, St Peter, once again you have done an excellent job,' said the Lord.

'Thank You, O Great One' replied St Peter. 'I am now ready to provide the brain, nerve endings and senses to this being, this woman. However, I require your assistance on this matter, O Lord.'

'You shall make her brain, slightly smaller, yet more intuitive, more feeling, more compassionate, and more adaptable than man's,' said the Lord.

'What about the nerve endings?' said St Peter. 'How many will I put in her hands?'

'How many did we put in Adam?' asked the Lord.

'Two hundred, O Mighty One,' replied St Peter.

'Then we shall do the same for this woman,' said the Lord.

'And how many nerve endings shall we put in her feet?' enquired St Peter.

'How many did we put in Adam?' asked the Lord.

'Seventy five, O Mighty One,' replied St Peter.

'Do the same for woman,' said the Lord.

'OK. And how many nerve endings should we put in woman's genitals?' inquired St Peter.

'How many did we put in Adam?'

'Four hundred and twenty, O Mighty One,' replied St Peter.

'Do the same for woman, said the Lord. 'Actually, no wait. I've changed my mind. Give her 10,000. I want her to scream my name out loud when she's enjoying herself!'

One day while walking down the street a highly successful executive woman was tragically hit by a bus and died. Her soul arrived in heaven where she was met at the pearly gates by St Peter himself.

'Welcome to heaven,' said St Peter.

'Before you get settled in though, it seems we have a problem. You see, strangely enough, we've never once had an executive make it this far and we're not really sure what to do with you.'

'That's a problem that can be solved. In the meantime just let me in,' said the woman.

'Well, I'd like to, but I have higher orders. What we're going to do is let you have a day in hell and a day in heaven and then you can choose whichever one you wish.'

'Actually, I think I've made up my mind. I prefer to stay in heaven,' said the woman.

'Sorry,' said St Peter, 'but rules are rules.'

And so saying, St Peter put the executive in an elevator and it went down, down, down to hell. The doors opened and the executive lady found herself stepping out onto the putting green of a beautiful golf course. In the distance was a country club and standing in front of that were all her friends, fellow executives that she had worked with. They were all dressed in evening gowns and were cheering for her.

They ran up and kissed her on both cheeks and talked about old times. They played an excellent round of golf and at night went to the country club where she enjoyed an excellent steak and lobster dinner.

She met the devil, who was actually a really nice guy (and kinda cute), and she had a great time telling jokes and dancing. She was having such a good time that before she knew it, it was time to leave. Everybody shook her hand and waved good bye as she got in the elevator.

The elevator went up-up-up and opened back at the pearly gates where she found St Peter waiting for her.

'Now it's time to spend a day in heaven,' he said.

So she spent the next 24 hours lounging around on clouds and playing the harp and singing. She also enjoyed this and before she knew it her 24 hours were up and St Peter came to get her.

'So, you've spent a day in hell and you've spent a day in heaven. Now you must choose your eternity,' he said.

The woman paused for a second and then replied, 'I never thought I'd say this, But although heaven has been really great and all, I think I had a better time in hell.'

St Peter escorted her to the elevator and again she went down-down-down back to hell. When the doors of the elevator opened she found herself standing in a desolate wasteland covered in garbage and filth. She saw her friends were dressed in rags and were picking up the garbage and putting it in sacks. The devil came up to her and put his arm around her.

'I don't understand,' stammered the woman. 'Yesterday I was here and there was a golf course and a country club and we ate lobster and we danced and had a great time. Now everything is a wasteland of garbage and all my friends look miserable.'

The devil looked at her and smiled. 'You know the business world. Yesterday we were recruiting you; today you're staff.'

We thought we were all going to die
When the minister raised his arms high
The benediction to say,
But it wasn't his day,
He'd forgotten to zip up his fly!

A 10-year-old Jewish boy was failing maths. His parents tried everything from tutors to hypnosis; but to no avail. Finally, at the insistence of a family friend, they decided to enrol their son in a private Catholic school.

After the first day, the boy's parents were surprised when he walked in after school with a stern, focused and very determined expression on his face. He went straight past them, right to his room and quietly closed the door. For nearly two hours he toiled away in his room with maths books strewn about his desk and the surrounding floor. He emerged long enough to eat, and after quickly cleaning his plate, went straight back to his room, closed the door and worked feverishly at his studies until bedtime.

This pattern of behaviour continued until it was time for the first quarter's report card. The boy walked in with it unopened, laid it on the dinner table and went straight to his room. Cautiously, his mother opened it and, to her amazement, she saw a large red 'A' under the subject of maths. Overjoyed, she and her husband rushed into their son's room, thrilled at his remarkable progress.

'Was it the nuns that did it?' the father asked.

The boy shook his head and said, 'No.'

'Was it the one-to-one tutoring?'

'No.'

'Or the peer-mentoring?'

'No.'

'The textbooks?'

'No.'

'The teachers?'

'No.'

'The curriculum?'

'No,' said the son. 'It was none of that.'

'Well, what was it?' chorused his parents.

'On that first day, when I walked in the front door and saw that guy nailed to the plus sign, I knew that they were serious about maths!'

Four Catholic mothers are sitting around bragging about their sons, each of whom is a priest.

The first mother says, 'My son is a monsignor, and when he walks in the room, people greet him with "Good morning, Monsignor".'

The second mother says, 'Well, my son is a bishop, and people greet him with "Good morning, Your Grace".'

The third mother says, 'Well, my son is a cardinal, and people greet him "Good morning, Your Eminence".'

The fourth mother pauses, and finally says, 'My son is six foot 10 and is 120kg of pure muscle. When he walks in the room, people greet him by saying, "Oh, My God!"'

An old rabbi, on seeing his son graduate from high school, wanted to know what the young man's plans were.

He called his son into his study and questioned him. 'Son, I vish to know, what kind of career are you going to have?'

The rabbi laid on a table three items, a $100 bill, a bottle of whisky and the good book.

He looked to the boy and said, 'Ve need to know your future. If you take the $100 bill, you will become a gambler, and that is very terrible. If you take the whisky, you will become a drunkard and that too is very, very bad. But . . . if you take the good book, you will become a rabbi, like you papa.'

The young lad's mind was blank. He was just out of high school and he did not yet know what he wanted to do with his life. After a few minutes of trying to think, he finally decided there was only one answer.

The boy took the $100 bill and put it in his pocket. He picked up the whisky in one hand and with the other grasped the good book, put it under his arm and quickly left the room.

The old rabbi was stunned. He could not understand what had just happened.

Then all of a sudden his eyes grew wide, he jumped to his feet, and slapping the side of his face he cried, 'Oi Vay . . . he is going to become a Catholic priest!'

God is talking to one of his angels.
He says, 'Boy, I just created a 24-hour period of alternating light and darkness on Earth.'

The angel says, 'What are you going to do now?'

God says, 'Call it a day.'

A monastery was perched high on an isolated cliff, and the only way to reach it was to ride in a basket which was hauled to the top by a team of monks. The ride up was not for the faint-hearted, and one visitor was looking exceedingly pale by the time he reached the summit. As he stepped trembling from the basket, he couldn't help noticing that the rope was old and frayed.

'How often do you change that rope?' he asked one of the monks.

The monk thought for a moment, then replied: 'Whenever it breaks.'

Two nuns are ordered to paint a room that is going to be redecorated in the convent for a visit by the pope. The last instruction from Mother Superior is that they must not get so much as a drop of paint on their habits. After conferring about this for a while, the two nuns decide to lock the door of the room, strip off their habits, and paint in the nude.

In the middle of the project, there is a knock at the door.

'Who is it?' calls one of the nuns.

'It's the blind man,' replies a voice from the other side of the door.

The two nuns look at each other and shrug, deciding that no harm can come from letting a blind man into the room. They open the door.

'Nice tits,' says the man, 'where do you want the blinds?'

Three guys get to heaven, but it's a little full.

St Peter says, 'OK, guys, I'll consider letting you in if you tell me how you died.'

The first guy says, 'OK, I'll go first. I thought my wife might be cheating on me, so one day I came home from work early to catch her in the act. Sure enough, when I get inside, there's this guy hanging from the balcony above mine. I grabbed his legs and started pulling, but he wouldn't fall. I yanked really hard, and finally, he fell off, but he was still alive when he hit the ground! I was so mad, I ran inside, picked up the refrigerator, and threw it on him. Then I died of a heart attack from the strain!'

The second guy comes forward and St Peter tells him that he has to tell him the story of how he died.

'Man, wait till you hear this! I was exercising on my balcony like I do every day, when suddenly, I slipped and fell over the railing! Lucky for me, I managed to snag the rail with my hand. I was just trying to get back up, when suddenly this lunatic on the balcony below mine starts yanking on my legs. I managed to hold on for a while, but I just couldn't hold on anymore, and I fell. But I was still alive when I hit the ground! Then the idiot drops a refrigerator on me, and, well, here I am.'

Finally, it's the third guy's turn to tell his story.

'Alright, I need to hear a story of how you died in order to let you in,' St Peter says.

'OK, picture this. I'm having an affair with a woman and her husband comes home unexpectedly. So I hide naked in the refrigerator . . .'

A gentle old lady I knew
Was dozing one day in her pew;
When the preacher yelled 'Sin!'
She said, 'Count me in!
As soon as the service is through!'

An old rich man was about to die and it was his wish that he take his fortune with him to the next life. He called together his doctor, his pastor and his lawyer.

He gave each of them a million dollars cash and told them that just as they were lowering his casket into the ground, he wanted each of them to throw the million dollars he had given them into the grave on top of the casket and to ensure that the money went with him to eternity.

They attended his funeral and appeared to do as asked. After the funeral, the three men were walking back to their cars when the doctor said he had a confession to make.

'I didn't throw in the whole million,' he said, 'I saved $250,000 of it for a new wing at the hospital.'

The pastor also had a confession. 'I saved $250,000 out of the million dollars for a new Sunday School at our church.'

The lawyer said, 'I'm shocked at the two of you! I threw in my personal cheque for the entire million dollars.'

The pope arrives in London for a meeting with Tony Blair. He is running late. As he comes out of the airline terminal he hails a cab.

He says to the Cockney cab-driver, 'I have to be at Number 10 in fifteen minutes.'

'Fifteen minutes, guv'nor? Leave it out. We're at Heathrow. This is London! It takes at least an hour. I can't do it!'

'Well, you get out and let me drive,' says the pope.

The cabbie is a bit taken back by this, but it's the pope, so he jumps into the back seat and the pope gets behind the wheel. The pope is enjoying the experience, flying along, dodging in and out of traffic, when he zooms past a policeman on a motorbike waiting in a side-street.

The cop jumps on his motorbike and pursues the speeding vehicle. Finally, he catches up with it, pulls it over, and asks the driver to wind down the window. When he sees who is driving, he gets on his radio.

'This is road patrol to base I need some help,' says the policeman.

'What's up?' asks headquarters.

'Well I've pulled someone over for speeding and he is obviously very important. What should I do?'

'How important is he? A local politician?' asks headquarters.

'No, bigger than that.'

'The Mayor of London?'

'No, bigger than that.'

'Michael Caine?'

'No, bigger than that.'

'Hell, not the prime minister?'

'No, bigger than that'

'Bigger than that?' asks headquarters in a bewildered tone, 'Bleedin hell, who is it?'

'I don't know,' replies the cop, 'but he's got the pope driving him around.'

An old Irishman is lying in bed, very ill. His son is sitting at his bedside, expecting the end to come at any moment. The old man looks up at the boy and says, 'Son, it's time for you to get me a Protestant minister.'

The son is astounded. 'But, dad!' he protests, 'You've been a good Catholic all you life! You're delirious. It's a priest ye be wanting now, not a minister.'

The old man looks up at him and says, 'Son, please. It's me last request. Get a minister for me!'

'But, dad,' cries the son, 'Ye raised me a good Catholic. You've been a good Catholic all your life. Ye don't want a minister at a time like this!'

The old man manages to croak out the words, 'Son, if you respect me and love me as a father, you'll go out and get me a Protestant minister right now.'

The son relents and goes out and gets the minister. They come back to the house, and the minister goes upstairs and converts him. As the minister is leaving the house, he passes Father O'Malley coming quickly through the door.

The minister stares solemnly into the eyes of the priest. 'I'm afraid you're too late, Father,' he says. 'He's a Protestant now.'

Father O'Malley rushes up the steps and bursts into the old man's room. 'Pat! Pat! Why did ye do it?' he cries.

'You were such a good Catholic! We went to St Mary's together! You were there when I performed my first Mass! Why in the world would ye do such a thing as this?'

'Well,' the old man says as he looks up at his dear friend. 'I thought if somebody had to go to hell, it was better a Protestant than one of us.'

Jesus walks into a Holiday Inn, tosses three nails on the counter and asks, 'Can you put me up for the night?'

Three nuns were driving down a highway one day when they lost control of their car and plunged off a cliff. They awoke and found themselves standing before the pearly gates.

St Peter walked toward them and, after greeting them, told them that they would have to answer one question each before they were admitted to the kingdom of heaven. This made the nuns very nervous. They had never heard of this requirement before.

Finally, one nun stepped forward and said, 'St Peter, I'm ready for my question.'

St Peter replied, 'Your question is: Who was the first man on Earth?'

The nun breathed a huge sigh of relief, and said, 'Why, it was Adam.'

The lights flashed, the bells tolled, and the gates of heaven opened. It was a cause of great relief to the others. The second stepped forward without hesitation.

St Peter said, 'And you must tell me who was the first woman on Earth.'

With another great sigh of relief, the nun replied, 'Eve.'

The lights flashed, the bells tolled, and the gates of heaven opened. The third nun was then brimming with excitement. 'I'm ready St Peter!'

St Peter said, 'All right, what was the first thing Eve said to Adam?'

The nun was shocked. 'My goodness, that's a hard one . . .'

The lights flashed, the bells tolled, and the gates of heaven opened.

St Peter is checking IDs outside heaven. He asks a man, 'What did you do on Earth?'

The man says, 'I was a doctor.'

St Peter says, 'Ok, go right through those pearly gates. Next! What did you do on Earth?'

'I was a school teacher.'

'Go right through those pearly gates. Next! And what did you do on Earth?'

'I was a musician.'

'Go around the side, up the freight elevator, through the kitchen.'

Noah's Ark lands after the flood and Noah releases all the animals, saying, 'Go forth and multiply.'

Several months pass and Noah decides to check up on the animals. All are doing fine except a pair of snakes.

'What's the problem?' asks Noah.

'We need help,' say the snakes. 'Could you cut down some trees for us and let us live in them?'

Noah follows their advice. Several more weeks pass and Noah checks up on the snakes again. He sees lots of little snakes; everybody is happy.

Noah says, 'So tell me how the trees helped.'

'Certainly,' reply the snakes. 'We're adders, and we need logs to multiply.'

Pat and Mick were doing some street repairs in front of a known house of ill repute in Boston. A Jewish Rabbi came down the street, looked to the left, looked to the right, and ducked into the house.

Pat paused a bit from swinging his pick and said 'Mick will you look at that! A man of the cloth, and going into a place like that in broad daylight!'

A bit later, a Baptist minister came down the street, looked to the left, looked to the right, and scurried into the house.

Mick laid down his shovel, turned to Pat and said 'Pat! Are you seeing what I'm seeing? A man of the church, and he's giving that place his custom!'

Just then, a Catholic priest came down the street, looked to the left, looked to the right, and slipped into the bawdy house.

Pat and Mick straightened up, removed their hats, and Mick says 'Faith, and there must be somebody sick in there.'

St Peter is checking IDs at the pearly gates, and up comes a Texan.

'Tell me, what did you do in your life?' says St Peter.

The Texan says, 'Well, I struck oil, so I became rich, but I didn't sit on my laurels. I divided all my money among my entire family in my will, so our descendants are all set for about three generations.'

St Peter says, 'That's quite something. Come on in. Next!'

The second guy in line has been listening, so he says, 'I struck it big in the stock market, but I didn't selfishly just provide for my own like that Texan guy. I donated five million to Save the Children.'

'Wonderful!' says St Peter. 'Come in. Who's next?'

The third guy has been listening, and says timidly with a downcast look, 'Well, I only made five thousand dollars in my entire lifetime.'

'Heavens!' says St Peter. 'What instrument did you play?'

Three women die together in an accident and go to heaven. When they get there, St Peter says, 'We only have one rule here in heaven, don't step on the ducks.'

So they enter heaven, and sure enough, there are ducks all over the place. It is almost impossible not to step on a duck, and although they try their best to avoid them, the first woman accidentally steps on one. Along comes St Peter with the ugliest man she ever saw.

St Peter chains them together and says 'Your punishment for stepping on a duck is to spend eternity chained to this ugly man!'

The next day, the second woman steps accidentally on a duck, and along comes St Peter, who doesn't miss a thing, and with him is another extremely ugly man. He chains them together with the same admonishment he gave to the first woman.

The third woman has observed all this and, not wanting to be chained for all eternity to an ugly man, is very, very careful where she steps. She manages to go months without stepping on any ducks, but one day St Peter comes up to her with the most handsome man she has ever laid eyes on. Very tall, long eyelashes, muscular and thin. St Peter chains them together without saying a word.

The woman remarks, 'I wonder what I did to deserve being chained to you for all of eternity?'

The guy says, 'I don't know about you, but I stepped on a duck!'

Jesus came across an adulteress crouching in a corner with a crowd around her preparing to stone her to death. He stopped the crowd and said, 'Let he who is without sin cast the first stone.'

Suddenly a woman at the back of the crowd fired off a stone at the adulteress.

Jesus looked over and said, 'Mother! Sometimes you really piss me off!'

So grimly the Abbot said, 'Look,
Wanking's a sin in my book,
Inadvertent or not.
Tie your dick in a knot
Or start sleeping with Annie the cook.'

Two Irish lads were shacked up with their girlfriends. One felt guilty and decided he should stop at the church and confess.

He went into the confession booth and told the Father, 'Father, I have sinned. I have committed fornication with a lady. Please forgive me.'

The Father said, 'Tell me who the lady was.'

The lad said he couldn't do that and the Father said he couldn't grant him forgiveness unless he did.

'Was it Mollie O'Grady?' asked the Father.

'No.'

'Was it Rosie Kelly?'

'No.'

'Was it that red-headed wench Tessie O'Malley?'

'No.'

'Well then,' said the Father, 'You'll not be forgiven.'

When the lad met his friend outside the friend asked, 'So, did you find forgiveness?'

'No,' said the other, 'but I picked up three good prospects!'

As soon as she had finished convent school, a bright young girl named Lena shook the dust of Ireland off her shoes and made her way to New York where, before long, she became a successful performer in show business.

Eventually she returned to her home town for a visit and on a Saturday night she went to confession in the church that she had always attended as a child.

In the confessional Father Sullivan recognised her and began asking her about her work. She explained that she was an acrobatic dancer, and he wanted to know what that meant. She said she would be happy to show him the kind of thing she did on stage. She stepped out of the confessional and within sight of Father Sullivan, she went into a series of cartwheels, leaping splits, handsprings and back-flips.

Kneeling near the confessional, waiting their turn, were two middle-aged ladies. They witnessed Lena's acrobatics with wide eyes, and one said to the other: 'Will you just look at the penance Father Sullivan is giving out this night, and me without me bloomers on!'

Moses, returning from the mountain, spoke to his people: 'The good news is that we got them down to 10. The bad news is that adultery is still one of them.'

A proud Irishman named Pat went to heaven and met St Peter at the pearly gates.

St Peter asked, 'Who are you?' and Pat replied, 'My name is Pat, I'm an Irishman, born on St Patrick's Day, died on St Patrick's Day, while marching in the St Patrick's Day parade.'

St Peter said to Pat, 'Yes, this is true, and a worthy claim! Here's a little green cloud for you to drive around heaven in and here is a harp that, when you push this button here, will play When Irish Eyes Are Smiling. Enjoy it, Pat. Have a good time in heaven.'

Pat jumps on his little green cloud, punches the button, and heads out with a smile on his face and a song in his heart.

He's having a wonderful time in heaven, driving his little green cloud around, but on the third day, he's driving down Expressway H-1 with the harp playing full blast when, all of a sudden, a Jewish man in a pink and white two-tone cloud with tail fins roars past him. And in the back of this cloud is an organ which is playing all sorts of celestial music. Pat makes a U-turn right in the middle of the Heaven Expressway and charges back to the pearly gates.

He says, 'St Peter, my name is Pat, I'm a proud Irishman. I was born on St Patrick's Day, died on St Patrick's Day, marching in the St Patrick's Day parade. I come up here to heaven and I get this tiny, insignificant little green cloud and this little harp that plays only one song, When Irish Eyes Are Smiling. But, there's a Jew over there. He's got a big, beautiful pink and white two-tone cloud and a huge organ that plays all kinds of celestial music and I, Pat the Irishman, want to know why!'

St Peter stands up from his desk. He leans over and motions Pat to come closer. Then he says, 'Pat, shush! He's the boss' son!'

RIDDLES

Q: Why did God invent whisky?
A: So the Irish would never rule the world.

Q: What do you call a beautiful, sunny day that comes after two cloudy, rainy ones?
A: Monday.

Q: Why don't sharks attack lawyers?
A: Professional courtesy.

Q: Why did the turtle cross the road?
A: To get to the Shell station.

Q: Why did the chicken scientist cross the road?
A: To invent the other side.

Q: Why did the chicken lawyer cross the road?
A: To corrupt the other side.

Q: Why did the chicken lawyer cross the road?
A: To get to the car accident on the other side.

Q: Why do birds fly south?
A: Because it's too far to walk.

Q: Which side of a chicken has the most feathers?
A: The outside.

Q: What do you get when you cross a parrot with a centipede?
A: A walkie-talkie, of course.

Q: Have you heard of that disease that you get from kissing birds?
A: Chirpies. It's one of those canarial diseases. I hear it's untweetable.

Q: Why don't they play poker in the jungle?
A: Too many cheetahs.

Q: What is the difference between a cat and a comma?
A: One has the paws before the claws and the other has the clause before the pause.

Q: What is the wettest animal in the world?
A: A reindeer.

Q: Where do dogs go when they lose their tails?
A: To the retail store.

Q: What kind of dog tells time?
A: A watch dog.

Q: What kind of fish do you find in a bird cage?
A: A perch.

Q: What is the best way to communicate with a fish?
A: Drop it a line.

Q: What happened to the fishing boat that sank in piranha-infested waters?
A: It came back with a skeleton crew.

Q: What's red, white and brown and travels faster than the speed of sound?

A: An astronaut's ham and tomato sandwich.

Q: Which cheese is made backwards?

A: Edam.

Q: What's small, round and white, and giggles?

A: A tickled onion.

Q: What is black and blue and found floating up side down in the Irish Sea?

A: Some dick-flop who tells a stupid Irish joke.

Q: Where do fish wash?

A: In a river basin.

Q: What has four legs and an arm?

A: A happy pit bull.

Q: Why is a tree like a dog?

A: Because they both lose their bark when they die.

Q: What colour is a hiccup?

A: Burple.

Q: Why was the broom late?

A: It overswept.

Q: Can you stand on your head?

A: No, my feet won't reach.

Q: Why did the cannibal live on his own?
A: He'd had his fill of other people.

Q: Why did the demon jump into the conserve?
A: Because he was a jammy devil.

Q: Why did the executioner go to work early?
A: To get a head start.

Q: Why did the vampire go to the orthodontist?
A: To improve his bite.

Q: What did the boa constrictor say to its victim?
A: I've got a crush on you.

Q: What did the bull say to the cow?
A: I'll love you for heifer and heifer.

Q: What did the cat say when it lost all its money?
A: I'm paw.

Q: Did you hear about the cowboy who got himself a dachshund?
A: Everyone kept telling him to get a long, little doggie.

Q: What is the difference between a Rottweiler and a social worker?
A: It is easier to get your kids back from a Rottweiler!

Q: Did you hear about the new breed in pet shops?
A: They crossed a pit bull with a collie. It bites your leg off and then goes for help.

Q: How do you know if there is an elephant under the bed?
A: Your nose is touching the ceiling.

Q: What do you get when you cross an elephant with a rhinoceros?
A: Elephino.

Q: Why did the trout cross the road?
A: Because it was the chicken's day off.

Q: What do you give a seasick elephant?
A: Lots of room.

Q: What kind of sea creature eats its victims two by two?
A: Noah's shark.

Q: How do you stick down an envelope under the water?
A: With a seal.

Q: What should you do if you find a shark in your bed?
A: Sleep somewhere else.

Q: Why did the salmon cross the road?
A: Because it was tied to the chicken.

Q: What is the difference between an introvert and extrovert mathematician?
A: An introvert mathematician looks at his shoes while talking to you. An extrovert mathematician looks at your shoes.

Q: Why do women have breasts?
A: So men will talk to them!

Q: Did you hear about the idiot who walked around the world?
A: He drowned.

Q: What's the quietest place in the world?
A: The complaint department at the parachute-packing plant.

Q: Did Monica like her job at the Pentagon?
A: The work was OK, but the benefits sucked.

Q: If the job was so boring, why didn't she quit?
A: She didn't want to blow another opportunity.

Q: What's the difference between Monica Lewinsky and the rest of us?
A: When we want some dick in the white house, we just vote.

Q: To which preacher did Bill go for advice?
A: Oral Roberts.

Q: How did Hillary Clinton feel?
A: She may have been the first lady, but she certainly won't be the last!

Q: Why doesn't Monica eat bananas?
A: She can't find the zipper.

Q: How did Bill reply regarding questions of 'coaching' Monica's testimony?
A: It wasn't words that I put in her mouth.

Q: How many times can you subtract 7 from 83, and what is left afterwards?
A: As many times as I want, and it always leaves 76.

Q: What is the difference between a psychotic, a neurotic and a mathematician?

A: A Psychotic believes that 2+2 = 5. A Neurotic knows that 2+2 = 4, but it kills him. A Mathematician simply changes the base.

Q: What is the difference between a chemist and a mathematician?
A: To mathematicians, solutions mean finding the answers. But to chemists, solutions are things that are still all mixed up.

Q: What do you call a small fish magician?
A: A magic carpet.

Q: What is the difference between philosophy and mathematics?
A: Philosophy is a game with objectives and no rules. Mathematics is a game with rules and no objectives.

Q: What is the difference between a statistician and an accountant?
A: A statistician is someone who is good with numbers but lacks the personality to be an accountant.

Q: What is the difference between an engineer, a mathematician and a physicist?
A: An engineer thinks that his equations are an approximation of reality. A physicist thinks reality is an approximation of his equations. A mathematician doesn't care.

Q: Why do musicians have to be awake by six?
A: Because most shops close by six thirty.

SPORT

RACING

Racehorse doping is not unknown in Ireland. One day, the clerk of the course spotted a trainer giving something to a horse just before the start of a race.

He went over and said, 'Doping?'

The trainer said, 'Indeed not, Sor. Tis just a lump of sugar. Look, I'll take a bit meself . . . see?'

The clerk of the course said, 'Sorry, but we have to be careful. As a matter of fact, I like a bit of sugar meself.'

So the trainer gave him a piece. When the clerk of the course disappeared, the trainer gave his jockey his last minute instructions.

'Don't forget the drill,' he said. 'Hold him in 'til the last four furlongs. And don't worry if anything passes ye. It'll either be me or the clerk of the course!'

BASEBALL

St Peter and Satan were having an argument one day about baseball. Satan proposed a game to be played on neutral grounds between a select team from the heavenly host and some of his own hand-picked boys.

'Very well,' said the gatekeeper of heaven. 'But you realise, I hope, that we've got all the good players and the best coaches.'

'I know, and that's all right,' Satan answered unperturbed. 'We've got all the umpires.'

SOCCER

A burglary was recently committed at the West Ham United ground and the entire contents of the trophy room were stolen. The police are looking for a man with a roll of claret and blue carpet.

Q: How does David Beckham change a light bulb?
A: He holds it in the air, and the world revolves around him.

The West Ham squad were offered an all-expenses paid holiday to Florida but they said they'd rather go to Blackpool so they could see what it's like to ride on an open-top bus.

The Fire brigade phones the manager of Tottenham Hotspur, in the early hours of Sunday morning.
'Boss, White Hart Lane is on fire!'
'The cups man! Save the cups!' cries the manager.
'Uh, the fire hasn't spread to the canteen yet, sir.'

A primary teacher starts a new job at a school on Merseyside and, trying to make a good impression on her first day, explains to her class that she is a Liverpool fan. She asks her students to raise their hands if they, too, are Liverpool fans. Everyone in the class raises their hand except one little girl.

The teacher looks at the girl with surprise and says: 'Mary, why didn't you raise your hand?'

'Because I'm not a Liverpool fan,' she replies.

The teacher, still shocked, asks: 'Well, if you're not a Liverpool fan, then who are you a fan of?'

'I'm a Manchester United fan, and proud of it,' Mary replies.

The teacher cannot believe her ears. 'Mary, why are you a United fan?'

'Because my mum and dad are from Manchester, and my mum is a United fan and my dad is a United fan, so I'm a United fan too!'

'Well,' says the teacher, in an annoyed tone, 'that's no reason for you to be a United fan. You don't have to be just like your parents all of the time. What if your mum was a prostitute and your dad was a drug addict and a car thief, what would you be then?'

'Then,' Mary smiles, 'I'd be a Liverpool fan.'

ACTUAL SPORTS QUOTES

'Nobody in football should be called a genius. A genius is a guy like Norman Einstein.'
- Football commentator and former player Joe Theismann 1996.

'You guys line up alphabetically by height.' and 'You guys pair up in groups of three, then line up in a circle.'
- Bill Peterson, a Florida state football coach.

'Why would anyone expect him to come out smarter? He went to prison for three years, not Princeton.'
- Boxing promoter Dan Duva on Mike Tyson hooking up again with promoter Don King.

'That's so when I forget how to spell my name, I can still find my bloody clothes.'
- Stu Grimson, Chicago Blackhawks left wing, explaining why he keeps a colour photo of himself above his locker.

'I can't really remember the names of all the nightclubs that we went to.'
- Shaquille O'Neal replying to a question about whether he had visited the Parthenon during his visit to Greece.

'He's a guy who gets up at 6am regardless of what time it is.'
- Lou Duva, veteran boxing trainer, on the Spartan training regime of heavyweight Andrew Golota.

'We can't win at home. We can't win on the road. As general manager, I just can't work out where else to play.'
- Pat Williams, Orlando Magic general manager, on his team's 7-27 record.

'My sister's expecting a baby, and I don't know if I'm going to be an uncle or an aunt.'
- Chuck Nevitt, North Carolina state basketball player, explaining to Coach Jim Valvano why he appeared nervous at practice.

'I'm going to send the injured reserve players out for the toss next time.'
- Mike McCormack, coach of the hapless Baltimore Colts after the team's co-captain, offensive guard Robert Pratt, pulled a hamstring running onto the field for the coin toss against St Louis.

'I'm not allowed to comment on lousy officiating.'

- Jim Finks, New Orleans Saints general manager, when asked after a loss what he thought of the refs.

'It's basically the same, just darker.'
- Alan Kulwicki, stock car racer, on racing Saturday nights as opposed to Sunday afternoons.

'I told him, "Son, what is it with you. Is it ignorance or apathy?" He said, "Coach, I don't know and I don't care."'
- Frank Layden, Utah Jazz president, on a former player.

'He treats us like men. He lets us wear earrings.'
– Torrin Polk, University of Houston receiver, on his coach, John Jenkins.

'Son, looks to me like you're spending too much time on one subject.'
– Shelby Metcalf, basketball coach at Texas A&M, recounting what he told a player who received four Fs and one D in his studies.

'I'd run over my own mother to win the Super Bowl.'
– Joe Jacoby of the Skins.

'To win, I'd run over Joe's mum too.'
– Matt Millen of the Raiders.

NOTICE TO THE MANCHESTER OLYMPIC COMMITTEE

In an attempt to influence the members of the international Olympic committee on their choice of venue for the games in the year 2004, the organisers of Manchester's bid drew up an itinerary and schedule of events. A copy has been leaked and is reproduced below.

Opening Ceremony

The Olympic flame will be ignited by a petrol bomb thrown by a native of the city, wearing the traditional balaclava. The flame will be contained in a large chip van situated on the roof of the stadium.

Events

In previous Olympic Games, Manchester's competitors have not been particularly successful. In order to redress the balance, some of the events have been altered slightly to the advantage of local Manchester athletes.

100m Sprint

Competitors will have to hold a video recorder and microwave oven (one in each arm) and on the sound of the starting pistol, a police dog will be released from a cage 10m behind the athletes.

100m Hurdles

As above, but with added obstacles (ie car bonnets, hedges, gardens, fences walls etc)

Hammer

Competitors in this event may choose the type of hammer they wish to use – claw, sledge etc. The winner will be the one who can cause the most grievous bodily harm to members of the public within the time allowed.

Fencing

Entrants will be asked to dispose of as much stolen silver and jewellery as possible in five minutes.

Shooting

A strong challenge is expected from the local men in this event. The first target will be a moving police van. In the second round, competitors will aim at a post office clerk, bank teller or a wages delivery man.

Boxing

Entry to the boxing will be restricted to husband and wife teams, and will take place on a Friday night. The husband will be given 15 pints of lager while the wife will be told not to make him any tea when he gets home. The bout will then commence.

Cycling Time Trials

Competitors will be asked to break into the university bike shed and take an expensive mountain bike owned by some mummy's boy from the country on his first trip away from home. All against the clock.

Cycling Pursuit

As above, but the bike will be owned by a visiting member of the Australian rugby team, who will witness the theft.

Modern Pentathlon

Amended to five new disciplines: Mugging, Breaking and Entering, Flashing, Joy-Riding and Arson.

Marathon

A safe route has yet to be decided, but the competitors will be issued with sharp sticks and bags with which to pick up litter on their way round the course.

Swimming

Competitors will be thrown off the bridge over the ship canal. The first three survivors to make it back will decide the medals.

Men's 50km Walk

Unfortunately this will have to be cancelled as the police can't guarantee the safety of anyone walking the streets of Manchester.

Closing Ceremony

Entertainment will include formation rave dancing in the community by a happy band of anti-drug campaigners, synchronised rock throwing and music by the Stockport Community Choir. The Olympic flame will be extinguished by someone dropping an old washing machine onto it from the top floor of the block of flats next to the stadium. The stadium will then be boarded up before the local athletes break into it and remove all the copper piping and the central heating boiler.

15 WAYS TO PREPARE FOR THE SKI SEASON

1. Throw away a $100 note – now.
2. Buy a new pair of gloves. Immediately throw one away.
3. Drive slowly for five hours – anywhere – as long as it's in a snowstorm and you're following a semi-trailer.
4. Find the nearest ice rink and walk across the ice 20 times in your ski boots carrying two pairs of skis, accessory bag and poles. Pretend you are looking for your car, while sporadically dropping things.
5. Go to McDonald's and insist on paying $18.50 for a hamburger. Be sure you are in the longest line.
6. Clip a lift ticket to the zipper of your jacket and ride a motorcycle fast enough to make the ticket lacerate your face.
7. Dress up in as many clothes as you can and then proceed to take them off because you have to go to the bathroom.
8. Visit your local butcher and pay $50 to sit in the walk-in freezer for a half an hour. Afterwards, burn two $100 bills to warm up.
9. Soak your gloves and store them in the freezer after every use.
10. If you wear glasses, begin wearing them with glue smeared on the lenses.
11. Place a small but angular pebble in your shoes, line them with crushed ice, and then tighten a C-clamp around your toes.
12. Secure one of your ankles to a bed post and ask a friend to run into you at high speed.
13. Fill a blender with ice, hit the pulse button and let the spray blast your face. Leave the ice on your face until it melts. Let it drip into your clothes.
14. Slam your thumb in a car door. Don't go see a doctor.
15. Go and see your mate with the yacht – it's the same sort of rich guy's sport – and ask him to sail you to Antarctica and dump you on an iceberg for three weeks.

RUGBY

An English family of Rugby supporters head out one Saturday to do their Christmas shopping. While in the sports shop, the son picks up a Scotland rugby shirt and says to his sister, 'I've decided to be a Scotland Supporter and I would like this for Christmas.'

His sister thinks the colours are cute, but is outraged by this, and promptly whacks him round the head and says, 'Go talk to Mum.'

So off goes the little lad with the blue rugby shirt in hand and finds his mother. 'Mum?'

'Yes My darling?' she says.

'I've decided I'm going to be a Scotland supporter and I would like this shirt for Christmas.'

The mother is outraged at this, promptly whacks him around the head and says, 'Go talk to your father.'

Off he goes with the rugby shirt in hand and finds his father. 'Dad?'

'Yes Johnny my boy?'

'I've decided I'm going to be a Scotland supporter and I would like this shirt for Christmas.'

The father is outraged and promptly whacks his son around the head and says, 'No son of mine is ever going to be seen in that!'

About half an hour later, they're all back in the car and heading towards home.

The father turns to his son and says 'Son, I hope you've learned something today?'

The son says, 'Yes, indeed I have dad.'

'Good son, what is it?'

The son replies, 'I've only been a Scotland supporter for an hour and already I hate you English bastards.'

A South African walks into a bar with his dog to watch a rugby game. The barman says no dogs allowed, but the man insists his dog should be allowed because it is well behaved.

The barman reluctantly agrees and shortly after, the South Africans score a field goal. The dog dances on the table, gives high fives to the drinkers and sings.

All the other people in the bar say 'Wow, that's really amazing. What happens if South Africa score a try?'

The South African replies, 'Dunno, only had him for three years!'

An Australian man was on the way to Wimbledon one Saturday, when he stepped into a pub just near Southfields tube station to watch the rugby. He considered himself a patriotic man, but watching rugby in England amongst a sea of red, it was sometimes better to be diplomatically silent.

However, a group of Aussies had already camped themselves in a corner and were gearing up for a bit of banter. A conversation between two Aussies followed, one of them obviously Victorian, and an Aussie Rules fan, as he didn't know anything about rugby.

'The team is made up of the best players from Ireland, England, Wales and Scotland,' his mate told him.

'So it's an all-star team then?'

'Not really.'

'But four countries, five countries if you count Northern Ireland as a separate country, against one. Is that fair?'

His mate looked around for help. Our friend told him about the tradition of the Lions and the enormous interest they create. As the game progressed, and the Aussie corner became more and more invisible, the Victorian spoke up again.

'If they're so good, how did we become the world champions?'

'They can't play in the World Cup,' came the reply.

'So, in the scheme of things, this means absolutely nothing.'

His mate looked like the straight man in a comedy duo. As the English became more and more rowdy, the Victorian became more and more patriotic.

One Englishmen threw a comment his way: 'You're getting killed, you dirty Aussie bastards!'

The Victorian launched into him.

'Five countries versus one. A country of 20 million, where only two states play the game. Even those two states divide the best players into rugby league and rugby union. What the hell are you so proud of?'

The last time the pope was in Australia he found himself contemplating the beauty of a river deep in the wilds of the Northern Territory when a sudden commotion on the far shore attracted his attention. There, in the jaws of a massive crocodile was a man wearing an All Black jersey, desperately struggling to get free.

Right at that moment, three blokes wearing Wallaby jerseys roared into view on a speedboat. The first bloke fired a harpoon into the crocodile's ribs, while the other two reached and pulled the Kiwi from the river and, using long clubs, beat the croc to death. They bundled the bleeding, semi-conscious man into the speedboat along with the dead croc and then prepared for a hasty retreat.

The pope was amazed by this, and summoned them to the shore. Curious, they went over, and the pope said to them: 'I give you my best papal blessing for your brave actions. I had heard that there is a racist xenophobic divide between Australia and New Zealand but now I have seen with my own eyes that this is not true. I can see that your two societies are true examples of racial harmony and could serve as a model for other nations to follow.'

He blessed them and drove off in a cloud of dust.

As he departed, the harpoonist turned to the other Aussies and asked: 'Who the bloody hell was that?'

'That', one answered, 'was his Holiness the Pope. He is in direct contact with God and has access to all God's wisdom.'

'Well,' the harpoonist replied, 'He knows nothing about croc hunting! Now,' he continued, pointing to the bloke in the All Black jersey, 'will this bait still work, or do we need to get another one?'

RUGBY WORLD CUP – ROUGH GUIDE FOR VICTORIANS

Every four years, 20 Rugby teams compete for the title of 'World Champions'. This is a bit like being AFL champions. Each of the 20 teams represents a different country. Most of the teams are very similar to one of the AFL teams, and they even have club songs (called 'national anthems').

Just think of the corresponding AFL club and you can't go wrong.

New Zealand = Collingwood. Appear to be top notch, and think it's their destiny to win - but rarely do, much to everyone's delight.

England = Port Adelaide. Chokers - most of the time.

Australia = Brisbane. Always seem to win the games that matter - somehow.

France = Sydney - Underestimated.

South Africa = Essendon. Not as good as they used to be.

Ireland = St Kilda. Sentimental favourites but never do much.

Wales = Hawthorn. Were good once - A long time ago.

Scotland = Geelong - Skirt wearers and too inconsistent to threaten.

Argentina	=	Fremantle. Better than they used to be, but not there yet.
Italy	=	Richmond. Long haired pretty boys.
Samoa	=	Melbourne. Mystery men.
Fiji	=	West Coast. Entertainers, and that's all.
Canada	=	Western Bulldogs. Love a scrap.
USA	=	Adelaide. Everyone wants to beat them.
Georgia	=	Kangaroos. No supporters.
Tonga	=	Carlton, in a hole but look neat in their strips.
Namibia	=	Carlton mark II.
Uruguay	=	Carlton mark III.
Japan	=	Carlton mark IV.
Romania	=	Carlton mark V.

Wiremoocow, a New Zealander, landed in England to watch the All Blacks and was not feeling well, so he decided to see a doctor.

'Hey doc, I don't feel so good, eh' said Wiremoocow.

The doctor gives him a thorough examination and informs Wiremoocow that he has prostate problems, and that the only cure is an immediate testicular removal.

'No way doc, I'm here for the rugby' replied Wiremoocow 'I'm gitting a sicond opinion. 'ey!'

The second English doctor gave Wiremoocow the same diagnosis and also advised him that testicular removal was the only cure.

Not surprisingly, Wiremoocow refused the treatment. He was devastated but, with only hours to go before the All Blacks opening game he found an expatriate Kiwi doctor and decided to get one last opinion from someone he could trust.

The Kiwi doctor examined him and said, 'Wiremoocow, you huv prostate suckness, 'ey'.

'What's the cure thin doc, 'ey?' asked Wiremoocow hoping for a different answer.

'Wull, Wiremoocow', said the Kiwi doctor 'Wi're gonna huv to cut off your balls.'

'Phew, thunk gud for thut!' said Wiremoocow, 'those Pommy bastards wanted to take my test tickets off me!'

POSITIONS IN RUGBY

Front Row

Without a doubt the manliest men on the pitch.

Large, often hairy, beer swilling carnivores that can and will smash anything in their path. Revelling in the violence inherent in the scrum, they are rarely considered 'nice' humans, and in fact to some they aren't even considered human at all.

This attitude is tolerated by front-rowers far and wide because they recognise their role at the top of the food chain and are used to suffering the fools that surround them. Accused by some of simply being dumb, it's more about being 'open to unconventional ways of thinking'.

Locks

Slightly below the front row on the food chain.

As with front row players it is inadvisable to be anywhere near them when they are in the feeding mode. This group of large, often foul-smelling brutes is also more than willing to relish the finer points of stomping on a fallen opponent's body.

While they tend to take the tag 'powerhouse of the scrum' a little too seriously, they can be useful if inured with the proper hatred of their fellow man.

Back Row Numbers 6, 7 & 8

These are fine fit fellows, confused as to what their role in life should be.

While they know they are undeniably linked to the forwards,

there are those among them who long for the perfect hair and long flowing gowns that come with being a back.

Some relish the forward role and will do anything to win the ball and there are others within this group that will break the prime directive of the forward and do anything to prance foolishly with the ball.

Scrum Half

Some like to think of this back as an honorary forward. The scrum half's presence is tolerated by the forwards because they know that he will spin the ball to the rest of the backline who will inevitably knock the ball on and allow them the pleasure of another scrum.

The scrum half can take pride in the fact that he is the lowest numbered back and that as such he can be considered almost worthwhile.

Fly Half

Primary role is the leader of the backs – a dubious honour at best.

Main responsibilities are the ability to throw the ball over people's heads and to provide something soft for opposing back rowers to land on.

The fly half is expected to direct the prancing of the rest of the backline. While some may argue that the fly halfs must be protected, it is hard to support anyone whose foot touches a rugby ball on purpose.

Centres

Usually come in two varieties – hard charger or flitting fairy. The hard charger is the one to acquire as he will announce his presence in a game with an authority rarely found. The flitting fairy is regrettably more common and will usually attempt to avoid contact at all costs.

Both types will have extensive collections of hair-care products in their kit bags and will be among the best dressed at the post-game festivities.

Back Three

Some people refer to this group as two wingers and a fullback.

How these three guys can play 80 minutes of rugby and stay clean and sweat free is beyond all reason.

These guys will be easy to spot after the game because they are the sweater-wearing, wine-sipping, sweet-talking, finely coifed guys in the corner avoiding the beer swilling at the bar.

The Wallabies were about to play the All Blacks at Eden Park. On the morning of the match, stand-in manager Ross Turnbull talked to the team, then asked the backs to leave him alone with the forwards.

'Look,' he said, waving an airy hand at the just-departed backs, 'those Phantom comic–swappers and mintie-eaters, those blonde flyweights are one thing, and we'll need them after the hard work is done. But the real stuff's got to be done right here by you blokes.'

Johnnie Wilkinson goes into the England changing room to find all his team mates looking a bit glum.

'What's up?' he asks.

'Well, we're having trouble getting motivated for this game,' says one guy. 'We know it's important but we've just beaten the All Blacks and Australia in consecutive weeks and let's be honest, it's only South Africa. They're shite and we can't be bothered.'

Johnnie looks at them and says 'Well, the way I've been playing recently, I reckon I can beat them by myself, you lads can go down the pub.'

So Johnnie goes out to play South Africa by himself and the

rest of the England team go off for a few jars. After a few pints they wonder how the game is going, so they get the landlord to put the telly on.

A big cheer goes up as the screen reads 'England 7 – South Africa 0 (Wilkinson – 10 minutes – Converted Try)'.

Wilkinson is beating South Africa all by himself! The telly goes off and a few more pints later the game is forgotten until someone remembers, 'It must be full time now, let's see how Johnnie got on.'

They put the telly back on.

'Result from the Stadium: England 7 (Wilkinson 10 minutes) South Africa 7 (Pause 79 minutes).'

They can't believe it, Johnnie has single-handedly got a draw against South Africa and maintained England's unbeaten run at home! They rush back to the Stadium to congratulate him. They find him in the dressing room, still in his gear, seated with his head in his hands. He refuses to look at them.

'I've let you down, I've let you down.' says Johnnie.

'Don't be daft, you got a draw against South Africa, all by yourself. And they only scored at the very, very end!' say the rest of the team.

'No, No, I have let you down,' says Wilkinson, 'I've let you and the whole country down . . . I got sent off after 12 minutes.'

RUGBY TERMS

Blind side:	The side of the pitch on which there is no action. It is where all the smart players retreat to avoid injury.
Dummy (silly dummy):	The person who replaces an injured hooker. It can also be a ruse whereby the player pretends to pass the ball, but in actual fact, doesn't. Dangerous, but clever.

Foul:	When the dirty bastards on the other side get physical. If your side gets physical it's just tough play and is to be admired.
Offside:	Something that not even the ref understands, something to do with the ball and the line of play and not going in front of it.
Possession:	When you have it and they don't. Very desirable.
Ruck:	The pack of big, ugly dangerous men that forms in anticipation of the ball being thrown in from the sideline.
Side step:	The smart person's way of stepping carefully aside to let the marauding crowd descend upon the ball.

Springbok rugby practice was delayed nearly two hours today after a player reported finding an unknown white powdery substance on the practice field. The head coach immediately suspended practice while police were called to investigate.

After a complete analysis, forensic experts determined that the white substance unknown to players was the try-line. Practice was resumed after special agents decided the team was unlikely to encounter the substance again.

Each member of a rugby union team was issued with an individual heart-rate monitor, similar to a watch, which, after exercise, could download data into a computer to measure resting heart rates, heart rates during exercise, rate of recovery etc.

In addition to the scheduled team training, each player was required to do a session by themselves each day, wearing the heart-rate monitor.

When one of the players, Johnny, handed in his monitor and the information was downloaded, the medical staff became seriously alarmed. They urgently called Johnny and asked if he had done his additional training.

'Yes.' he replied, looking a little strained.

'What did you do?' they asked.

'A big sprint session down at my local park,' he replied. 'Why, what's the problem?'

'The monitor reported 300 beats per minute – at that rate the human body cannot survive.'

'What do you mean the human body? I strapped the monitor on my Rottweiler and made him chase balls for the session.'

BACKYARD CRICKET

Rules

1a. You can't get out on the first ball.

1b. Caught behind – Since no one has the desire or the reflexes to stand in the slips cordon, an edge onto the back fence constitutes instant dismissal.

1c. One hand, one bounce – A fielder can dismiss a batsman by catching the ball in one hand on the first bounce. Note that this rule only applies when the fielder is holding a beer in their other hand.

1d. No LBW: When no umpires are available (or trustworthy), the only option is to can the LBW rule altogether.

1e. Six and out (then fetch it).

1f. Standard over – All veteran backyard bowlers know that the standard length of an over in backyard cricket ranges from anything between 10-12 balls. You only relinquish the bowling duties when questioned by any fielders or opposing team members. But only after the standard response of 'two to come'.

Essential Gear & Equipment

2a. Esky – Strategically placed at the bowler's end, the esky is the shrine of backyard cricket – because it holds the beer.

2b. Balls – A minimum of three tennis balls is advised, as there's always some smart-arse who takes delight in whacking them over the fence.

2c. Dog – Preferably of kelpie or heeler extraction, so it can field every ball, including those that disappear under the house or into thorny bushes.

2d. Rubbish bin – It would be nice to think you can clean up your own mess, but in reality the bin makes a perfect set of stumps.

2e. Bat – It's usually old and battered, with no grip and boasting a fake signature of Merv Hughes.

Code of Ethics

3a. Stumps – The game draws to a close when your host finally cooks the snags after the barbie has run out of gas or the last ball is hit onto the road and it disappears down the drain or you can't get that batsman out with any type of bowling pace or spin or your girlfriend cracks the shits and wants to go home.

3b. Flower damage – All members of both your own and the opposing team will help hide the fact that you have just topped your girlfriend's roses.

3c. Spilt Beer – Ideally, the offending batsman should apologise profusely and offer to replace the stubbie. He will be required to get one for everyone else while he is there.

3d. No running between wickets – The words fun and run don't go together. How the hell are you supposed to run in thongs?

3e. Courtesy call – Always invite the chicks to have a bat. They usually say no, but if they say yes get them out and send them back to making the salads.

TELEPHONE TALES

ANSWERING SERVICE AT A MENTAL INSTITUTE

Hello, and welcome to the mental health hotline.
If you are obsessive-compulsive, press one repeatedly.

If you are co-dependent, please ask someone to press two for you.

If you have multiple personalities, press three, four, five and six.

If you are paranoid, we know who you are and what you want. Stay on the line so we can trace your call.

If you are delusional, press seven and your call will be transferred to the mother ship.

If you are schizophrenic, listen carefully and a small voice will tell you which number to press.

If you are manic depressive, it doesn't matter which number you press, no one will answer.

If you have a nervous disorder, please fidget with the hash key until someone comes on the line.

If you are dyslexic, press 6969696969.

If you have amnesia, press eight and state your name, address, phone number, date of birth, social security number, and your mother's maiden name.

If you have post-traumatic-stress disorder, slowly and carefully press 000.

If you have bipolar disorder, please leave a message after the beep, or before the beep, or after the beep. Please wait for the beep.

If you have short-term memory loss, press nine. If you have short term memory loss, press nine. If you have short term memory loss, press nine. If you have short term memory loss, press nine.

If you have low self esteem, please hang up. All our operators are too busy to talk to you.

TELEMARKETER TORTURE 2004

What to do when your dinner is interrupted by a keen telemarketer on the phone:

Go absolutely silent.

Breather slowly and heavily into the phone.

Mumble: 'I like to watch.'

Pretend that this is a call that you are expecting from the child psychologist in relation to your troubled and disruptive teenage son.

Ask them if they are selling beer.

Start speaking in another language.

Tell them the person they want doesn't live here anymore. Give them the number of a phone sex line and tell them that it is the new number.

Tell them that you're not here right now.

Start selling them something else.

Tell them you're poor and ask for money.

Start preaching your religion to them.

Try to hypnotise them.

Put on some really annoying music and put the phone up to the stereo.

Ask the telemarketer if s/he is single. Then try hitting on him/her. Be sure to mention your various medical problems and your fascination with odd smells.

Use a voice changer to disguise your voice.

Rap all your replies to the telemarketer's questions.

Ask the telemarketer if s/he minds if you talk to him/her on the toilet. Then take a plastic sauce bottle and squeeze out sauce repeatedly.

Try to rhyme with everything the telemarketer says.

Sell them on the 'value of high colonics'. Explain your 'dedication to good health' in your most convincing, passionate voice.

Start talking about your many medical ailments and don't allow the telemarketer to get a word in.

TOILET HUMOUR

SOME THINGS TO PONDER ON THE LOO

- If all the world is a stage, where is the audience sitting?
- If all is not lost, where is it?
- If God dropped acid, would he see people?
- What's the speed of dark?
- If you're in hell and mad at someone, where do you tell them to go?
- What happens if you were scared half to death twice?
- How is it possible to have a civil war?
- If only the good die young, what does that say about senior citizens?
- How can you be alone with someone?
- If corn oil comes from corn, where does baby oil come from?
- What do sheep count when they can't get to sleep?
- If it's tourist season, why can't we shoot them?
- Why do they call it instant credit, when it actually means instant debt?
- If we're not supposed to eat late-night snacks, why is there a light in the refrigerator?
- Why is it called a TV set, when you only get one?
- Did God create man before woman, because He didn't want any advice?
- Isn't it scary that doctors call what they do 'practice'?
- Why do they sterilise needles for a lethal injection?
- Can a blonde play an AM radio in the evening?
- Why are they called 'apartments', when they're all stuck together?

- Does a heavy voice on the phone mean I should not go to bed with that person?
- How come wrong numbers are never busy?
- If a word in the dictionary was misspelled, how would we know?
- If space is a vacuum, who changes the bags?
- Where do they keep daylight savings time?
- Why do banks charge you an 'insufficient funds' fee when they know you don't have any funds?
- If the No 2 pencil is the most popular why is it still No 2?
- Can a stupid person be a smart-arse?
- Why is the time of day with the slowest traffic called rush hour?
- Since Australians throw rice at weddings, do Asians throw meat pies?
- When God rested on the seventh day, what did He do?
- And if He played golf, did he set a course record?
- If man evolved from monkeys and apes, why are there still monkeys and apes?
- Do they give pilots crash courses in flight school?
- Is killing time a crime?
- When I erase a word with a pencil, where does it go?
- How do you get off a non-stop flight?
- If you're sending someone Styrofoam, what do you pack it in?
- How do you write zero in Roman numerals?
- Can you buy a full chess set in a pawn shop?
- Why is the third hand on a watch called the second hand?
- Why don't people in Australia call the rest of the world 'up over'?
- If all those psychics know the winning lottery numbers, why are they still working for a living?
- How did a fool and his money get together in the first place?
- Why doesn't the fattest man in the world become a goalie?
- How can someone draw a blank?

- Before they invented drawing boards, what did they go back to?
- How come Superman can stop a bullet with his chest but always ducks when someone throws a gun at him?
- Why do we wait till a pig is dead before we cure it?
- When everything is coming your way, are you in the wrong lane?
- If tin whistles are made out of tin, what are fog horns made out of?
- Can vegetarians eat animal crackers?
- Is Santa always jolly because he knows where all the bad girls live?

MORE THINGS TO PONDER ON THE LOO

- All those who believe in psychokinesis raise my hand.
- Ambition is a poor excuse for not having enough sense to be lazy.
- Beauty is in the eye of the beer holder.
- Black holes are where God divided by zero.
- Corduroy pillows – they're making headlines!
- Drink 'til she's cute, but stop before the wedding.
- Eagles may soar, but weasels don't get sucked into jet engines.
- Energizer Bunny arrested, charged with battery.
- Everyone has a photographic memory, but some don't have any film.
- Excuses are like arses – everyone's got em and they all stink.
- For Sale: Parachute. Only used once, never opened, small stain.
- Give a man a free hand and he'll run it all over you.
- How do you tell when you run out of invisible ink?
- I almost had a psychic girlfriend but she left me before we met.
- I couldn't repair your brakes, so I made your horn louder.
- I drive way too fast to worry about cholesterol.
- I intend to live forever – so far, so good.
- I love defenceless animals, especially in good gravy.
- I poured Spot remover on my dog. Now he's gone.

- I used to have an open mind but my brains kept falling out.
- If Barbie is so popular, why do you have to buy her friends?
- If everything seems to be going well, you have obviously overlooked something.
- If I worked as much as others, I would do as little as they do.
- If you ain't making waves, you ain't kicking hard enough!
- If you choke a Smurf, what colour does it turn?
- Join the army, meet interesting people, kill them.
- Laughing stock – cattle with a sense of humour.
- Many people quit looking for work when they find a job.
- Quantum Mechanics – The dreams stuff is made of.
- Shin – a device for finding furniture in the dark.
- Support bacteria – they're the only culture some people have.
- The early bird gets the worm, but the second mouse gets the cheese.
- The only substitute for good manners is fast reflexes.
- Wear short sleeves – support your right to bare arms!
- When I'm not in my right mind, my left mind gets pretty crowded.
- Who is General Failure and why is he reading my hard disk?
- Why do psychics have to ask you for your name?

EVEN MORE THINGS TO PONDER ON THE LOO

- A planetarium puts on all-star shows.
- A plastic surgeon's office is the only place where no one gets offended when you pick your nose.
- If a cow laughed, would milk come out her nose?
- If a no-armed man has a gun, is he armed?
- If a shop is open 24 hours a day, 365 days a year, why are there locks on the doors?
- If a turtle doesn't have a shell, is he homeless or naked?
- If nothing ever sticks to Teflon, how do they make Teflon stick to the pan?

- If swimming is so good for the figure, how then do you explain whales?
- If you cross a four-leaf clover with poison ivy, would you get a rash of good luck?
- If you crossed an electric blanket with a toaster, would you pop out of bed quicker in the morning?
- If you feed gunpowder to a chicken do you get an eggsplosion?
- If you get into a taxi and the driver starts driving backwards, does s/he owe you money?
- If you tied buttered toast to the back of a cat and dropped it from a height, which way would it end up?
- Is it is bad luck to be superstitious?
- Is it OK to use your AM radio in the afternoon?
- Is it true that cannibals won't eat clowns because they taste funny?
- Is there another word for synonym?
- Smoking kills, and if you're killed, you've lost a very important part of your life.
- The trouble with most referees is that they don't care who wins.
- What do people in China call their best plates?
- What do you call a male ladybird?
- What was the best thing before sliced bread?
- When dog food is new and improved, who tested it?
- Who says nothing is impossible? Some people do it every day.
- Why didn't Noah swat those two mosquitoes?
- Why doesn't glue stick to the inside of the bottle?
- Why is a carrot more orange than an orange?
- Why is abbreviated such a long word?
- Why is it that when a door is open, it's ajar, yet when a jar is open, it's not a door?
- Why isn't phonetic spelled the way it sounds?
- Why isn't there mouse-flavoured cat food?
- Would a fly without wings be called a walk?

As the elevator car left our floor,
Big Sue caught her tits in the door;
She yelled a good deal,
But had they been real,
She'd have yelled considerably more.

A crooner who lived in Lahore
Got his balls caught up in a door.
Now his mezzo soprano
Is rather piano
Though he was a loud basso before.

There was a young fellow of Chiselhurst
Who never could piss till he'd whistled first.
One evening in June
He lost track of the tune,
'Dum-da-dee' was all, then his bladder burst!

There was a young man of Loch Leven
Who went for a walk about seven.
He fell into a pit
That was brimful of shit,
And now the poor bugger's in heaven.

Three lunatics were walking down the road when they came
across a huge pile of shit.
The first loony put his eye in it and said, 'Look's like shit'.
The next one put his nose in it and said, 'Smell's like shit.'
The last one put his tongue in it and said, 'Taste's like shit.'
They all looked at each other and said, 'Lucky we did not
stand in it!'

DIFFERENT TYPES OF POO

Clean poo: The kind you poo out, and see it in the toilet, but there is nothing on the toilet paper.

Corn poo: Self explanatory.

Gassy poo: It's so noisy, everyone within earshot is giggling.

Gee-I-wish-I-could-poo-poo: The kind where you know you want to poo but all you can muster are a few farts.

Ghost poo: The kind where you feel the poo come out, you hear the splash but there is no trace of the poo in the toilet.

Log pooh: The kind of poo that is so huge you are afraid to flush it for fear of blocking the S-bend.

Mexican poo: It smells so bad that even you gag.

Pop-a-vein-in-your-forehead-poo: The kind where you strain so much to get it out, you practically have a stroke.

Second-wave poo: This happens when you think you are all done, you've pulled up your pants and then you realise that there is an encore.

Surprise poo: You didn't even know that you wanted to poo! You were just here on other business.

Upper-class poo: The kind that doesn't smell at all.

Wet cheeks poo: The power dump! The kind that propels itself out with such force that the splash hits your cheeks. On your face.

Wet poo: The kind where you wipe your bottom 50 times and it still ain't clean.

A man had been admitted to the local hospital with dysentery after a safari trip to Africa. He had spent three miserable days on a liquid diet trying to recuperate, and smile as best he could while visitors stopped in to wish him well and hope he didn't have an attack of diarrhoea.

The nurse knocked on his door, peeked in, and informed him that he had more visitors on the way up. As he lay in bed and readied himself for the visit, a sudden onslaught of diarrhoea caught him by surprise, making a mess of his hospital gown and bed sheets.

Not wanting to be embarrassed when his visitors showed up, he quickly took off his hospital gown and ripped the sheets off the bed, tossed them out the window, and ran into his bathroom to clean up and put on another hospital gown.

Unbeknownst to him, Tim Murphy had just left the local pub and was staggering along the street below his window, when the hospital gown and sheets fell on top of him.

Thinking he had been attacked, Tim spun around, covered by the sheets, swinging his arms and punching out at his 'attacker'. When he finally managed to knock the sheets off, he fell backwards on his behind and sat staring at the pile of sheets in awe.

Just then, a city policeman happened along. Trying to comprehend the sight before him, he asked Murphy, 'And, just what in the hell happened here?'

Murphy replied, 'I don't know, sir; but, I think I just beat the shit out of a ghost!'

Two beggars, Seamus and Niall, were walking along the road at dusk. Being the more amateur of the two, Niall complained loudly, 'I'm famished! How will we get something to eat this night?'

'Worry not,' said Seamus, 'I'll show you how it's done.'

As they approached a farmhouse, he picked up a dried cow pat from the field and went to the door. He knocked on the door, and the missus answered.

'Yes?' she said.

'Forgive me missus,' begged Seamus, 'I am but a humble beggar with nought to eat but this dried old cow pat. Could I trouble you for some salt to go with it?'

'Why that's no fit meal for a man,' the woman exclaimed. 'Come in here and sit down, I'll feed you proper.'

A half hour later, Seamus emerged from the house stuffed with lamb and potatoes and smiling ear to ear.

'Wow,' shouted Niall, 'I can do that!'

He ran to the next farmhouse, grabbing his own cow pat along the way. He knocked on the door, and the missus answered.

'Forgive me missus,' he begged, 'I am but a humble beggar with nought to eat but 'this dried-up old cow pat. Could I trouble you for some salt to go with it?'

'Sakes alive,' she cried 'that's no fit meal for a man. That things all horrible and dried up. Go on out back and get yourself a fresh one.'

THE ART OF THE FART

Woe, alack, and alas!
I'm held together by gas!
Each time I fart,
Something falls apart.
See! There's a crack in my ass!

A sparkling young farter from Sparta,
His fart for no money would barter.
He could roar from his rear
Any scene from Shakespeare,
Or Gilbert and Sullivan's Mikado.

Q: Why do farts smell?
A: So that deaf people can appreciate them as well.

A very attractive young lady was sitting in a fine restaurant one night. She was waiting for her special date and she wanted to make sure everything was perfect. As she bent down in her chair to get the mirror from her purse, she accidentally farted quite loudly just as the waiter walked by. She sat upright, embarrassed and red faced, knowing that everyone in the place had heard her.

To cover her embarrassment she turned to the waiter and demanded loudly, 'Stop that!'

'Sure lady, which way is it headed?' said the waiter.

There was a young royal marine,
Who tried to fart God Save the Queen.
When he reached the soprano
Out came only guano
And his britches weren't fit to be seen.

Q: Did you hear the joke about the fart?
A: It stinks.

Q: Someone stole all the toilet seats from the police station.
A: The officers have nothing to go on.

A man has a serious problem. Every time he takes a step, he farts. He goes to the doctor and when he walks in, 'Parp! Fumph! Toot! Poop!' go his bowels.

He sits down and the doctor tells him to walk across the room. He walks across the room and again his arse explodes with each stride, 'Parp! Fumph! Toot! Poop!' He walks back to his seat, 'Toot! Fumph! Parp! Poop! Rumble.'

'I know what I'm going to do!' says the doctor.

He goes to his cupboard and brings out a giant pole with a great big hook on the end of it.

The fellow looks in horror and says, 'Jeez, Doc, what the hell are you gonna do with that?'

'I'm going to open the window, of course. This place stinks!'

YOUR MOTHER

- Your mother's so old she farts dust.
- Your mother's so fat, fat people run around her for exercise.
- Your mother's so fat that when she jumps in the sea all the water jumps out.
- Your mother's so fat that when she gets her shoes shined she has to take their word for it.

Woman: Your son is terribly spoiled.
Mother: How dare you. He's not spoiled at all.
Woman: Yes he is. He just got hit by a bus.

Mummy, mummy, why are we pushing the car off the cliff?
Shut up or you'll wake your father.

Mummy, mummy, why can't we give Grandma a proper burial?
Shut up and keep flushing.

Mummy, mummy, dad has been run over by a steamroller.
Shut up and slide him under the door.

Mummy, mummy, daddy's on fire.
Hurry up and get the marshmallows.

Mummy, mummy, my head hurts.
Shut up and get away from the dart board.

Mummy, mummy, why is dad running in zig zags?
Shut up and keep shooting.

Mummy, mummy, why can't we buy a garbage disposal unit?
Shut up and keep chewing.

Mummy, mummy, dad's going out.
Shut up and throw some more petrol on him.

Mummy, mummy, daddy just put Rover down!
I'm sure he had a good reason for it.
But he promised I could do it.

Mummy, mummy, daddy's hammering on the roof again.
Shut up and drive a bit faster.

Q: Is it possible to kill a mother-in-law with newspaper?
A: Yes, but only if you wrap an iron in it.

AND FINALLY . . .

CONFUCIUS SAY

- Woman who wear G-string, high on crack!
- Woman who pounce on dead rooster go down on limp cock.
- Woman who cooks carrots and peas in same pot is unsanitary.
- While others are inside sitting down, you will be outstanding.
- War doesn't determine who's right, war determines who's left.
- Virgin like balloon. One prick, all gone.
- Secretary not permanent until screwed on desk.
- Put rooster in freezer to get a stiff cock.
- Penis put in vacuum cleaner get sucked off.
- Panties not best thing on earth, but next to it.
- OK for shit to happen. It will decompose.
- Never eat yellow snow.
- Naked man fears no pick pocket.
- Man with one chopstick go hungry.
- Man with no legs bums around.
- Man with hole in pocket feels cocky all day.
- Man with hand in pocket is having a ball.
- Man with an unchecked parachute will jump to conclusion.
- Man who tell one too many light bulb jokes soon burn out.
- Man who stand on toilet is high on pot.
- Man who speaks with forked tongue should not kiss balloons.
- Man who sneezes without tissue takes matters into his own hands.
- Man who smoke pot choke on handle.
- Man who sit on tack get point.

- Man who sink into woman's arms soon have arms in woman's sink.
- Man who scratches ass should not bite fingernails.
- Man who put head on railroad track to listen for train likely to end up with splitting headache.
- Man who put face in punchbowl gets punch in nose.
- Man who piss into wind get wet.
- Man who paints on toilet door is a shithouse painter.
- Man who masturbate only screwing himself.
- Man who masturbate into cash register, soon come into money.
- Man who keep feet firmly on ground have trouble putting on pants.
- Man who go to bed with diarrhoea wake up in deep shit.
- Man who fart in church sit in own pew.
- Man who eat many prunes get good run for money.
- Man who drop watch in toilet have shitty time.
- Man who drive like hell bound to get there.
- Man who chase cars will soon get exhausted.
- Man who bounce woman on bedspring this spring have offspring next spring.
- Man trapped in sewer, eat shit and die.
- It takes many nails to build crib, but one screw to fill it.
- Is good to learn how to masturbate, may come in handy.
- Hockey player on ice have big stick.
- He who stands in corner with hands in pocket doesn't feel crazy, feels nuts.
- He who sleeps with itchy bum, will wake with smelly thumb.
- He who sits on an upturned tack shall surely rise.
- He who lives in glasshouse dresses in basement.
- He who eats crackers in bed gets crummy sleep.
- He who crosses the ocean twice without washing is a dirty double crosser.
- Girl laid in tomb may soon become mummy.
- Fly who sit on toilet seat get pissed off.

- Butcher who back into meat grinder get a little behind in his orders.
- Boy who go to bed with sex problem wake up with solution in hand.
- Best way to prevent hangover is to stay drunk.
- Baseball is wrong. Man with four balls can't walk!
- Baby conceived on back seat of car with automatic transmission grow up to be shiftless bastard.
- A bird in hand makes hard to blow nose.